The Heart of **Giving**

The Heart of **Giving**

Discovering the Freedom of Giving through Grace

Dr. Steven W. Hough

Changing Lives Publishing
Updated Third Edition

Published by Changing Lives Publishing

Cover design by David Munoz

Published in the United States of America ISBN: 9781549921612
Religion / Christian Life / Stewardship & Giving

Acknowledgements

I wish to personally thank the following people for their contributions to my inspiration, knowledge and other help in creating this book:

To my wife Catherine, my high school sweetheart, life partner, inspiration and love. You have been such a great encouragement for me as we embarked on this path of discovery together. Your editing insights have been keen. I can't thank you enough. You truly are the "wind beneath my wings." We have journeyed this book together!

To our family Tiffany, Brittney, Brad, Justin and Jake who reflect such a love towards us and toward our grandchildren. You have inspired me with hope to reach your generation with this message.

To my parents Bonnie and Charlie who instilled in me a heart of giving at an early age. You trained me up well, and I have not departed from it.

To Catherine's parents Betty and Walter who have supported and encouraged us in so many ways through the years. You are great examples of selfless giving.

To my good friend Pastor Femi Omiye who listened, learned, stepped out in faith and became a great mentor when you heard this message. Thank you for your inspiration and encouragement to me to press on to bring this book to fruition.

To my good friend Pastor Larry Cooke whose life, ministry, and love for the Lord coupled with the spiritual understanding of this truth have inspired me to greater heights in knowing our heavenly Father.

To my good friend Pastor Kingsley Walker, for your unconditional love and friendship. You have a true heart for God.

To my friend David Munoz, for waiting on and listening to Holy Spirit for the artistic cover design that captured the heart and intention of this book.

To our Abba Father God: You have shown an uncontainable love towards us and have captured my heart forever. To Jesus for His Ultimate Sacrifice that allowed me the chance to get to know Him and to know the heart of our heavenly Father.

To Holy Spirit who guides and leads us into all truth; You have stirred my heart to dig deep into God's amazing Word, more deeply understand His heart and to reach the lost and hurting world with this message.

"But the moment one turns to the Lord with an open heart, the veil is lifted and they see. Now, the "Lord" I'm referring to is the Holy Spirit, and wherever he is Lord, there is freedom."

(2Corinthians 3:16-17 TPT)

Contents

Introduction

I was sitting at my table studying God's Word when a pastor friend of mine was at our house. I said to him, "I need to bounce something off you. God is really showing me something in His Word about tithing. Actually, it reveals that as Christians, we are not required to tithe. But I would like you to look at this information and see what you think."

When he returned to our house a couple weeks later he was very excited. He said his life was changed. Later, my friend shared with me that when I first asked him to examine this topic, he thought I was crazy. Everyone knew that tithing was biblical and was expected by God. But he agreed to look at the information to humor me, and out of respect for our friendship, he was compelled to approach it with an open mind. As he studied, he not only discovered God's truth but also stepped into a new joy of giving, not out of fear or obligation but through the grace of God in Jesus Christ.

There has been an ever-growing emphasis on the need to bring the tithe to the church to receive the blessing of God and prevent God from sending a curse to His people. This book is intended to help the Christian walk in the fullness of grace that God has extended to all people and which is upon all who believe; to rest in the confidence of knowing that we are so loved by God and that He has already poured out His blessing upon us through Christ. The misunderstanding of scripture has placed fear into many Christians, stirred an unsubstantiated hope in others, and chased and kept many others away from experiencing God's love and connecting with the church. This book is intended to bring clarity to His Word and reveal the true heart of a giving Father.

This book is for the Christian and the non-Christian alike. It is an in-depth biblical study coupled with revelation and insights that will help you discover the true freedom that all Christians have to give through God's grace.

It is for the Christian who has received Christ as Lord and Savior yet still walks with uncertainty. In gaining a greater understanding of God's giving heart the hope is you will come to know His intimate love for you. Christians are freed from all the law of sin and death, and the blessing of God is freely given to those who trust and follow in Him.

It is for the non-Christian, so many of whom have turned away from God because they think all the church wants is their money. In realizing that as one chooses to be a follower of Christ, the act of giving becomes a response to His love for us and not a requirement. The hope is that one sees the door open to receive this free gift of salvation through Christ and seizes the opportunity to enter into an amazing relationship with the one true and living God.

It is my prayer that the reader lay down any preconceived understanding regarding tithing and giving to look openly and afresh at what God's Word says regarding this issue. I believe as you discover the truth of God's Word, you will know this by no means suggests Christians stop giving. Rather, I believe, you will find a greater joy in giving through a personal relationship with our heavenly Father. As this truth sets you free, I pray your hearts will be stirred towards a kingdom mentality of giving. All we have is from God. As His children, kings, ambassadors and priests, when we ask Him what to do with the gifts and provision He has entrusted to us, He will surely direct our path.

How to read this book:

First of all, I request that you read this book with an open heart, open mind, and open spirit to hear what the Word of God is saying.

Secondly, while many authors may not subscribe to "jumping ahead", it may be beneficial to skip to different sections. Some find it beneficial to know the story behind the book first before they read. Also, there is a chapter near the end, "What God is Saying Today About This Message" which some may find important as they grasp the understanding and importance of this message.

Finally, I request that once you start, you commit to finishing the entire book. I'm not suggesting that this be done in one setting. Take your time; there is a lot of information to take in. However, the message in this book is only complete as you read all sections. Likely you will have some beliefs and understandings that will be challenged. So it is important not to reach conclusions of what is presented without exploring everything that this book contains.

In addition and after great feedback, I have designed "The Heart of Giving Workbook and Discussion Guide" to assist in going through this material. Many have found this a helpful tool to assist in self-study, bible study groups and for teaching this material.

So come, let us reason together and find the love that is so great that it casts out all fear and requires nothing in return. Yet this love stirs us to give abundantly out of His overflowing love and mercy for us. May you be blessed as you read.

A Firm Foundation

As we embark on the discovery to understand the true heart of giving, it is important that we build on the proper foundation. Where we begin, our understanding and our beliefs, will ultimately influence our future understanding and beliefs. It will guide what we look for and how we interpret things. My heart is for all to be on the correct side of what Jesus has done, but I know that all that can be shaken will be shaken. God will have His way, and wrong foundations will be taken down so that His kingdom will be established on the sure foundation of Jesus.

Many are aware that there are two basic positions or arguments regarding tithing in the church today. We either believe we are to bring a tithe (ten percent) of our money to the church (or Jesus), or we believe that as Christians we are not required to tithe. In this discussion please don't misinterpret the position of "not tithing" to mean "not giving". Nothing is farther from the truth. Giving is important for the individual and the church. It is performed solely out of love, wanting nothing in return, as both God and Jesus have taught us (John 3:16 and John 14:27). Tithing, however, is done in expectation of an exchange. This is readily verified in all tithing teachings. Traditionally, tithing teaches we must bring one tenth of our income in order to access God's blessing and to prevent a curse (Malachi 3:8-10). Other teachings regarding tithing suggests we are to bring a tithe of money to honor God in the same manner that Abraham honored Melchizedek. In addition, more recently, the traditional tithing teaching has taken on a newer position, suggesting the need to bring a tithe to a heavenly "trading floor", done through worship, where we trade our money for things or currency of God. This "honoring God through our tithes" suggests that it gives us access to His glory realm and that we are the ones who then "open the windows" to release blessing from heaven and to gain kingdom authority on earth. Still others teach that if we don't tithe, we won't get into heaven, suggesting that by not tithing we are "robbing God". And, suggesting as Jesus taught, thieves will not enter the Kingdom of Heaven.

Both positions can't be correct. It is either one or the other. We are either supposed to tithe or we are not. There is a difference, and it does matter to God. I believe it is extremely important, even vitally and critically important, that we get this right. The stakes are too high to get it wrong.

When people look at things through the wrong filter they can be misled into following wrong thinking and understanding. Whatever filters are used to "listen through" tend to let through only those things that fit the model or experience. This is because the "filter" is based on the wrong foundation. For example over the years people have argued that the world is flat. Even today there are "flat earthers". They can make a very persuasive argument of why the earth is flat. They claim facts and describe conspiracy theories that can mislead, bringing false evidence against those that suggest the earth is round. In spite of insurmountable evidence that shows the earth is 'round', these people choose to ignore the evidence and hold onto their belief. This is built on the wrong foundation. But if you ask one simple question you can clear this up: if the earth is flat then the sun should rise and set on everyone at the same time. Obviously, this doesn't happen, so the whole argument can be dismissed because it is built on a faulty foundation.

In a similar way, the theory of evolution has long been taught as truth. But, in reality, it is still just the "theory" of evolution. This theory is built on a wrong foundation. Charles Darwin writes, "I am sorry to have to inform you that I do not believe in the Bible as a divine revelation & therefore not in Jesus Christ as the son of God. Yours faithfully Ch. Darwin". Because of this faulty belief, he argues that we must have evolved over millions of years spontaneously without the help of an intelligent designer. Over the years there are many persuasive and scientific arguments in favor of evolution, yet people must ignore the very basic foundational errors to cling to this false doctrine. Darwin himself stated that the only way this theory could be proven true was if there was ample fossil evidence to support it. However, there has not been one credible finding that would support this theory. Scientists, archeologists, physicists and others are discovering inarguable truths that there is an "intelligent design" to our universe, our earth, and life itself. However they must continually shift their "theory of evolution" to match their findings. Many of these findings contradict the basic foundation of evolution: that there is no God (or intelligent designer). Everything taught regarding evolution is suggested as truth and fact. But since the foundational premise is incorrect, all evidence to support this theory cannot stand. In other words, without the proper foundation the whole theory fails. Evolution, as Darwin suggested, is not true. The only way to properly understand life and the universe is to build it on the proper foundation: God created all things.

Now, let's look at tithing. The foundational understanding and teaching regarding tithing today is that our tithe is about our money. The "filter" that is used to understand this is not accurate because the foundational understanding is incorrect.

While there have been a great number of teachings to suggest that we are to tithe our money, teachers and students alike must ignore the basic premise that tithing is not about money in order to support their position. Scriptures are misinterpreted to support this foundation. The book of Malachi, the book of Hebrews, Genesis 14:18-20, Mark 4:13:25, and Luke 6:18-20 and more have all been used to support the need and/or requirement for tithing money. Even the gospel of grace has to be ignored or altered in order to support the requirement of tithing money. Evidence is accumulated and shared in an attempt to claim the benefits of tithing. Other evidence is ignored that doesn't match this "model of thinking". Those that bring forward an "opposing view" are often dismissed, chastised, and ridiculed.

I believe that you will see that this entire platform is built on the "wrong foundation". Again, please understand, this is not my opinion, but rather is founded in proper Biblical understanding and truth. As you read, you will come to understand that the biblical tithe was never about bringing money to God. While it was used and exchanged in the synagogues and temples, money was never directly brought as a tithe. The tithe's ultimate purpose was always about bringing a blood sacrifice and offering to the altar of the Lord. Specifically, it was about Jesus and His blood. It was about gaining access and restoring a relationship between God and His people.

If the foundation is not of God and established on His Word, what is the foundation built on? It's either God or not. And if it is not God, it is either flesh (our sinful nature) or the enemy (Satan). Because this false foundation is built on the premise surrounding money as the tithe, it is reasonable to surmise that this comes from the spirit of Mammon. It is also linked to the spirit of Baal. We understand that the spirit of Baal has been exposed as the strongman over America (Dutch Sheets, John Benefiel, etc.). To break away from this spirit there have been legal documents and declarations written for and spoken by the body of Christ to divorce the spirit of Baal and remarry / recommit to God. There are even 'writs' delivered and spoken to call for a returning of what the enemy has stolen. However, even though many in the church have ceremonially divorced Baal and remarried Christ, the truth is that if you maintain a mistress you are still in adultery. While many have divorced the major spirit of Baal, they maintain the mistress of mammon by continuing to try to gain access through the tithe (money). It is the wrong foundation. Knowing that the tithe is not money allows us to establish our footing on the proper foundation. This is the only true foundation: the blood of Jesus has accomplished it all. We are called to not walk and war according to the flesh, but in the Spirit, for our weapons are not carnal (money) but "mighty in God for pulling down strongholds, casting down arguments and every high thing that exalts itself against the knowledge of God, bringing every thought into captivity to the obedience of Christ." (2Cor. 10:5-6) Tithing is one of those "high things".

As you continue to read, you will discover much more about this subject and about true giving. But, as you can see, there is a choice to make. Which path will you follow. Believing in something does not make it true. Only truth is true. Information built on the wrong foundation leads down a crooked path. Evidence that is built on the sure foundation leads to the truth. I pray for wise choices. My heart is that all may come to know the truth and experience the fullness and freedom that Jesus' precious blood bought for us.

True giving, giving as God and Jesus have shown, is from the heart. As Christ followers, with "Christ in us, the hope of glory" we should undoubtedly reflect His love for God and those around us. Giving is the heartbeat of every Christian. If we don't give of ourselves, our time, and our possessions we grow weak. So be encouraged to give as God stirs in your heart. Give without expectation or anticipation of a return. Give through the heart of the true giver that says, I (God) so loved the world that I (God) gave My only begotten Son so that all who believe in Him shall not perish but have everlasting life. (John 3:16) Give as Jesus gave, not as the world gives, but freely and only in love. (John 14:27) Give through a heart of giving and discover the freedom that brings joy and frees us from the bonds of tithing.

The Simple Message

The most important thing I hope the reader captures is how much God the Father, Son, and Holy Spirit deeply love you. He spared no expense to show that love. As Jesus willingly laid down His life for us He freed us from the depths of Hell and death. He poured out His Spirit upon all flesh so that we may live together with Him forever through Christ. While it is sometimes hard to grasp the fullness and depth of His love for us, know that it is a deep and everlasting love.

As you read, my hope is that you will grasp this love that the Father, Son, and Holy Spirit has for you. This is a message of love, hope and freedom. While it will undoubtedly be challenging and perhaps convicting to many, please know that this is not a message of condemnation or judgement. Rather it is a message of love and freedom. It is God's heart that all come to the fullness of the knowledge of Jesus Christ and step into the freedom that He alone extends to us through His sacrifice on the cross.

God is love. And God is a giver. It is His nature, and it flows from Him because that's who He is. Giving is a natural outpouring of God. As believers, Christ is in us. The character of His nature should become more and more evident in our lives, including the evidence of giving. So giving is not the question, but rather what motivates our giving and what is at the heart of why we give. For God does not look at the outward appearance of a man's actions but the intent of his heart.

With that in mind the message is simple: give. Give as you purpose in your heart, not according to a formula that someone tells you or out of fear or obligation, or out of what you think you might "owe" God, but simply give. Give out of love, the love that God has shown us and the love that we have both for God and for others. God loves a cheerful giver.

It's a simple message and it's also a hard message at the same time. God makes it simple because of His love and grace towards us through Jesus Christ. But our flesh makes it difficult to simply trust and rest in this grace. The flesh and mind say we can't get something for nothing, especially such a valuable gift. The flesh says we must certainly do something to obtain such a favored position with God. But this message cannot be received by the flesh, because the flesh is working against God. It can only be received by and through the Spirit of God, by grace through faith working in us and speaking to our spirit; because His Spirit is one with the Father. So we must listen and inquire by our spirit through faith as we engage His Spirit, which leads us into all truth (John16:13).

God is a good God, and He loves His children. He gives good gifts to His sons and daughters, gifts that are just that—gifts. These are not something that would need to be returned to Him (either in full or a portion, such as ten percent) or that He charges an interest or a tax upon. This gift is not something that can be earned, as if it would be paid like a wage by doing good deeds. It is not a debt that we owe or an obligation that we could fulfill. Jesus paid our debt in full. The debt of the law is cancelled. We are free. And who the Son sets free is free indeed!

In a similar manner, true giving is not motivated by greed or duty but rather out of love. True giving does not expect a return nor is it contingent upon the actions of another. It is not used to manipulate, such as trying to obtain blessing or favor from another (even God). True giving does not say, "If I give you this, then you do this for me." True giving is simply and wholly motivated by love.

Financial support is certainly critical to help spread the Gospel of Jesus Christ, and it depends upon the faithful giving of members of the body of Christ. So give. Give as you purpose in your heart. Support the work of those who spread the Gospel, care for widows and orphans and help those in need. If God stirs your heart to give a certain percentage or an amount, cheerfully do so. But don't be obligated to give a tithe because you're taught that you are required to fulfill this commandment of the law. We are freed from the law and its requirements. The message in this book is by no means suggesting that one should stop giving. On the contrary, this message is to give in the freedom that Christ has afforded us through His sacrifice on the cross. But don't give out of fear, for we are children of a loving Heavenly Father, and we have not been given a spirit of fear but of power and love and of a sound mind.

To understand the difference and why it even matters, it becomes important (and even critical) to examine what is being taught about giving in the church. To be more exact, it calls out to examine tithing and to bring about a more complete understanding of giving as it relates to God's Word as we live in the fullness of the grace that He has extended to us through Jesus Christ.

As one reads this book, it is the intention that the reader will hear what I believe is the heart cry of Jesus, proclaiming, "Look, see what I have done for you. I have freed you from the law of sin and death. Come, rest in the fullness of the grace that the Father has given to you because of Me and do not place yourself again under the bondage of the law that exposed sin and lead to death." However, I also believe there is a cry of the Father who would say, "Beware those of you who teach and believe that you can obtain My blessing through any action of your own, as you make the blood of

Christ of no effect and must keep the entire law" (see Gal. 5:4). "See that I have made you holy only through the sacrifice of the body and blood of Jesus Christ once, for all" (see Heb. 10:10). "But it is much worse to dishonor God's Son and to disgrace the blood of the promise that made us holy. And it is just as bad to insult the Holy Spirit, who shows us mercy. (Heb 10:29, CEV).

With these "cries" in mind, this book is intended both to make a plea from the heart of God, whose kindness leads us to repentance, and a warning to those who would attempt to take His children back into bondage. It is the prayer that none take offense, but rather each one fully examines the truths laid forth and come to the greater understanding of what it means to "give through grace" and to bring freedom to the believer from the bondage of a misunderstanding of scripture. Even more, I believe God wants people to more fully comprehend the love that He has for us and the extent He has gone through to bring us back to Him as children, heirs, and coheirs with Christ, taking us out from under the burden of the law, even the burden of the tithe.

So I pray, "Lord, open our eyes and give us a greater understanding of Your scriptures as you did in Luke 24:45 and have Your Spirit lead us into all truth" (John 16:13). Come let us reason together as we investigate His Word and discover the heart of giving from the heart of the True Giver Himself. As Paul charged Timothy, let us "do [our] best to present [ourselves] to God as one approved, a workman who does not need to be ashamed and who correctly handles the word of truth" (2 Tim. 2:15amp). Let us not be "carried about with divers and strange doctrines. For it is a good thing that the heart be established with grace." (Heb 13:9a KJV).

Confusion in the Church

I heard a comment on a Christian radio station from a caller that said, "Your station has taught me that the only person who can give me unconditional love is Jesus Christ." This is so true! However, as the church teaches tithing, it teaches that the fullness of God's love is conditional. The condition is that we must bring our tithe to receive God's full blessing or risk receiving God's curse. Bill Johnson has said that "in the absence of experience, bad theology is formed, and any revelation that does not bring us into greater encounter only trains us to be more religious. (Johnson, 2015)[1]"

Much of the church is in confusion today. We serve a loving God and Father in heaven, yet when it comes down to our money, we are told that He would somehow curse us if we don't bring His tithe (one-tenth of our money) to the church. We know that Jesus paid our debt in full, but somehow, we still have a debt to pay God, and we do so by bringing Him the tithe. God gives freely and supplies all our needs, but we must return ten percent to Him (through the church) to fulfill an obligation to him. Jesus is the sacrificial Lamb of God, the final and complete offering for our sins, yet we must still continually bring an "offering" of our tithe before the Lord to satisfy Him. Christ took away the curse that was upon us, but we must continually bring our tithe to keep from being cursed. Christ has set us free from the law of sin and death, but we are still bound and obligated to continually bring a tithe (which is part of the law He has set us free from). I am blessed beyond measure, but I am not blessed financially unless I bring my tithe.

It's easy to see how people can be confused. We don't serve a gangster-type god who would strong arm us with a threat like "give me your money or I'll break your arm (or put a curse on you)". This confusion is perhaps the biggest stumbling block that has turned more people away from the Church (and away from God) in this time. At the very least, there is a great misunderstanding of the truth of God's Word and the new covenant that we have in Christ. At worst, there is a manipulation by church leadership to place pressure, guilt, and fear in people to give money to the church.

However, as we examine more closely, we see that even Paul says, regarding giving, "I am not commanding you" (2 Cor. 8:8a). Bible scholars write in the footnotes of The Reformation Heritage KJV (King James) Study Bible regarding 2 Corinthians 8 and 9 and New Testament giving:

> 2 Corinthians 8:8-13 KJV: (8) I speak not by commandment, but by occasion of the forwardness of others, and to prove the sincerity of your love. (9) For ye know the grace of our Lord Jesus Christ, that, though he was rich, yet for your sakes he became poor, that ye through his poverty might be rich. (10) And herein I give my advice: for this is expedient for you, who have begun before, not only to do, but also to be forward a year ago. (11) Now therefore perform the doing of it; that as there was a readiness to will, so there may be a performance also out of that which ye have. (12) For if there be first a willing mind, it is accepted according to that a man hath, and not according to that he hath not. (13) For I mean not that other men be eased, and ye burdened:
>
> 8:8 *I speak not by commandment.* Giving ought to be voluntary. *forwardness.* Earnestness and diligence of others in giving. *To prove.* To

> test or try.
>
> 8:9 *For ye know the grace of our Lord Jesus Christ.* God's grace to believers ought to move them to be gracious to others; in this case, it ought to move them to give to others' needs.
>
> 8:12 *a willing mind...accepted according to that a man hath.* Paul does not stipulate an exact amount each person is to give. The giver must have a willingness to give and should give according to what he is able to give
>
> 8:13 *not that other men be eased, and ye be burdened: But by an equality.* Fairness in the gathering of funds for the saints, not to enrich some at others' expense, but to care for all.
>
> 2 Corinthians 9:7 KJV Every man according as he purposeth in his heart, so let him give; not grudgingly, or of necessity: for God loveth a cheerful giver.
>
> 9:7 *Every man according as he purposeth in his heart.* Paul does not demand a specific percentage of one's income, but urges voluntary giving. Not *grudgingly, or of necessity.* Christians should not feel forced into giving, nor should they give while still desiring to hold on to their money. *cheerful.* Joyful, glad, not angry. God delights in cheerful giving, and that alone should motivate Christians to give cheerfully. (Reformation Heritage Books, 2014)

Similarly, in the footnotes of the NIV Life Application Bible, the bible scholars write regarding 2 Corinthians 8 and 9:

> 2 Corinthians 8:8-12 NIV 8 I am not commanding you, but I want to test the sincerity of your love by comparing it with the earnestness of others. 9

For you know the grace of our Lord Jesus Christ, that though he was rich, yet for your sake he became poor, so that you through his poverty might become rich.10 And here is my judgment about what is best for you in this matter. Last year you were the first not only to give but also to have the desire to do so. 11 Now finish the work, so that your eager willingness to do it may be matched by your completion of it, according to your means. 12 For if the willingness is there, the gift is acceptable according to what one has, not according to what one does not have.

(8:7, 8) The Corinthian believers excelled in everything—they had faith, good preaching (speech), much knowledge, much earnestness, and much love. Paul wanted them to also be leaders in giving. Giving is a natural response of love. Paul did not order the Corinthians to give, but he encouraged them to prove that their love was sincere. When you love someone, you want to give him or them time and attention and to provide for his or her needs. If you refuse to help, your love is not as genuine as you say. (8:10–15) The Corinthian church had money, and apparently, they had planned to collect the money for the Jerusalem churches a year previously (see also 9:2). Paul challenges them to act on their plans. Four principles of giving emerge here: (1) your willingness to give cheerfully is more important than the amount you give; (2) you should strive to fulfill your financial commitments; (3) if you give to others in need, they will, in turn, help you when you are in need; (4) you should give as a response to Christ, not for anything you can get out of it. How you give

> reflects your devotion to Christ.
>
> (8:12) How do you decide how much to give? What about differences in the financial resources Christians have? Paul gives the Corinthian church several principles to follow: (1) each person should follow through on previous promises (8:10, 11; 9:3); (2) each person should give as much as he or she is able (8:12; 9:6); (3) each person must make up his or her own mind how much to give (9:7); and (4) each person should give in proportion to what God has given him or her (9:10). God gives to us so that we can give to others.
>
> 2 Corinthians 9:7 Each of you should give what you have decided in your heart to give, not reluctantly or under compulsion, for God loves a cheerful giver.
>
> (9:7) Our attitude when we give is more important than the amount we give. We don't have to be embarrassed if we can give only a small gift. God is concerned about how we give from the resources we have (see Mark 12:41-44).According to that standard, the giving of the Macedonian churches would be difficult to match (8:3) (Life Application Bible, 1991)

These passages themselves should settle the issue regarding a tithing requirement for followers of Christ. It's easy to see why people become confused. Bible scholars confirm that Paul's instructions do not command a certain amount or percentage (including a tithe) but rather to give freely as one chooses in his or her own heart. It should not be out of lack so that no one would go through hardship. Yet much of the church insists that giving ten percent of one's income is biblical, and it carries both the chance for blessing and curse. Furthermore, it is often taught that it becomes more important to give the minimum of a tithe of one's income when someone is facing hardship in order to procure the blessing.

Be sure, though, that we do serve a loving God. Jesus did pay it all. He is the pure sacrificial Lamb that has taken away the sin of the world. Christ has taken away the curse completely by being hanged on the cross, and He has set us free from the law of sin and death so that we are no longer bound to sin, but to righteousness that is of faith through Jesus. We are blessed beyond measure as God has extended His grace to us through faith in His Son. And we have full and complete right standing (righteousness) with God through Jesus. While we owe Him everything, we owe Him nothing, because it is a debt that we cannot pay. It has been paid in full by Jesus. He has not given us a spirit of fear but of power and love and a sound mind. So let's not be double-minded but rather be firm and secure in the truth of God's great love, that His Son has set us free. For whomever the Son has set free is free indeed!

So, I pose this question: What if tithing, which is intended to honor God, is actually a strategy of the enemy to dishonor God as it cheapens and brings insult to the blood of Jesus; and actually makes the blood of Jesus for naught? As we uncover the truths about this issue you may agree that this is a valid question. Remember, Satan's schemes have not changed. From the beginning of time he has attempted to deceive and mislead God's children:

> Now the serpent was more cunning than any beast of the field which the Lord God had made. And he said to the woman, "Has God indeed said, 'you shall not eat

> of every tree of the garden'?" and the woman said to the serpent, "We may eat the fruit of the trees of the garden; but of the fruit of the tree which is in the midst of the garden, God has said 'You shall not eat it, nor shall you touch it, lest you die.'" Then the serpent said to the woman, "You will not surely die. For God knows that in the day you eat of it your eyes will be opened and you will be like God, knowing good and evil." (Gen. 3:1–5 NKJV)

If Eve truly understood who she was (she was created in God's image, and so was already like God), she would not have been persuaded or tempted to do something that would cause her to be something like she already was. In a similar way, I believe, God would say, "Through Jesus I have brought the righteous offering that I spoke about in Malachi and have opened the windows of heaven and poured out My blessing that can't be contained." But I suggest Satan also says, "Didn't God say you were robbing Him and you need to bring your tithe to activate your blessing, and if you don't bring your tithe, you will be cursed?" Be careful not to be caught up in Satan's deception. God's Word says Jesus has fulfilled the law and those that are in Him are no longer bound to the law. But those who try to gain righteousness (and blessing) through part of the law must keep the whole law and have lost all effect from Christ. They have fallen from grace. Paul writes in Galatians 5:

> Stand fast therefore in the liberty with which Christ has made us free, and do not again be held with the yoke of bondage. Behold, I, Paul, say to you that if you are circumcised, Christ shall profit you nothing. For I testify again to every man that is circumcised, that he is a debtor to do all the Law, you who are justified by Law are deprived of all effect from Christ; you fell

from grace. (Gal. 5:1–4)

If we were to truly understand the fullness of God's grace extended to us through Jesus, we would not be deceived into thinking that we need to do something further to gain God's blessing. Jesus paid the price in full and when we receive Him into our hearts we are walking in the fullness of God's blessing. There is nothing more that needs to (or can be) done. We already are. So don't be deceived into thinking that we must do something to obtain what is already ours.

I am discovering that one of the greatest enemies to spreading the Gospel today, especially to the younger generation, is the message of tithing. This message, first of all, is not consistent with the message of Grace, so it does not settle well in a Christian's spirit. When the young believer, or someone who is considering the love that God has for us, hears the message of tithing which bears both a blessing and a curse, it brings fear and confusion. They can't reconcile the message of unconditional love with the requirement of having to give something to obtain a blessing. Particularly when one hears that God will curse them if they do not tithe, they run from the church. This is not a message of a loving God that is trying to capture the heart of a generation. And the perception is that the church is all about trying to get money.

To add to the confusion in the church, there are many testimonies that will proclaim that tithing has worked, and a blessing has resulted from the giving of the tithe. Why does tithing work for some yet doesn't work for everyone? Why is there poverty in the church of tithers? If tithing was God's true plan, then it should work for everyone and every tither should be blessed beyond measure. It seems, however, that tithing taps into the principle of giving. This principle is much like the principle or law of gravity. Just like when throwing an object up it must come down, some will experience a return on the investment of a tithe. But Paul tells us this: "Now to the one who works, his wages are not counted as a gift but as his due. And to the one who does not work but believes in him who justifies the ungodly, his faith is counted as righteousness" (Rom. 4:4–5, ESV). If you challenge God to "repay you" (bless you) out of your act of tithing, this principle will make that happen, but you have received your reward in full (financial) as it was paid to you as a debt owed. But if you believe in Him and trust in Him who has completed the work (through faith) and rely not on your own efforts, your reward will be great in heaven and on earth. There is much evidence that financial blessing occurs to those who give without adhering to the tithing principle and give without expecting anything in return, but just simply give out of love.

In addition, there is confusion because some prophets today preach the tithing message and miracles happen in their ministry. So why would God allow these things to happen if tithing is an incorrect teaching? It is written,

> The Lord is merciful and gracious, slow to anger and abounding in steadfast love. He will not always chide, nor will he keep his anger forever. He does not deal with us according to our sins, nor repay us according to our iniquities. For as high as the heavens are above the earth, so great is his steadfast love toward those who fear him; as far as the east is from the west, so far does he remove our transgressions from us. As a father shows compassion to his children, so the Lord shows compassion to those who fear him. (Ps. 103:8–13 ESV)

God's compassion for His people to share His heart through prophecy and to heal freely surpasses man's flaws, inadequacies, and even wrong understanding. It is very clear that prophecy and healings occur often in ministries where tithing is not accepted as a principle in the church today. So, miracles, healings and blessings are not dependent upon the giving of a tithe but, rather, on God's love, grace and mercy. The problem with deception is that you don't know you are being deceived. Consider this: As a Christian, is there anything that we can do or not do that could make God love us? Those that truly understand God's Word know that God loves us not by what we do or have done. He loves us just the way we are (and He loves us so much not to leave us where we are). An equal question can be posed if there is anything that would cause God to withhold, remove, or pull back His blessing, peace, or love from us. The answer again is no. God's promises are yes and amen. However, one can ask if there is anything we can do to block that blessing coming from God to us. I believe the answer here is yes. While these blessings are obtained by faith alone, if we do not receive it by faith but attempt to obtain it by works, it may actually block these blessings and promises from God.

I believe tithing is part of a bigger scheme of the religious spirit which is to tie the individual to works and not grace through faith. Staying with a "works" mind-set keeps one always aware of our weakness and inability to fulfill God's requirements. This keeps one "sin conscious" and therefore in bondage rather than awakening to the freedom that we have in Christ. Religion says that we "must do," but Christ says, "I have done." Christ did not come into the world to establish a religion but to restore the relationship of man to God and God to man. Religion establishes a set of rules and regulations (like tithing) to operate out of as a way to reach God. Christianity, however, is about God reaching out to man. Jesus was very stern with the Pharisees who were in this established religion of rules and regulations. These regulations kept the people from seeing who God really was. Jesus came so that we might have life and have it to the full.

Bill Johnson has said: "God never violates His Word. But He's quite comfortable violating our understanding of His Word." (Johnson, 2015) Many in the church are camped on the wrong side of the cross. Law requires. Grace enables. God's judgment is aimed at whatever interferes with His love.[4]" One of the biggest concerns I have heard from pastors when considering this message is that without tithing, "How will I get my members to give to the church?" This in itself, is revealing. First of all, whose church is it, God's or the pastor's? Whose work is the money supporting, God's or the pastor's? If it is God's church and God's work, He will supply what is needed. In other words, if it's God's will, it's God's bill. When pastors reveal and people experience the great love that God has for us they are moved and inspired to give without the pressure of a tithe. It will cause one to place their trust in God and not the people.

For those ascribing to tithing, the misunderstanding may be rooted in two things. Fear is a great motivator, and a fear of displeasing God with the consequence of being cursed by Him motivates a lot of people to give (even beyond their ability and resources). In addition, the church and society are taught that our worth is based on our performance. The better we perform, the more we are worth. If we do well in school, if we have a high-paying job, if we, if we, then we are worth more. If we give more, then somehow, we are worth more to the church and/or to God. But our worth in Christ is not based on our performance, but rather it is based on God's love for us alone. We are a treasured possession to God not because of anything we have or have not done. He has created us in His own image. He loves us so much that He sent His Son to redeem us from the law and our sin. While we were yet sinners, He sent His Son to die for us. So our worth is not based on our performance but on our relationship with Him. And when we have a relationship based in truth, love, and respect, we not only enjoy being together, but we will do whatever is in our ability to help each other. So out of our relationship first with God and second with others, we are inspired (not convicted) to give when and where it is needed.

A friend reminded me of a story in history. In the late 1500s, Galileo, one of the leading thinkers in that time, was trying to disprove one of the old theories of Aristotle being taught in the universities. Aristotle's theory on gravity was that the heavier the object, the faster it would fall. However, Galileo discovered that gravity had the same effect on objects regardless of their weight.

So Galileo assembled the scientists in Athens University and in their presence dropped two stones from the Leaning Tower of Pisa at the same time. One was large and heavy the other much smaller and lighter. To their surprise, both stones landed at the same time, which proved Galileo's point: the pull of gravity does not discriminate according to weight. The scientists all saw the results, but rather than accepting them and changing their thinking, they went back to their classrooms and continued teaching the old doctrines and theory set forth by Aristotle.

My friend's point was this: no matter how accurate and true this revelation of giving is presented, many of the teachers of today will not accept it and will continue to teach a requirement of tithing despite the overwhelming evidence to the contrary. They will read it and ignore the evidence like the scientists in the case above. However, there will be those whose spirit will delight in the truth, and they will be set free, free to give as they would purpose in their heart, not as a requirement but out of love, being firmly established in the grace of God through Jesus Christ (Heb. 13:9a). God will not share the credit for His glory or the glory of His Son with any man. While I believe it is not the intention of any Christian to take glory away from Christ or what He has done for us, believing that it is necessary to bring a tithe to receive His blessing is, in essence, declaring that Jesus's sacrifice was not sufficient for us to enter into God's blessing and favor. One day, we will all stand before the Lord. If He were to ask what have we done to be worthy of His blessing, how will you respond? If we think that in keeping the tithe God will be pleased, we must remember that our "works are as filthy rags" (Isa. 64:6). As for me and my house, we completely trust in the finished work of Jesus, knowing that we have entered our blessing fully by grace through faith in Him, apart from any works we could or could not do (including the tithe).

A Love Story for the Ages

God's Word is rich in so many ways. As Christians, we have heard of (and hopefully experienced) the depth of God's love for us through Jesus Christ. Of course, depending on how one views God, there will be greater emphasis on certain aspects of the Bible than others. It is easy to read in the Torah/Old Testament of God's strong hand, judgment, disappointment, and wrath on both the Jews and the Gentiles, speaking blessings and curses over people. When the Jews did not follow God and His law, there were certain consequences and judgments that followed. And God's strong action against the enemies of the Jewish people could suggest a merciless God against those that are not His own.

A friend of mine made a great observation: Our view of our Heavenly Father is skewed by the relationship and view we have with and of our earthly father and is influenced by the teachings of religion. Regardless of the relationship we have with our earthly father, our Heavenly Father's love is perfect. However, as life's experiences unfold with our earthly fathers, we may be led to have another picture of what a father's love is like. Even the best of fathers has weaknesses. Many have grown up with a broken father, or no father at all.

If a father raises a child with an iron fist, always judging, the child may see our Heavenly Father as one who always has a gavel in His hand, only here to condemn or pass judgment rather than a Father who loves us and is our best friend. If a father is absent, the child may see our Heavenly Father as one who is distant and does not care for us in our daily lives and that we have to "go it alone" rather than seeing our Father as one who "knows the hairs on our head" and wants to have an intimate relationship with us. If a father raises a child with the emphasis on performance being the way to please the father, then the child may view our Heavenly Father as one who is only pleased by what we do or don't do (including how we give or don't give) instead of seeing our Father who loves us, meets us, and accepts us just as we are.

The "Orphan Spirit"

While the other views of our earthly fathers listed above can influence our view of our Heavenly Father, the view from an orphan's eyes are much different. As a child is orphaned, whether by losing both parents or just one (especially a father), their perception of fathers can be drastically changed. Other situations would lead a child to attempt to gain their father's love and affection by perceived acts, holding on to a hope that somehow, some way, they will gain their father's love. However, as an orphan, there is no hope of ever gaining that relationship back with their father. The father is nowhere in the picture. To never have a chance of gaining a relationship, approval, or blessing with their father leaves an emptiness which has no hope of being fulfilled. We have a generation that is dominated by this "orphan spirit". Physically, many are 'fatherless', being abandoned at a young age. Often unknowingly, they spend their entire lives searching for that fatherly connection, looking for love in all the wrong places. When this individual comes to find our Heavenly Father (or rather find that our Heavenly Father has been calling out to them through Christ), their lives, like many, are radically changed. However, they may become especially susceptible to a spirit that would suggest they have to "do something" to please God, to gain a right standing with Him, or to earn His love and blessing. Since they had once been orphaned, they may be susceptible to the fear of being orphaned again. Out of fear of losing their fatherly relationship they may hold on to anything that would suggest the risk of them losing this relationship. This is particularly true when it comes to giving. As an orphan hears that they must give a certain percentage to either gain their Heavenly Father's blessing (or even worse is to prevent His curse and rejection) they hang on tightly even if it's not a true reflection of their Father's heart for them. While the absence of a father leads to these things listed above, it is also the absence of those things a good father brings and gives to his children. These includes physical, mental, and spiritual things, especially the absence of a father's blessing. This absence leads to a wounded heart.

However, as we look back from the cross of Christ, we can see the love and plan that God had from the beginning. It was necessary for God to be firm to establish His plan. It is also important to remember that we are no longer in a time where we live with "an eye for an eye" mentality. Jesus says pray for your enemies, and if your enemy would strike you in the cheek, give him the other cheek. The life of Jesus and the cross of Jesus have changed everything. Jesus is the revelation of the love the Father has for humanity. "But God commendeth his love toward us, in that, while we were yet sinners, Christ died for us." (Rom 5:8, KJV). "In this the love of God was manifested toward us, that God has sent His only begotten Son into the world, that we may live through Him. In this is love, not that we loved God, but that He loved us and sent His Son to be the propitiation of our sins" (1 John 4:9–10 NKJV). In Christ is revealed a love story for the ages, of whom Moses in the law, and the prophets, did write (John 1:45).

In the beginning, God created all things. Then He created mankind, and He saw that it was good. He blessed Adam and Eve and gave them dominion over all the earth (quite a gift!). There was only one command from God: "But you shall not eat of the tree of knowledge of good and evil. For in the day that you eat of it you shall surely die" (Gen. 2:17).

So man had a choice, and in that choice, Eve was deceived, and Adam disobeyed God. In that act of disobedience, it brought sin into the earth and all creation and gave Satan authority over the earth. But God still loves, because He is love. From the beginning, He had a plan that would restore that intimate relationship He created between God and man (Gen. 3:15). He chose Abram while he was an idol worshipper. Abram believed God, and it was counted to him as righteousness, and he became Abraham, a God follower and the father of many nations. God made a covenant with Abraham and, knowing the weakness of the human flesh, God made an oath to Himself that was not dependent upon Abraham or man to fulfill (Gen. 15, Heb. 6:13). In the same manner, God made a covenant with Moses and established the law (Exod. 34:27) knowing that man could not (nor would not) perfectly keep the law. So in God's plan, He established that a seed would spring up from the branch of Jesse that would be the Savior of the world. He (Jesus) would fulfill the law and thus establish a new covenant with both Jew and Gentile as one new man.

But the enemy also knew that God had a plan. While Satan did not know the fullness of God's plan, in His infinite wisdom God established this plan that only He could fulfill. This plan was established in love, for God knows the thoughts

He has for us, and they are plans for peace and not to harm or bring evil but to give us a future and a hope (Jer. 29:11). So to accomplish this, God first had to protect this established seed until the fullness of time had been reached. He knew that the enemy would try his best to extinguish the line of Abraham, Isaac, Jacob, and Jesse that would bring forth the Messiah. So God, in his love for humanity, dealt very hard blows to the enemy and to those that would oppose Him. History shows how the enemies of God have tried to eliminate His chosen people, the Jewish nation. Therefore, it was necessary for God to give strict instructions in those times on how to deal with the "enemies" of the "People of Promise." While these instructions may seem harsh, it is out of the love that God has for mankind that He gave such instructions. And it was necessary in order to preserve the promised seed to come forth in the fullness of time, when God would send His only begotten Son, not to condemn the world, for the world was already condemned, but to save the world through Him (John 3:16–17). And so the wisdom and plan of God was hidden in a mystery which God Himself set in place before the beginning of time. None of the rulers of that time knew of or understood this mystery. If they had, they would not have crucified Jesus. (1 Cor. 2:7–8).

Of course, in the beginning, there were consequences for Adam's disobedience (sin).

> Therefore, just as through one man sin entered the world, and death through sin, and thus death spread to all men, because all sinned—for until the law sin was in the world, but sin is not imputed when there is no law. Nevertheless death reigned from Adam to Moses, even over those who had not sinned according to the likeness of the transgression of Adam, who is a type of Him who was to come. But the free gift is not like the

> offense. For if by the one man's offense many died, much more the grace of God and the gift by the grace of the one Man, Jesus Christ, abounded to many. And the gift is not like that which came through the one who sinned. For the judgment which came from one offense resulted in condemnation, but the free gift which came from many offenses resulted in justification. For if by the one man's offense death reigned through the one, much more those who receive abundance of grace and of the gift of righteousness will reign in life through the One, Jesus Christ. Therefore, as through one man's offense judgment came to all men, resulting in condemnation, even so through one Man's righteous act the free gift came to all men resulting in justification of life. For as by one man's disobedience many were made sinners, so also by one Man's obedience many will be made righteous. Moreover the law entered that the offense might abound. But where sin abounded, grace abounded much more, so that as sin reigned in death, even so grace might reign through righteousness to eternal life through Jesus Christ our Lord. (Rom. 5:12–21 NKJV)

Jesus changed everything. In the fullness of time, God sent His Son to be born of a virgin and to bring peace to earth (which is Jesus, the Peace and Light of the world). Jesus did not come to abolish the law or the prophets but to fulfill them (Matt. 5:17). And in His fulfilling of the law, He established a new covenant and way to the Father, through faith in Christ (not through the law). This way is not achieved by any action of our own doing. For (as those who believe) we are now established in Christ not by any work of our own but only by the work of Jesus Christ. If we die with Christ and thus sin dies in us, we live for God as a new creation, a true son and/or daughter of God, established in His new covenant through the blood of Jesus. This is the ultimate representation of the love God has for us, that "God so loved the world, that He gave His only begotten Son, that whosoever believeth in him should not perish, but have everlasting life" (John 3:16, KJV). And this everlasting life is a life in communion with God, walking as Adam once did before the fall and as Jesus does now, with a clear conscience, without spot or blemish. This is not only a promise for future but for this moment as well. "Greater love hath no on than this, that a man lay down one's life for his friends" (John 15:13, KVJ). This is the love that God has for us!

It is not about what we can do for God to keep Him satisfied. He knows that we could never do enough to fulfill the requirements of the law. It is fully and only about what Christ has done for us. It is not about striving to try to please God, for He is pleased with His Son and all that are in His Son. It is about receiving the love that He has shown us and accepting the free gift of salvation made possible through Christ so that we may be with our loving Father now and throughout eternity. It is about walking in kingdom authority with a kingdom mentality to share and spread His love throughout the earth and thus expressing His kingdom that has come to earth as it is in heaven.

Religion is formed on earth as a way for "man" to reach out to a god, trying to please or appease a god in order to obtain favor or blessing. This is evident in all religions of the world. Even in the covenant with Moses, a law was established that appeared to have man reaching to God to remain in His favor. Tithing was a part of the law, which was a "heavy yoke" to bear and showed that no man could keep the fullness of the law, not even this portion. But God Himself promised to bring the unblemished offering as spoken about in Malachi, and through this offering, He made a way for the windows of heaven to be opened. God poured out a blessing so great that no man could contain it. This blessing is Holy Spirit and so much more. And it came through Jesus, in which is the fullness of all blessing. It is God's Glory, which is "Christ in you, the hope of Glory. Jesus did not come to establish a religion but rather to restore a relationship between us and the Father. Christianity, in the true sense, is the only faith where we don't have to strive to meet God. Through Christ God reaches out to show how much He loves us and calls us back into a loving relationship with Him.

The point is this. Do you know how much God loves you? Do you really know? He is deeply in love with you. He desires to be with you. He wants to have a relationship with the ones He created. Sure, the relationship was broken by us, but He made a way for that relationship to be restored. This relationship is not founded in rules and regulations that we must keep in order to satisfy Him. He knows all our flaws, our weaknesses, and our shortcomings, and He loves us still. He says, "Come all you who are heavy laden and I will give you rest." It is my prayer that you see and experience the deep and complete love of Abba Father. It is not conditional on doing or not doing anything, nor is it conditional on giving or not giving. It is a love that goes beyond explanation. But be careful though. When you experience His love, you will be wrecked for life…for a new life that is abandoned to the One who loves you so much. You don't need to change because He loves you just the way you are. But you will be changed in a radically awesome way. You won't need anyone to tell you that you should do this or that, or to give this amount or that amount because the lover of your soul is within you, and in Him, you will live and move and have your being. So get ready, freedom waits in the loving arms of your Heavenly Father! In Him, live. In Him, give. In Him, love. But most importantly, know that you are loved deeply by Him.

So as you read further, know that it is the Father's heart for you to know His deep and unfailing love that He has for you, a love story that He established from the beginning. It was made manifest in the person of Jesus Christ, Son of God and Son of Man, and is reaching out to you in this very moment to say, "Receive this free gift that I have given, established in My love. This love is unconditional; simply believe on Him [Jesus]." He has removed the yoke of slavery of the law. Know and rest in His love. Come boldly before His throne with confidence and be of full confidence in the love He has for you.

A Lesson from the Story of the Prodigal Son

God's love for us is personified in the parable of the Prodigal Son. This parable, told by Jesus, is so rich in meaning. At the heart of it is a picture of God's love for us in spite of what we have done. When we turn back to our Heavenly Father, He not only is there to welcome us, but He runs to meet us where we are. This parable also speaks to us with regard to the requirement of tithing.

> Jesus continued: "There was a man who had two sons. The younger one said to his father, 'Father, give me my share of the estate.' So he divided his property between them. Not long after that, the younger son got together all he had, set off for a distant country and there squandered his wealth in wild living. After he had spent everything, there was a severe famine in that whole country, and he began to be in need. So he went and hired himself out to a citizen of that country who

sent him to his fields to feed pigs. He longed to fill his stomach with the pods that the pigs were eating, but no one gave him anything. When he came to his senses, he said, 'How many of my father's hired men have food to spare, and here I am starving to death! I will set out and go back to my father and say to him: Father, I have sinned against heaven and against you. I am no longer worthy to be called your son; make me like one of your hired men.' So he got up and went to his father. But while he was still a long way off, his father saw him and was filled with compassion for him; he ran to his son, threw his arms around him and kissed him. The son said to him, 'Father, I have sinned against heaven and against you. I am no longer worthy to be called your son.' But the father said to his servants, 'Quick! Bring the best robe and put it on him. Put a ring on his finger and sandals on his feet. Bring the fattened calf and kill it. Let's have a feast and celebrate. For this son of mine was dead and is alive again; he was lost and is found.' So they began to celebrate. "Meanwhile, the older son was in the field. When he came near the house, he heard music and dancing. So he called one of the servants and asked him what was going on. 'Your brother has come,' he replied, 'and your father has killed the fattened calf because he has him back safe and sound.' The older brother became angry and refused to go in. So his father went out and pleaded with him. But he answered his father, 'Look! All these years I've been slaving for you and never disobeyed your orders. Yet you never gave me even a young goat so I could celebrate with my friends. But when this son of yours who has squandered your property with prostitutes comes home, you kill the fattened calf for him!' 'My son,' the father said, 'you are always with me, and everything I

> have is yours. But we had to celebrate and be glad, because this brother of yours was dead and is alive again; he was lost and is found." (Luke 15:11–32 NIV)

Jesus shows that as the prodigal son asked for his share of the estate, the father freely gave it to him. There were no strings attached. In particular, there was no instruction that he was to return a portion of what the father had freely given to him. There weren't instructions on how the son should or shouldn't use his portion (nor did the son ask for any guidance on this). The son went away and squandered it all on foolish things. In desperation and when he had come to his senses, the son returned to his father. As he returned, the father, full of love, ran to meet him. He received him freely and lovingly with no questions (just joy). His father did not let him become a servant but rather welcomed him back as his son. He wasn't required to repay or give any portion back that he squandered away. When the son returned, the father did not put a stipulation on giving back one-tenth of the things the father was now providing after the son's return. The son had nothing, but the loving father provided for the son's needs with love and compassion and without requirement of the son. The father was "giving" his son good things.

The other brother became angry. He had been working (slaving) for his Father and therefore felt he deserved something (out of his works). The father told his son in the passage above, "You are always with me, and everything I have is yours." This son was working to gain his father's blessing. The father said that his blessing is always there, and he didn't have to work for it. He was his son as well. As this son was busy "working," he failed to see the fullness of the blessing and provision that the father had available for him all along.

As sons (and daughters) of God, He makes everything ours: we are heirs and coheirs with Christ (Gal. 4:7). Even if we make foolish or bad decisions, He receives us as His children. It is without stipulation or the need to repay. It's a free gift that no one can earn. "For by grace are ye saved through faith; and that not of yourselves: it is the gift of God: Not of works, lest any man should boast (Eph 2:8-9, KJV).

In working to obtain our blessing, we can lose sight of the fact that our blessing, which God has given freely to us, is already there without any work on our part. It is simply because our Father loves us. As we receive, it pleases our Father's heart.

On the other hand, if we take the position of the other brother, declaring that we have worked for and so have earned His blessing (especially in bringing the tithe), our Father reminds us that His blessing has always been there for us.

This story of the prodigal son embraces all that God is and wants to be for us. In the passage above we read: "But while he was still a long way off, his father saw him and was filled with compassion for him; he ran to his son, threw his arms around him and kissed him." Know that your Heavenly Father loves you so much and does not require anything for that love, only that you believe on Him. Yet that love will inspire and spur us all on to good deeds and actions, and a heart of giving.

Giving and Tithing; What's the Difference and Why Does It Matter?

Tithing and giving are the same, right? What's the big deal? I'm giving my tithe. Aren't they the same thing? While the appearance of giving and tithing may look the same (a transfer of money), the truth is they are very different. As a friend of mine likes to say, "it is very important to place the emphasis on the correct syll·à·ble." Tithing is religious in nature; giving reflects God's heart, love, and the kingdom. When one declares themselves to be a "tither," one becomes aligned with a mind-set and thinking that is different than one who declares themselves to be a "giver." Therefore, it is important to understand what we align ourselves with and to know the difference between the two. In addition, your perception on the matter will affect your behavior, your mind-set, and your reality. As a loving parent, if you give your child a gift, would you require them to pay ten percent of the gift back to you? If you gave them something and required a return, was it really a gift, or was it more like a loan that you were expecting a return on? Even if you would require partial repayment, as a loving parent, would you curse your child if they didn't pay back the complete ten percent? At the very least, it is hard to imagine a loving father ever cursing his child any matter, let alone a ten percent requirement of return. How much more would your loving Father in heaven not curse His children if He gives us a gift.

Parents who love their children will give them good gifts and provide for their needs. As they grow, the parents teach responsibility and help them mature as they learn to go into the world. They help them develop the skills to make a good living and flourish while teaching them right from wrong and consequences that may occur when making undesirable choices. These are all things a loving parent will do "free of charge."

In a similar manner as a child who has been loved by his parents mature, he learns to give unselfishly to others, especially his parents, if they are in need. It is a "God system" of loving and giving, not a worldly system of giving expecting a return.

A friend of mine told me a story about his dog which he would often become upset with. He would unknowingly "curse" the dog, saying things like, "Stupid dog," "You are always in the way", and "You're a bad dog," etc. Of course, the dog lived up to his speaking, expectation, and cursing. Then God quickened his heart and asked, "Why do you curse your dog? I have given him to you. You should bless your dog." The man started speaking blessing over the dog like, "You are a good dog," "You are loved," etc., and lo and behold, the dog changed his behavior to match the words spoken over him! If we have a God who is always ready to curse us, our response will be reflected in our behavior, which could be fear, guilt, trepidation, or even impotency. But if we have a Father who loves us unconditionally, our response will be one of confidence and assurance that we cannot fail in His eyes, and while trying to please Him, we know that He has our back no matter what happens.

I read another story of a pastor who, early in his ministry, went to a small group gathering in which there was a young child who was acting "off the wall." She would climb all over furniture at the hosts' home, acting wild and not listening to the parents' instructions/corrections. They would say, "Tiger, don't do that," or "Tiger, do this," but the young girl did not pay much attention. As the pastor observed, he thought, *What an unruly child. She is certainly living up to her nickname—Tiger.*

A few months went by and there was another small group gathering in which this family was there again. However, this time, the young girl was quite different. She was quiet, sitting in the chair, and very well mannered. The pastor, having noticed such a marked change in the girl, approached the parents and asked, "As a young man, I anticipate having children, and I couldn't help but notice how well-mannered your child is. Can you share some of your pointers on how you are raising her?" The parents responded, saying that they came to the realization that as they had nicknamed her "Tiger," she was actually acting out just like a tiger. They decided to change her nickname to "Lamb," and that's when they started to see the change in her behavior.

The lesson here is that your name, or how you view yourself, and even how others view you, is significant in how you "show up" and in your actions. Remember, "Death and life are in the power of the tongue: and they that love it shall eat the fruit thereof" (Prov. 18:21, KJV). Do you see yourself as a "sinner" or a "sinner saved by grace," always trying to appease God or trying to climb your way out of sin? Or do you see yourself as a "child of the One True King," righteous and holy in His eyes because of Jesus? This question of itself could invoke a longer conversation, but in the context here, we act and focus on how we see ourselves, whether it be constantly reminded of sin or walking forward in the power and fullness that Christ has completed and given through his death and resurrection. So if you see yourself as a tither, you tie yourself to a certain belief and understanding of the law which is different than if you see yourself as a giver. And if you see yourself as a tither, you subject yourself to the fear that if you do not keep up your end of tithing, God (according to popular teachings) will curse you. In addition, if you do tithe, you will be expecting a reward and financial blessing from God because you have met His expectations. However, if you see yourself as a giver (as God is a giver), you give freely and unconditionally with a cheerful heart and clear conscience not out of fear but out of love. There is freedom for God to do whatever He wants to do with your gift if we are not expecting anything in return.

In addition, consider the Divine exchange of Jesus on the cross. He provided His blood as an exchange so that we who believe can be free and welcomed into God's family. Whenever there is an exchange or trade one party gives up something they have in exchange for what they want. God wanted fellowship with mankind, so he exchanged His only begotten Son. Because of this trade we are able to come back into relationship with our heavenly Father. When we bring our tithes, offerings and/or first-fruits to God in an attempt to get a greater blessing or favor with God we are actually trading away our grace for the works of the flesh/law (See Galatians 5: 1-6). Remember when Esau traded away his blessing for a meal (Genesis 27). Esau could never get his blessing back and was actually hated by God (Malachi 1:3 and Romans 9:13). However, when you truly give (freely and without expectation of a return) we are actually honoring the Devine Exchange by giving the way God gives. We are giving God's love for more of God's love, His heart for more of His heart.

Moreover, it is important (and wise) to view yourself as God sees you. And God sees you as His child, loved, spotless in Christ, blessed, a priest, a king, and an ambassador, and He receives you as you are. To suggest otherwise (either by your own view or that of another) would make God a liar, and it is impossible for Him to lie about you!

As our heavenly Father, God reveals Himself to us through His many names. These names reveal His nature and who He declares He is to those who love and follow Him. With the understanding of our relationship with God, or rather, God's relationship with us, through the new covenant, let's examine some of the names of God.

God declares He is the "Great I Am." As He shows Himself to be "I Am," He is also saying that He is our "All in All." Anything we need, He is. And He supplies for all our needs.

- Yahweh (Lord, Jehovah)
- Jehovah Nissi (The Lord My Banner)
- Jehovah Raah (The Lord My Shepherd)
- Jehovah Rapha (The Lord Who Heals)
- Jehovah Tsidkenu (The Lord Our Righteousness)
- Jehovah Mekoddishkem (The Lord Who Sanctifies You)
- Jehovah Jireh (The Lord Will Provide)

When you realize that we have obtained all these attributes (God is my Banner, my Shepherd, my Healer, my Righteousness, my Sanctifier) *only* and *completely* through the blood of Jesus, not by any act of our own, to think that we are required to gain access to Jehovah Jireh (our Provider) through the act of tithing, one should wonder how this can be. This is not consistent with the rest of the Word of God based on the redemption of the cross. Even in thinking that we have the ability to earn this provision suggests that the blood of Jesus is not complete in its redemptive value.

A "Slippery Slope"

While at a pastor's conference I was listening to a well know pastor who has a very large congregation and following. He made this statement: "The Bible says in 1 Corinthian 6:10 that thieves and robbers won't get into the Heaven. Malachi says that if you're not paying your tithe you are robbing God. So if you're not paying your tithe you will not get into heaven." I was shocked and very troubled as he made this statement. But what broke my heart even more was the number of pastors and others in the room that shouted "Amen" to what he said.

Of course, if these people would truly reflect on this pastor's statement they more than likely would realize that this assessment isn't accurate. Thank God, we are "saved by grace through faith, not by works", so our access to heaven is dependent upon the work of Jesus, not our tithing. But this is a dangerous and slippery slope that many go down when they don't have the correct understanding of the book of Malachi. There is a difference between giving and tithing, and it does matter. Take care not to follow someone down this "Slippery Slope" of misconception. If we have a "rules" relationship it develops a heart of rebellion. However, if we have a love relationship it will develop love relationships.

Tithing and the Modern Church

How Did This Happen?

As some grasp the fullness of grace afforded to us by faith in Christ, the question comes about as to how this teaching became so prevalent in the church today. I'm reminded of the story of the Korean Airline Flight KAL 007. On September 1, 1983, the passenger airliner was scheduled to fly from New York City to Seoul, Korea, by way of Anchorage, Alaska. As the plane left Anchorage, as it was later discovered, it had strayed off course by only fifteen degrees. This was such a small degree of being "off course" that it went unnoticed by the pilots. They continued on this course for over five hours. However, this small degree of being off target caused the plane to enter into Russian air space where it was shot down and all 269 passengers and crew were killed. The lesson here is that even a very small deviation from the correct path (which may not even be detectable at first) can lead to dire and even deadly consequences.

I heard a speaker share a story of how four generations ago there was virtually no mortgage debt in our country. This was the norm. In addition, there were no credit cards, and people were accustomed to living within their means and not going into debt. However, in this speaker's observation, the Spirit of Mammon arose and led people to enslave themselves into bondage by becoming a borrower and a servant to the institution of money.

This started very innocently with just a few people. Then a

few more started the practice of borrowing money to purchase houses with mortgage payments. Then parents started to teach their children, and soon it became a widely accepted and expected practice.

Proverbs 22:6–7 says, "Train up a child in the way he should go; and when he is old, he will not depart from it. The rich rules over the poor, and the borrower is servant to the lender." The children today are now being taught at an early age the practices of borrowing to obtain what they want. The unfortunate thing is that they will not readily depart from these ways. In the same way, Jesus warned, "Take heed and beware of the leaven of the Pharisees and of the Sadducees, (Mat 16:6, KJV)." Of this he was not speaking of the leaven (yeast) of bread but of the doctrine of the Pharisees and Sadducees. Jesus knew that false doctrines were being taught and that they would continue to be taught to God's followers. He knew it was important to warn the disciples not to be misled by these false teachings because they work their way into affecting the truth.

The spirit of this world continually works his way into all that he can. Consider these important institutions. Government was initially established to protect the people. While it has this as an element, a major focus has become about getting more money. In the same way, the health-care industry was established to heal and care for people. While this continues, a strong driving force has become the focus on getting money. The educational system was established to help teach people but has also become greatly focused on getting money. The church has not been immune to this. While the original purpose of the church was to care for and minister to God and people, it has also become greatly focused on how to get more money.

While tithing may seem to be a small or insignificant issue

as compared to giving, if not understood and corrected, it may lead to dire consequences for those that are "off target." As any false doctrine, if it is taught long enough through the generations, it becomes accepted and goes unquestioned. A little leaven (yeast) will ruin the entire lump (Gal. 5:9).

As one reads the New Testament, one will discover that there is no instruction given on the requirement of tithing. Tithing is mentioned twice; once when Jesus was speaking to the Pharisees and then again in the book of Hebrews. But as we will discuss later in this book, neither were intended to establish the requirement of tithing; rather they were addressing other issues. The early church understood there was no requirement to bring a tithe, offering, or first fruit offering to the temple or the church. Giving, however, was described as a condition of the heart and indicated the genuineness of one's love, as Paul writes, "I say this not as a command, but to prove by the earnestness of others that your love also is genuine" (2 Cor. 8:8) and "Each one, as he purposes in his heart, let him give; not of grief, or of necessity, for God loves a cheerful giver" (2 Cor. 9:7).

Paul did not seek favor of man through the act of the law (including tithing), as he wrote, "For now do I persuade men, or God? Or do I seek to please men? For if I yet pleased men I would not be a servant of Christ" (Gal. 1:10 KJV). Saul (as a Pharisee) followed the law. Paul (as his name was changed by God) was bound to grace. However, we find much like the requirement of circumcision tried to creep its way back in to the early church, the requirement of tithing has moved back in to the church today.

Again, tithing was not found to be taught or performed in the first church. However, a Catholic Encyclopedia establishes that tithing came back in to the church around 567 A.D:

> The payment of tithes was adopted from the Old Law, and early writers speak of it as a divine ordinance and an obligation of conscience. The earliest positive legislation on the subject seems to be contained in the letter of the bishops assembled at Tours in 567 and the canons of the Council of Maçon in 585. In course of time, we find the payment of tithes made obligatory by ecclesiastical enactments in all the countries of Christendom. (Fanning, William. "Tithes." The Catholic Encyclopedia. Vol. 14. New York: Robert Appleton Company, 1912. [Accessed September 26, 2015). http:// www.newadvent.org/cathen/14741b. html)

There could be much discussion regarding this implementation, including asking the question if this was truly biblical or was it to support the early Catholic view that included a "work-based" salvation (discussed later). As Protestants left England to gain religious freedom, there was no tithing requirement in the early church of the United States.

In his book *Should the Church Teach Tithing?* Russell Earl Kelly, PhD, shares his research regarding the history of tithing in the church. In his writing, he speaks of the book *In Pursuit of the Almighty's Dollar*, in which James Hudnut-Beumler of Vanderbilt University outlines the methods of financing the church in the United States, showing that tithing was not suggested in the church until 1873. Tithing was first introduced to the Southern Baptist Convention on May 11, 1895. The convention urged state conventions to educate the people. This system was initially *rejected* by the people (http://www.tithing-russkelly.com).

Gary J. Arnold writes in his paper "Church History and Tithing,"

A study of church history will show that at some point, probably around the year 600, the churches brought back the teaching of tithing, but only as voluntary giving, and still just on the crops, herds, and flocks, right out of the Old Testament. Since they didn't teach it as a "biblical tithe," they were able to change the rules to make it fit the needs of the church. By the middle of the 13th century, the Church's claim to tithes was extended to include the poultry of the yard and the cattle of the stall, to the catch of fish and the game of the forests. Had tithing in the Old Testament been on everything as some have claimed, there would have been no need to expand the definition.

My research shows that tithing was first taught and collected by churches in the United States during the second half of the 1800s. Had tithing always been required, why was it not until the late 1800s that the churches in the United States started collecting tithes? And even then, the teaching of tithing was not consistent between churches. It wasn't until recent years that churches started teaching that you tithe on your income, or gross income.

My research shows that during the late 1800s some churches taught that men were to tithe a larger amount than women, that no tithing was required for those under the age of 18, and once you reached the age of 65 you no longer were required to tithe. At times tithing was based on the value of property owned. Those who didn't own property didn't tithe. They gave freewill offerings. In one case I found the church council members voted to change tithing to income because it would bring in twice as much money. The problem is, all this was taught as biblical. (Arnold, 2009)

As tithing was not a requirement or part neither of the early Christian church nor of the early American church, one should consider that this alone would raise questions to the validity of the tithing requirement as the modern church would so forcefully ascribe to today.

Completing the "Reformation"

While some may declare there may be other topics that need to be addressed in order to complete the "reformation" of the church, tithing is certainly one practice that requires reformation.

In 1517, Martin Luther wrote his *Ninety-Five Theses*, attacking the Catholic Church's corrupt practices of selling "indulgences" to absolve sin. These theses addressed two main beliefs: The Bible is the main religious authority and salvation is reached only by grace through faith and not by works (Eph. 2:8–9). The practice of selling indulgences suggested (and required) that if one would bring money to the church, he or she would be given "a partial remission of the temporal punishment, especially purgatorial atonement, that is still due for a sin or sins after absolution." (Houghton Mifflin Company, 2005) There was also a great fear that was instilled to those who did not bring the money for indulgences, that their sins would not be repudiated. In other words, bring your money and you will be forgiven—don't bring your money, and you will be in sin. It was Luther's stance that "for by grace you are saved through faith, and that not of yourselves, it is the gift of God, not of works, lest anyone should boast" (Eph. 2:8–9). The requirement of buying "indulgences" was not only unbiblical but also manipulative and kept people in fear and bondage. They were taught that by bringing money to the church, they would be freed from the curse of sin.

There were many rules and regulation that Christians were to follow to prevent God's wrath and to prevent the judgment of sin from being imposed. Paying for indulgences was required to keep a proper standing with God and the church. With this understanding in mind, translations would be tempered to reflect this doctrine of requiring a certain offering. This doctrine stood for a long time (and still does in many churches) until Martin Luther stepped forward with his revelation of the *Ninety-Five Theses*, proclaiming, among other things, that we are saved by grace through faith alone, not by works, so that no man can boast. The doctrine of tithing brings on the same bondage. It is a doctrine based in works and is implemented (at least in part) through fear. It declares that if you bring your money to the church, you will be blessed, but if you don't bring your tithe, you will be cursed. Just as in the days of Martin Luther, today there is a cry to complete the reformation of the church and restore it back to God's original intent. To do this, it is necessary to come out from the bondage of tithing and into the freedom that Christ has afforded us to live and operate which is free from the law of sin and death.

The Modern-Day Circumcision

Clearly, as one reads the letters written by Paul, we can see that one of greatest challenges he faced was the fact that there were many who were attempting to bring Christians back into the bondage of the law, including the requirement of circumcision.

Paul (formerly Saul) was a Pharisee, and as a Pharisee, he knew the law as well or better than most. This included the law of tithing. Yet after Jesus came to Paul on the road to Damascus and showed him the truth, Paul unswervingly preached the good news of entering God's kingdom by grace through faith in Christ.

The issue that Paul battled regarding circumcision was about the freedom of not having to keep the law. Circumcision was the beginning of the law for the Jews. It was the first act of keeping all the law, and it was the first act of keeping the old covenant with God. It was established between God and Abraham and was a sign of God's everlasting covenant withhim.

But as Jesus revealed Himself, Saul (Paul) received the revelation that Jesus fulfilled the law and that only by relying on and having faith in His work could one enter in to a right standing (righteousness) before God. Not only was it not necessary to keep the law but to do so would insult the blood sacrifice of Jesus. In addition, Jesus revealed to Paul that He established a new covenant, not of circumcision of the flesh but of circumcision of the heart (Rom. 2:28–29) and that this new covenant, established in His blood, is better than the blood of goats (Heb. 8:6, 9:23).

Paul spoke clearly on circumcision:

> Stand fast therefore in the liberty with which Christ has made us free, and do not again be held with the yoke of bondage. Behold, I, Paul, say to you that if you are circumcised, Christ shall profit you nothing. For I testify again to every man that is circumcised, that he is a debtor to do all the Law, you who are justified by Law are deprived of all effect from Christ; you fell from grace. For we through the Spirit wait for the hope of righteousness out of faith. For in Christ Jesus neither circumcision nor uncircumcision has any strength, but faith working through love. (Gal. 5:1–6)

The issue of circumcision has clearly been "laid to rest" in Paul's writings. In addition, the issue of the requirement to follow the law (of Moses) has also been laid to rest, as we are now free from having to keep these requirements. There are those, however, as in the days of Paul's writings who would continue to have us go back to the law by means of the tithe. But clearly, this is not from the heart of God, as He has set us free from the bondages of the law, as it is written:

> But now a righteousness of God has been revealed apart from Law, being witnessed by the Law and the Prophets; even the righteousness of God through the faith of Jesus Christ, toward all and upon all those who believe. For there is no difference, for all have sinned and come short of the glory of God, being justified freely by His grace through the redemption that is in Christ Jesus; whom God has set forth to be a propitiation through faith in His blood, to declare His righteousness through the passing by of the sins that had taken place before, in the forbearance of God; for

> the display of His righteousness at this time, for Him to be just and, forgiving the one being of the faith of Jesus. Then where is the boasting? It is excluded. Through what law? Of works? No, but through the law of faith. Therefore we conclude that a man is justified by faith without the works of the Law. (Rom. 3:21–28)

Paul writes further,

> For I want you to know what a great conflict I have for you and those at Laodicea, and for as many as have not seen my face in the flesh, that their hearts might be comforted, being knit together in love, and to all riches of the full assurance of the understanding, to the full knowledge of the mystery of God, and of the Father, and of Christ; in whom are hidden all the treasures of wisdom and knowledge. And I say this that not anyone should beguile you with enticing words. For though I am absent in the flesh, yet I am with you in the spirit, rejoicing and beholding your order and the steadfastness of your faith in Christ. Therefore as you have received Christ Jesus the Lord, so walk in Him, rooted and built up in Him, and established in the faith, as you have been taught, abounding in it with thanksgiving. Beware lest anyone rob you through philosophy and vain deceit, according to the tradition of men, according to the elements of the world, and not according to Christ. For in Him dwells all the fullness of the Godhead bodily. And you are complete in Him, who is the Head of all principality and power, in whom also you are circumcised with the circumcision made without hands, in putting off the body of the sins of the flesh by the circumcision of Christ, buried with Him in baptism, in whom also you were raised through the faith of the working of God, raising Him from the dead. And you, being dead in

> your sins and the uncircumcision of your flesh, He has made alive together with Him, having forgiven you all trespasses, blotting out the handwriting of ordinances that was against us, which was contrary to us, and has taken it out of the way, nailing it to the cross. (Col. 2:1–14)

Anything that would suggest that we must perform, act or work to either establish or maintain a right standing with God to receive from Him is opposite the message of grace. Paul battled this in the early church as those from the "circumcision" group came to persuade new (and established) Christians to perform the law of circumcision and the Law of Moses to please God. Tithing is of the same persuasion as it was in the day that Paul battled the circumcision issue. It has just taken on a different name.

Jesus is the vine, we are the branches (John 15:5). Originally it was just Israel that were the branches. These branches were held to the vine not because of works, especially works of the law. Israel was a stiff-necked people and were often and continually falling away in rebellion of the heart. It has always been God's love that held the branches to the vine. And now it is His love shown through Grace and mercy that, through faith, we are attached to that vine. This is the forming of one new man, not by what we do, but by God's love, grace and mercy. It may look like we are doing something, because our positions change (physically, mentally, and spiritually), but it is God's heart that orchestrates it all.

Ephesians 5:27 tells us that Christ is returning for a "Glorious church", without spot or wrinkle, holy and without blemish. However, when we look at the church and see the imperfections we often times think that we must do something that would make the church spotless and acceptable to Jesus for His return. The only way the church can be spotless is when it is immersed and covered by the blood of Jesus. This is the only way we can be seen as spotless before God. Yet we are led to think that we are to be about making ourselves spotless before the Lord's return when, in fact, when we try to do something to make ourselves spotless, it takes us out of the blood covering and exposes us again as blemished and sinful. This is what happens when we try to gain our righteousness through any works of our own, including the work of tithing. Step back into the righteousness that is by faith alone and we again become spotless before the Lord.

Right now much of the church is unclean and exposed because of the deception of the teaching of tithing. For the church to be spotless for His return we must put off this way of thinking and renew our minds to the revelation that Christ has paid the price in full, we no longer have a requirement to fulfill. We only trust fully and completely in the finished work of the cross, entering into our rest in Him. In this position alone will God see a pure and spotless church, honoring the sacrifice of Jesus and standing ready for His return.

Don't be misled however. This is not suggesting that we have a "license to sin". We are called to a higher calling, to live according to the Spirit, not according to the flesh. Paul writes in Galatians, "For you, brethren, have been called to liberty; only do not use liberty as an opportunity for the flesh, but through love serve one another" (Gal 5:13 NKJV). So live a life that reflects Jesus, and trust that He has made you spotless. John Bevere states, "Grace gives us the power to live a holy and Godly life. Without this power we try to obtain our holiness and righteousness by our own power." Don't be caught in this "modern-day circumcision".

The Heart of the Matter

God's Word

There are many persuasive arguments that would entice one to believe that tithing is a requirement set before us by God and should be maintained and fulfilled in order to please God and/or to obtain blessing and favor before Him. While tithing was required under the law, the cross of Christ has changed everything. To assist in understanding this issue, it is critical to examine the tithe within the complete context of God's Word as well as examine what His Word says specifically about tithing. Examining these Scriptures without the proper contexts could lead to a misunderstanding of God's Word.

Contexts used to examine tithing:

1. Jesus Christ and His finished work through the cross—that we are saved by grace through faith and not by works (as written in Eph. 2:8-9) being established in the new covenant that is for those who believe and follow Him.

2. The scriptures surrounding the passage, including the meaning of the original words used in a passage.

3. The scriptures that relate to these passages.

4. God's love and the Father's heart for His children.

In addition, it is also important to keep in mind that biblical translations were done by man. These translations were and are sometimes "tempered" by the translator's understanding and/or intentions at the time. Specifically, regarding the King James translation as stated earlier, the translation was completed under the influence of the Catholic Church. At that time the Church was steeped in the misunderstanding of scripture that kept them more focused on "work-based" salvation rather than "grace-through-faith-based" salvation.

As we discover the heart of giving, it is first important to understand the heart that God has for us. Let's examine the covenants that God has made with His chosen ones over time.

God's Covenants

God is a covenant-making and covenant-keeping God. Throughout time, God has made a number of covenants with man. With each new covenant, He does not forget the older covenant but rather makes a way for the covenant to be fulfilled, which leads to restored relationship with Him.

God's Covenant with Mankind

God made a covenant with mankind from the beginning of creation:

> And God created man in His image; in the image of God He created him. He created them male and female. And God blessed them. And God said to them, Be fruitful, and multiply and fill the earth, and subdue it. And have dominion over the fish of the sea and over the fowl of the heavens, and all animals that move upon the earth. And God said, Behold! I have given you every herb seeding seed which is upon the face of all the earth, and every tree in which is the fruit of a tree seeding seed; to you it shall be for food. And to every beast of the earth, and to every fowl of the heavens, and to every creeper on the earth which has in it a living soul every green plant is for food; and it was so. (Gen. 1:27–30)

This is the original covenant and plan that God has for mankind. After God had spoken everything above, it was then said, "And it was so," which affirms the agreement (or covenant) that God had just spoken for mankind. It was God's heart to walk with man in relationship and love to bless and to keep him. Through Jesus, God has made a way for us to return to Him in this relationship. While this restoration is completed now, it will be fully expressed on the earth and in mankind when Jesus returns again in His glory.

When Adam fell into sin, God made a covenant to assure that He would make a way to bring mankind back to the proper place of dominion and relationship with God:

> And Jehovah God said to the serpent, "Because you have done this you are cursed more than all cattle, and more than every animal of the field. You shall go upon your belly, and you shall eat dust all the days of your life. And I will put enmity between you and the woman, and between your seed and her Seed; He will bruise your head, and you shall bruise His heel. And for Adam and his wife Jehovah God made coats of skins, and clothed them. (Gen. 3:14–15, 21)

In this covenant, God has promised that He will put enmity between Satan and the woman and between their seeds. Note that while it is God that is making this covenant, it is also God promising to fulfill this covenant as well when He says,"I [God] will put."

God's Covenant with Noah

After "cleansing" the earth through the flood, God made a covenant with Noah:

> And God spoke to Noah, and to his sons with him, saying, Behold! I, even I, establish My covenant with you and with your seed after you; and with every living creature that is with you, of the birds, of the cattle, and of every animal of the earth with you; from all that go out from the ark, to every animal of the earth. And I will establish My covenant with you. Neither shall all

> flesh be cut off any more by the waters of a flood. Neither shall there anymore be a flood to destroy the earth. And God said, This is the token of the covenant which I make between Me and you and every living creature with you, for everlasting generations: I set my rainbow in the cloud. And it shall be a token of a covenant between Me and the earth. And it shall be, when I bring a cloud over the earth, that the rainbow shall be seen in the cloud. And I will remember My covenant which is between Me and you and every living creature of all flesh; and the waters shall no more become a flood to destroy all flesh. And the rainbow shall be in the cloud. And I will look upon it that I may remember the everlasting covenant between God and every living creature of all flesh that is upon the earth. And God said to Noah, This is the token of the covenant which I have established between Me and all flesh that is upon the earth. (Gen. 9:8–17)

Again, God makes the covenant, and God also is the one promising that He will fulfill this covenant: "I, even I, establish My covenant with you."

God's Covenant with Abraham

God made a promise to Abram: "And I will make you a great nation, and I will bless you, and make your name great; and you shall be a blessing: and I will bless them that bless you, and curse him that curses you, and in you shall all families of the earth be blessed" (Gen. 12:2–3). Abram "believed in the Lord; and He counted it to him for righteousness" (Gen. 15:6). God made covenant with Abram and swore an oath by Himself to keep that covenant (Gen. 15:17–18). "For when God made promise to Abraham, because He could swear by no greater, He swore by Himself, saying, 'Surely in blessing I will bless you, and in multiplying I will multiply you'" (Heb. 6:13–14).

We read further:

> And God said to Abraham, And you shall keep My covenant, you and your seed after you in their generations. This is My covenant, which you shall keep, between Me and you and your seed after you. Every male child among you shall be circumcised. And you shall circumcise the flesh of your foreskin. And it shall be a token of the covenant between Me and you. (Gen. 17:9–11)

It is interesting to study this passage in more detail. When simply read, this translation appears to place the responsibility on Abraham and his seed after him to "keep" this covenant. However, in closer examination, we see a different meaning consistent with God establishing and fulfilling His covenants. "And I will establish My covenant between Me and you and your seed after you in their generations for an everlasting covenant, to be a God to you and to your seed after you" (Gen. 17:7). Here, God is declaring that He Himself will (again) establish His covenant as an everlasting covenant. God sealed His covenant with Abram, changed his name to Abraham and instructed all males to be circumcised. Then, in the passage above, God says that Abraham "shall keep" His covenant.

This word *keep* comes from the Hebrew *shâmar* (shaw-mar'), which means to hedge about (as with thorns), that is, guard; generally to protect, attend to, etc. It also means beware, be circumspect, take heed (to self), keep (-er, self), mark, look narrowly, observe, preserve, regard, reserve, save (self), sure, (that lay) wait (for), watch (-man).

In context here, God is not telling Abraham that it is up

to him to keep the covenant through circumcision, but rather that Abraham and his seed will guard, take heed, observe, wait for, and watch for this covenant as it is established as an everlasting covenant (in his seed Jesus). Again, the responsibility of keeping the covenant is upon God, not Abraham. Circumcision, similar to the rainbow, is so that all will be reminded, take heed, watch, and wait for God keeping this covenant. In this sense, it was important for those in the lineage of Abraham to continually be circumcised so that the covenant would always be remembered.

God's promise and blessing came before "seal of the covenant" of circumcision as God instructed. "Abram was very rich in cattle, in silver, and in gold" (Gen. 13:2) prior to his offering of a tithe of war spoils to Melchizedek (Gen. 14:20), and Abraham's righteousness (right standing before God) was because of faith, not of works (Gen. 15:6 and Rom. 4:13).

God's Covenant with Moses

God made a covenant with the Israelites through Moses that was conditional upon them keeping covenant:

> You have seen what I did to the Egyptians, and I bore you on eagles' wings and brought you to Myself. And now if you will obey My voice indeed, and keep My covenant, then you shall be a peculiar treasure to Me above all the nations; for all the earth is Mine. And you shall be to Me a kingdom of priests and a holy nation. These are the words which you shall speak to the sons of Israel. (Exod. 19:4–6)

Here, again, we see God, in keeping His covenant with Abraham and his seed, was the one who "bore" them on eagle's wings and brought them to Himself. Then, after

God performed this, He instructed them that if they would obey His voice and keep His covenant, then they shall be a treasure to Him above all nations. This word *keep* is the same word as used in Genesis 17:9 and described above, which means to be reminded, take heed, watch, and wait for. Even though this was conditional, it did not make the covenant that God made with Abraham conditional. The covenant would remain as promised, and it now would be fulfilled through these Israelites coming out of Egypt. God knew, however, that these were a "stiffed neck people" (Deut. 31:27, Jer. 17:23) and would lose sight of God, so He established additional requirements for them to keep (to watch and be reminded of) His covenant. Out of this came the law and instructions for the people to follow and obey so they would continually be reminded to watch for the covenant that God had established and would fulfill through His Son Jesus. In keeping watch, those who had eyes to see and ears to hear received Jesus as He came to earth as God's Son, as it was recorded in John 1:45: "Philip found Nathanael and said to him, We have found Him of whom Moses wrote in the Law and the Prophets, Jesus of Nazareth, the son of Joseph."

When we see a rainbow, we are reminded of God's covenant with Noah that He will never again destroy the earth. In a similar manner, as Abraham's seed, the Israelites were to constantly look at the "rainbow" of circumcision and the law to be reminded and watchful of God's covenant that He made and that He would keep with Abraham. Jesus is the one who they were to be watching and waiting for as it was written by Moses as God's instruction to hear His voice and "keep"His covenant.

God's "New Covenant" with Mankind through Jesus

God's Word tells us: "But when the fullness of the time came, God sent forth His Son, coming into being out of a woman, having come under Law, that He might redeem those under Law, so that we might receive the adoption of sons" (Gal. 4:4–5). Through Jesus, the long-awaited and watched for promise of God's covenant was fulfilled. In this fulfilling, a new covenant was established with mankind. This covenant was made possible through Jesus fulfilling the Law of Moses (Matt. 5:17, Exod. 19:5) and reestablished a way for us to be part of the covenant God made with Abraham, a covenant that was not based upon condition of the law but established by grace through faith: "Therefore it is of faith so that it might be according to grace; for the promise to be made sure to all the seed, not only to that which is of the Law, but to that also which is of the faith of Abraham, who is the father of us all" (Rom. 4:16).

This covenant established by grace through faith is confirmed again in Ephesians:

> For by grace you are saved through faith, and that not of yourselves, it is the gift of God, not of works, lest anyone should boast. But now in Christ Jesus you who were once afar off are made near by the blood of Christ. For He is our peace, He making us both one, and He has broken down the middle wall of partition between us, having abolished in His flesh the enmity (the Law of commandments contained in ordinances) so that in Himself He might make the two into one new man, making peace between them; and so that He might reconcile both to God in one body by the cross, having slain the enmity in Himself. (Eph. 2: 8–9, 13–16)

Again Paul establishes this as he writes to the Galatians:

> O foolish Galatians, who bewitched you not to obey the truth, to whom before your eyes Jesus Christ was written among you crucified? This only I would learn from you: Did you receive the Spirit by works of the law, or by hearing of faith? Are you so foolish? Having begun in the Spirit, do you now perfect yourself in the flesh? Did you suffer so many things in vain, if indeed it is even in vain? Then He supplying the Spirit to you and working powerful works in you, is it by works of the law, or by hearing of faith? Even as Abraham believed God, and it was counted to him for righteousness. Therefore know that those of faith, these are the sons of Abraham. And the Scripture, foreseeing that God would justify the nations through faith, preached the gospel before to Abraham, saying, "In you shall all nations be blessed." So then those of faith are blessed with faithful Abraham. For as many as are out of works of the Law, these are under a curse; for it is written, "Cursed is everyone who does not continue in all things which are written in the Book of the Law, to do them." But that no one is justified by the Law in the sight of God is clear, for, "The just shall live by faith." But the Law is not of faith; but, "The man who does these things shall live in them." Christ redeemed us from the curse of the Law, being made a curse for us (for it is written, "Cursed is everyone having been hanged on a tree"); so that the blessing of Abraham might be to the nations in Jesus Christ, and that we might receive the promise of the Spirit through faith. Brothers, I speak according to man, a covenant having been ratified, even among mankind, no one sets aside or adds to it. And to Abraham and to his Seed the promises were spoken. It does not say, And to seeds, as of many; but as of one, "And to your Seed," which

> is Christ. And I say this, A covenant having been ratified by God in Christ; the Law (coming into being four hundred and thirty years after) does not annul the promise, so as to abolish it. For if the inheritance is of Law, it is no more of promise; but God gave it to Abraham by way of promise. Why then the Law? It was added because of transgressions, until the Seed should come to those to whom it had been promised, being ordained through angels in the Mediator's hand. But the Mediator is not a mediator of one, but God is one. Is the Law then against the promises of God? Let it not be said! For if a law had been given which could have given life, indeed righteousness would have been out of Law. But the Scripture shut up all under sin, so that the promise by faith of Jesus Christ might be given to those who believe. But before faith came, we were kept under Law, having been shut up to the faith about to be revealed. So that the Law has become a trainer of us until Christ, that we might be justified by faith. But faith coming, we are no longer under a trainer. For you are all sons of God through faith in Christ Jesus. For as many as were baptized into Christ, you put on Christ. There cannot be Jew nor Greek, there is neither bond nor free, there is no male nor female; for you are all one in Christ Jesus. And if you are Christ's, then you are Abraham's seed and heirs according to the promise. (Gal. 3:1–29)

Paul is instructing the Galatians not to be misled and fall back into the bondage of the law but rather to rely on faith in and through Jesus for justification before God to enter into the covenant and promises that God had given Abraham. It is according to God's promise that we enter in through faith rather than through the works of the law.

In Hebrews, it is emphasized that this new covenant established in and by Jesus is greater than the old covenant:

> But now He has obtained a more excellent ministry, by so much He is also the Mediator of a better covenant, which was built upon better promises. For if that first covenant had been without fault, then no place would have been sought for the second. For finding fault with them, He said to them, "Behold, days are coming, says the Lord, and I will make an end on the house of Israel and on the house of Judah; a new covenant shall be, not according to the covenant that I made with their fathers in the day I took hold of their hand to lead them out of the land of Egypt," because they did not continue in My covenant, and I did not regard them, says the Lord. "For this is the covenant that I will make with the house of Israel after those days, says the Lord: I will put My Laws into their mind and write them in their hearts, and I will be their God, and they shall be My people. And they shall not each man teach his neighbor, and each man his brother, saying, Know the Lord, for all shall know Me, from the least to the greatest. For I will be merciful to their unrighteousness, and their sins and their iniquities I will remember no more." In that He says, A new covenant, He has made the first one old. Now that which decays and becomes old is ready to vanish away. (Heb. 8:6–13)

This new covenant is different than the covenant God made through Moses when He led them out of Egypt. Even though the people did not continue in God's covenant, God stayed true to His word when He spoke that "after those days," He would make a new covenant, and this new covenant is without the regulations of the old (including tithing).

In all of this, we see that God is indeed a covenant-keeping God. It is out of His love for us that He keeps His covenant(s). And it is out of His love for us and His knowledge of our weakness that He fulfills His covenants even when we cannot fulfill the requirements of the covenant on our own. God has not only made the covenant(s) between Himself and man, but He has made a way to keep and fulfill them by and through Himself apart from the works of any man.

Understanding God's Law

With the limitations of the English language, there can be confusion regarding the full meaning and direction of some of the words and language used in God's Word. This can be true even when discussing and hearing about God's law. Often, the mention of the law brings confusion or comingles Moses's law with God's law of the Ten Commandments and even Christ's commandment(s). But they are very different. This explanation comes from preparingforeternity.com. (preparing for eternity, 2015)

> Many people often confuse or comingle the Law of Moses with God 's Law or the 10 Commandments. However they are quite different and distinct. Moses' law was the temporary, ceremonial law of the Old Testament. It regulated the priesthood, sacrifices, rituals, meat and drink offerings, etc., all of which foreshadowed the cross. This law was added "till the seed should come," and that seed was Christ (Galatians 3:16, 19). The ritual and ceremony of Moses' law pointed forward to Christ's sacrifice. When He died, this law was fulfilled and thus the fulfilling of God's covenant with Abraham and his seed. But the Ten Commandments (God's law) "stand fast for ever and ever" (Psalm 111:7, 8).

As described earlier, the Mosaic Law was established not as much to "keep" the covenant but rather to watch for and remember constantly the covenant that God had established and promised that He would keep.

God's law (the Ten Commandments) is summed up in what Jesus said: "Jesus said to him, You shall love the Lord your God with all your heart, and with all your soul, and with all your mind. This is the first and great commandment. And the second is like it, You shall love your neighbor as yourself. On these two commandments hang all the Law and the Prophets" (Matt. 22:37–40).

This is clearly and distinctly different from the Law of Moses, which is the ceremonial law spoken of when Jesus said to them, "And He said to them, These are the words which I spoke to you while I was still with you, that all things must be fulfilled which were written in the Law of Moses and in the Prophets and in the Psalms about Me. And He opened their mind to understand the Scriptures" (Luke 24:44–45). The act of not following the law of Moses brought a curse on the people as it is written in the law of Moses. This curse was removed when "Christ redeemed us from the curse of the Law, being made a curse for us (for it is written, 'Cursed is everyone having been hanged on a tree')"(Gal. 3:13).

When Jesus says to "keep my commandments," He is referring to the Ten Commandments. These commandments are summed up in the two: love God and love others. He is not suggesting that we keep the commandments or Law of Moses, which Jesus did not come to destroy but rather to fulfill. Through Him we would no longer be held to the requirement of this Mosaic law. Again, to clarify, when Jesus instructed to keep the law, He was referring to the commandments of loving God and loving others. It is important to keep these two laws separate, as the one law remains while the other is fading away.

The Purpose of the Mosaic Law

We know the Law of Moses held many purposes. While this is a simplified explanation, it provided for the Levitical tribe so they could continually tend to the temple and sacrifices required by God. It was a continual reminder to God's people of the sacrifice required for the atonement of sin. It was also in place to show that no one man (except for Jesus) could fully keep the law that would be pleasing to God, and if you broke one part of the law, you broke the whole law. The law abounded so that sin would be exposed. The law was to be kept until it would be fulfilled by Messiah, God's sent and chosen one. Jesus said, "Do not think that I have come to destroy the Law or the Prophets. I have not come to destroy but to fulfill" (Matt. 5:17).

As stated above, through Jesus fulfilling the law, He has made a better way and a way for us to enter in to this new covenant with God. However, as stated in Heb. 8:12, the old covenant with its laws and regulations is "ready to vanish." Being "ready" also indicates that it has not gone away as of yet. So if it has not vanished, it must still have a purpose. We read:

> But we know that the law is good if a man uses it lawfully, knowing this, that the law is not made for a righteous one, but for the lawless and disobedient, for the ungodly and for sinners, for unholy and profane, for murderers of fathers and murderers of mothers, for manslayers, for fornicators, for homosexuals, for slave-traders, for liars, for perjurers, and anything else that is contrary to sound doctrine, according to the glorious gospel of the blessed God, which was committed to my trust. (1 Tim. 1:8–11) But we know that whatever things the Law says, it says to those who are under the Law; so that every mouth may be stopped and all the world may be under judgment before God, because by the works of the Law none of all flesh will be justified in His sight; for through the Law is the knowledge of sin. But now a righteousness of God has been revealed

> apart from Law, being witnessed by the Law and the Prophets; even the righteousness of God through the faith of Jesus Christ, toward all and upon all those who believe. For there is no difference, for all have sinned and come short of the glory of God, being justified freely by His grace through the redemption that is in Christ Jesus; whom God has set forth to be a propitiation through faith in His blood, to declare His righteousness through the passing by of the sins that had taken place before, in the forbearance of God; for the display of His righteousness at this time, for Him to be just and, forgiving the one being of the faith of Jesus. Then where is the boasting? It is excluded. Through what law? Of works? No, but through the law of faith. Therefore we conclude that a man is justified by faith without the works of the Law. (Rom. 3:19–28) "But the Law entered so that the offense might abound. But where sin abounded, grace did much more abound, so that as sin has reigned to death, even so grace might reign through righteousness to eternal life by Jesus Christ our Lord" (Rom. 5:20–21).

In other words, the law remains to show that no man can be justified by the law. Again, we are reminded in Ephesians 2:8 that we are saved by grace through faith and not by works. However, if one would choose to try to gain a "right standing" with God through the keeping the law, there is a warning:

> Stand fast therefore in the liberty with which Christ has made us free, and do not again be held with the yoke of bondage. Behold, I, Paul, say to you that if you are circumcised, Christ shall profit you nothing. For I testify again to every man that is circumcised, that he is a debtor to do all the Law, you who are justified by Law are deprived of all effect from Christ; you fell

from grace. (Gal. 5:1–4)

Jesus tells us that nobody puts new cloth with an old garment because it will make it worse than it was. In the same way we are not to put new wine in an old wineskin, but rather new wine should only go into new wineskins so that both the old wine (in the old wineskin) and the new wine are preserved. (Matt. 9:16–17). In the same manner, the new and the old covenants cannot be mixed. While both are preserved, they must remain separate in order to have their value and purpose. The old covenant (the covenant of Moses) was established and remains to show that no man can be justified by the law. This leads to Jesus, the way, the truth, and the life that is established in the new covenant.

The Law of the Covenant (through Jesus)

For one to fulfill the law of the covenant through Jesus is much different than fulfilling the law of Moses. Moses and the people of Israel were given a book of laws to follow in order to maintain watch over the covenant and favor with God (Deut. 28:58–63). However, no man was able to fulfill the "heart" of the law on his own. Jesus came, not only to fulfill the law (and thus fulfill the instruction of the covenant) but to make way for a greater covenant. "But the Law entered so that the offense might abound. But where sin abounded, grace did much more abound, so that as sin has reigned to death, even so grace might reign through righteousness to eternal life by Jesus Christ our Lord" (Rom. 5:20–21). "In that He says, 'A new covenant', He has made the first one old. Now that which decays and becomes old is ready to vanish away" (Heb. 8:12).

Of course, the only way to enter into this new covenant (and not be under the instructions of the law) is by the grace of God through faith in Jesus. It is written, "Jesus said to him, I am the Way, the Truth, and the Life; no one comes to the Father but by Me" (Joh 14:6). Likewise it is written "And it shall be that everyone who shall call upon the name of the Lord shall be saved" (Acts 2:21). The commandment that Jesus gives in this new covenant is to love one another: "I give you a new commandment, that you love one another. As I have loved you, you should also love one another" (John 13:34). "If you fulfill the royal Law according to the Scripture, 'You shall love your neighbor as yourself,' you do well" (James 2:8). "Bear one another's burdens, and so you will fulfill the Law of Christ" (Gal. 6:2). "But the end of the commandment is love out of a pure heart, and a good conscience, and faith unfeigned" (1 Tim. 1:5). "But the fruit of the Spirit is: love, joy, peace, long-suffering, kindness, goodness, faith, meekness, self- control; against such things there is no law" (Gal. 5:22–23). Here we see that in the new covenant established through Jesus there are no requirements, only love. There is no requirement to tithe or bring a certain amount or percentage of money.

However, when true love abides in us the natural outpouring is to give, not out of necessity, but out of love. This relates to Paul's instruction to give as you purpose in your heart (2 Cor. 9:7).

The Tithe Defined

In light of the new covenant and God's attributes, let's explore tithing, how it is taught and how it relates to the new-covenant Christian. A tithe, by definition, is one-tenth of something. To better understand what the biblical tithe is referring to, it is important to see what God's Word says regarding this.

There are basically three types of tithes mentioned throughout Scripture:

1. Abramic tithe
2. Jacob's tithe
3. Levitical tithe

It is important to understand that tithing is mentioned before the law. However, as one will see, tithing before the law is quite different than tithing established in the Law of Moses and as in the Levitical tithe, which is the type of tithe referenced in the book of Malachi.

Tithing before the Law

There are two mentions of a tithe before the implementation of the Mosaic Law and Levitical tithe. These tithes are associated with Abraham (Abram) and Jacob.

The Abramic tithe

In Genesis 14 we read the account of Abraham that includes his tithe to Melchizedek:

> And the king of Sodom went out to meet him after his return from the slaughter of Chedorlaomer, and of the kings that *were* with him, at the valley of Shaveh, which *is* the king's dale. And Melchizedek king of Salem brought forth bread and wine: and he *was* the priest of the most high God. And he blessed him, and said, Blessed *be* Abram of the most high God, possessor of heaven and earth: And blessed be the most high God, which hath delivered thine enemies into thy hand. And he gave him tithes of all. And the king of Sodom said unto Abram, Give me the persons, and take the goods to thyself. And Abram said to the king of Sodom, I have lift up mine hand unto the LORD, the most high God, the possessor of heaven and earth, That I will not *take* from a thread even to a shoelatchet, and that I will not take any thing that *is* thine, lest thou shouldest say, I have made Abram rich: Save only that which the young men have eaten, and the portion of the men which went with me, Aner, Eshcol, and Mamre; let them take their portion. (Gen 14:17-24 KJV)

This passage is often referenced to establish the importance of tithing today. One reason given is that because Abram tithed it has become part of the covenant with God. Because this occurred before the law was given to Moses, it is taught to be a lasting requirement even though Jesus has come and fulfilled the law. The law of first mention is often applied to this tithe, suggesting that when something is first mentioned in God's Word, it holds additional "weight" and shows God's heart in a matter. In addition, it is used as an example that there is blessing in tithing.

But as we examine the entire context, we see specifically that Abram brought forward a tenth of only the spoils of war (not of his own possessions) (see Heb. 7:4, discussed later). Of additional interest is the examination of the word "all" as it reads "he gave him tithes of all". In the Hebrew, this word "all" is actually represented by two words, H4480 and H3605. The first Hebrew word for this combined word means "a part of". The second portion of the word "all" means "whole". This word "whole" (H3605) is the same word used in Malachi 3:10 and, as we will discuss later, can indicate a condition rather than an amount (meaning whole, complete, perfect, unblemished). So, if we were to better translate this sentence it would read "he gave him a tithe of "the part of the best unblemished, perfect".

Also, note that the blessing came first, then the gift. The gift was not required but was given as a "free will" gift. It is important to note that it was not an offering but rather a gift. An offering in itself suggests the giving of something to appease or expect a return while a gift is free with no expectation in return. Also, note that Abram kept none of the spoils for himself. After he gave a tithe to Melchizedek, he gave the rest of the spoils away. He allowed his men to have their share and gave the rest to the king of Sodom. Also, note that there is no indication that the men who received their share were asked, required, or even compelled to give a tithe of their portion to either king. In addition, there is no other mention in the scriptures of Abram (or Abraham) returning to bring a tithe to Melchizedek after any other victory, blessing, gain, harvest, sale, increase, or after receiving any income. And there is no other indication in Scripture that Abram (or Abraham) gave a tithe to anyone else at any other time. It is sometimes taught that the tithe (ten percent) was the king's portion. However the king of Sodom apparently received a much greater portion than did Melchizedek.

As a law of first mention, it is clear that this tithe is a free-will gift, expecting nothing in return. Rather, it was a response to the blessing that Melchizedek first gave Abram. Therefore, if we are to put a greater weight on this first mention of tithing in Scripture, it would follow that we are not instructed by God, priest, or man to give a tithe but to rather give freely without expectation out of the blessing that God has given us.

It is clear that God's promise was to bless Abram even before Abram did anything to deserve such a blessing:

> The Lord had said to Abram, "Leave your country, your people and your father's household and go to the land I will show you." I will make you into a great nation and I will bless you; I will make your name great, and you will be a blessing. I will bless those who bless you, and whoever curses you I will curse; and all peoples on earth will be blessed through you." So Abram left, as the Lord had told him; and Lot went with him. Abram was seventy-five years old when he set out from Haran. (Gen. 12:1–4, NIV)

Furthermore, there is no indication that this sets a precedent for this type of tithing to continue beyond the law or that Abraham ever spoke of or taught his son Isaac the requirement of tithing. And there is no mention of Isaac ever tithing. Isaac was also greatly blessed of God as described in Genesis 26:13-14 where he had a great number of flocks, herds, and servants; so much that even the Philistines were envious of him.

If tithing was viewed to be a critically required and established principle set forth by God at that time (as was circumcision), surely, Isaac would have been instructed on this, and there would be record of him keeping this requirement. In addition, if this type of tithe were to continue, it would stand that it should be only of the spoils, and it would be a free-will gift, not one that God requires. Similarly, if this were a valid argument, then it would stand to reason that circumcision should also continue beyond the law since it was the actual sign of the covenant God made with Abraham before the law. God even gave instruction that circumcision should continue throughout the generations (Gen. 17:9–11). However, Paul specifically addressed this issue of circumcision in the New Testament as not being a requirement for the Gentiles (Christians) to be burdened with (Acts 15:28–29).

The other place that we read about the account of Abraham's tithe is in the New Testament book of Hebrews. We will discuss this in greater detail later in the book, but it is helpful to mention it here as well. However, as we read about this account it is important to understand that as the writer of Hebrews talks about Abraham's tithe he is using this to establish the position and greatness of Jesus, not to establish the need or requirement to tithe today. Nevertheless, we can glean some additional information regarding this tithe that Abraham brought to Melchizedek.

We read in Hebrews:

> For this Melchisedec, king of Salem, priest of the most high God, who met Abraham returning from the slaughter of the kings, and blessed him; To whom also Abraham gave a tenth part of all; first being by interpretation King of righteousness, and after that also King of Salem, which is, King of peace; (Heb 7:1-2 KJV)

Again, while this description is being used to establish Jesus, we read the account that “Abraham gave a tenth part of all”, which is consistent with the scripture in Genesis. The word “gave” is from the Greek word “merizo” (G3307 Strong’s Concordance) which actually means “give part”. The words written as “tenth part” are from G1181 meaning tenth or tithe, and the word all (from G3956) means “all or whole”.

We read in Hebrews 7:4 that “Abraham gave the tenth of the spoils”. This word “spoils” is from the Greek word “akrothinian” (G205 Strong’s Concordance) which means “the top of the heap, that is, the best of the booty”. The understanding of this word also supports that fact that this tithe was not simply a tenth of “all” of the spoils of war, but it was the best part, the unblemished and perfect part of the spoils.

So placed in proper order, this scripture would read, “To whom also Abraham gave part of a tenth/tithe of the whole (unblemished, perfect condition) top of the heap, best part of the booty”. When written like this the passage is an accurate match to what was written in the book of Genesis and brings about a different understanding about what this tithe represented.

As we read further we find the author stating,

> “And if I may say so, Levi, also, who receives tithes, paid tithes in Abraham. For he was still in the loins of his father when Melchizedek met him.” (Heb 7:9-10 MKJV)

Now, considering the tithes that Levi both received and paid, these were specific through the law of Moses. These tithes (as we will discuss in greater detail later) were only tithes of the things from the land, like livestock and grain; they were never money. So the tithe that Abraham brought had to be consistent with the tithe that Levi would bring, otherwise it would not be a valid comparison that the author brought forth in this passage. In other words Abraham's tithe would have been the same type of tithe that the Levites received and paid. It would have been livestock and grain, which had the purpose to be used for a sacrifice for the Lord. In addition, as we understand the Levitical tithe, the Levites received tithes from the people. These tithes were generally a random tenth part of livestock and grain. However, the tithe that the Levites were to present to the Lord was to be an unblemished, spotless tenth portion of all the tithes they received from the people. In other words, the tithes the Levites presented were to be "the top of the heap, the best of the tithes". This is consistent with what Abraham would have presented to Melchizedek.

Abraham's tithe was a free will gift and came after the blessing. If applying the law of first mention, we see that Abraham's tithe would not be required by any of Abraham's seed. Rather it was initiated by the giver as a free-will gift. This pattern shows clearly that a requirement that would carry over to the followers of Christ. By definition, if it were a requirement, it would not be by one's free will. If anything, it shows an example of giving out of the abundance and blessing of what God has done first, not as a requirement. In other words, this gift would be done as one would purpose in his/her heart.

Jacob's tithe

In Genesis 28 we read of Jacob's encounter when he vowed to pay a tithe:

> And he dreamed. And behold! A ladder was set up on the earth, and the top of it reached to Heaven! And behold! The angels of God *were* ascending and descending on it! And behold! Jehovah stood above it, and said, I *am* Jehovah, the God of Abraham your father, and the God of Isaac! The land on which you lie I will give to you and to your seed. And your seed shall be like the dust of the earth, and you shall spread abroad to the west, and to the east, and to the north, and to the south. And in you and in your Seed shall all the families of the earth be blessed. And, behold, I *am* with you, and will keep you in every *place* where you go, and will bring you again into this land. For I will not leave you until I have done that which I have spoken of to you. And Jacob awakened from his sleep. And he said, Surely Jehovah is in this place, and I did not know. And he was afraid, and said, How fearful *is* this place! This *is* nothing but the house of God, and this *is* the gate of Heaven! Early the next morning Jacob took the stone he had placed under his head and set it up as a pillar and poured oil on top of it. He called that place Bethel, though the city used to be called Luz. Then Jacob made a vow, saying, "If God will be with me and will watch over me on this journey I am taking and will give me food to eat and clothes to wear so that I return safely to my father's house, then the Lord will be my God and this stone that I have set up as a pillar will be God's house, and of all that you give me I will give you a tenth." (Gen. 28:12–22 NIV)

This passage is also used to teach that there is blessing in the tithe, and one must tithe to gain access to God's blessing. In addition, it is suggested that this tithe is a continuation of the tithe given by Abram (Abraham), supporting the argument that it is to continue even past the law of Moses.

However, we see that Jacob's tithe was a conditional tithe,- as he specifically said, "And of all that You shall give me, I will surely give the tenth to You." This requires more investigation to gain understanding about what Jacob has promised. Before we look at this tithe, let's look closer at these vows that Jacob made.

In Jacob's dream the Lord spoke to him, saying, "The land on which you lie I will give to you and to your seed. And your seed shall be like the dust of the earth, and you shall spread abroad to the west, and to the east and to the north, and to the south. And in you and your Seed shall all the families of the earth be blessed." (Gen 28:13-14). Here, it is clear that God is showing Jacob His plan and promise for his future; for the land that God will give him and the blessing that Jacob's lineage will be on earth. Then God makes a promise for 'the now': "And behold, I am with you, and will keep you in every place where you go, and will bring you again into this land. For I will not leave you until I have done that which I have spoken of to you." (Gen 28:15)

We can see that Jacob understood these as two separate promises from God by the way Jacob responds. As he awakens and realized that the place he rested was "the House of God" he "vowed a vow, saying, If God will be with me, and will keep me in this way that I go and will give me bread to eat and clothing to put on, and I come again to my father's house in peace, then shall Jehovah be my God." (Gen 28:20-21) Jacob is responding to the second part of God's promise for him. As Jacob was greatly afraid to face his brother again (as we read in Genesis 32). As we read above, God declares, "I *am* Jehovah, the God of Abraham your father, and the God of Isaac!" It's interesting to note that God is not yet seen as the God of Jacob. But as God promised that He would be with Jacob, Jacob responded by saying if you will be with me, take care of me, and bring me back to "my father's house in peace" then You shall be my God. This is the first vow that Jacob makes with God, and it is a conditional vow; if You (God) will, then I (Jacob) will respond.

In reading further of the account of Jacob we see clearly that God was with Jacob as he flourished. After "wrestling with God, God changed Jacob's name to Israel and brought him back to his father's house, where Esau was. And there was peace between he and his brother. As God showed himself to fulfill this promise to Jacob (now Israel), he built an altar and declared that the Lord was now his God: "And he [Jacob] bought a parcel of a field, where he had spread his tent, at the hand of the children of Hamor, Shechem's father, for a hundred pieces of money. And he erected there an altar, and called it Elelohe-Israel [which means God of Israel].(Gen 33:19-20 KJV) It is also confirmed that Jacob new that God had kept his promise as he states in Genesis 35:3, "And let us arise, and go up to Bethel; and I will make there an altar unto God, who answered me in the day of my distress, and was with me in the way which I went."

After such a great encounter with God and knowing how God fulfilled his promise to take care of Jacob, one would think that Jacob would surely keep his vows to God. Of course, we just read how he kept his first vow, which was that God would be his God. But what about Jacob's second vow to give a tithe? Surely Jacob would not keep this part of his vow to God after all that the Lord had done for him. Yet there is no account of Jacob giving a tithe to the Lord. However, as we look closer we gain a proper understanding of this part of the vow and its fulfillment.

First of all, it is important to understand that Jacob's vow of giving a tithe was based on a different condition that stated earlier. Jacob was likely aware of the promise that God made to Abraham: "And Jehovah appeared to Abram and said, I will give this land to your seed. And he built an altar there to Jehovah who appeared to him." (Gen 12:7 MKJV) The land God was referring to, as stated in Gen 12:5, was the land of Canaan. This is the same land that God promised to Isaac's seed as well. We find, however, that as God continued to promise Abraham and Isaac, that He would give this land of Canaan to them and their seed, they never possessed this land. They were only sojourners in this land. And now God is declaring that He will keep the promise He made to Abraham and Isaac through Jacob, declaring again that "the land on which you lie I will give to you and your seed." (Gen 28:14)

After Jacob vows a vow conditional upon God fulfilling the second part of His promise (as discussed earlier), Jacob now makes another vow to the Lord: "all that You shall give me, I will surely give the tenth to you". When Jacob says, "all that You shall give me" he is referring to "the land on which you lie on I will give to you and to your seed". This was an additional 'vow' and separate to the other vow. And it was also conditional in that he said, "all that you shall give me (of the promised land) I will surely give the tenth to You."

We have discussed earlier how this promise to Jacob was a promise looking to the future. In addition, as we read throughout the book of Genesis, we find that Jacob never directly received the inheritance of the land God promised to him and his forefathers Abraham and Isaac. While Jacob would have surely kept his vow to give a tenth (because it was conditional upon God giving him the land) Jacob never saw the condition fulfilled that would cause him to give his tithe. God's promise to give the land to Abraham, Isaac, and

Jacob only began to come to fruition as God brought the Israelites out of Egypt through Moses. As Jacob's seed prepared to enter into the "promised land" God remembered the vow that Jacob made to Him and put the regulation in place for Jacob's seed to keep this vow. The Mosaic Law was formed, which included bringing a tithe of those things from the land. Specifically it was of those things from "the promised land", the land which God said He would give to His people. We read in Leviticus, "And all the tithe of the land, *whether* of the seed of the land, *or* of the fruit of the tree, *is* the LORD'S: *it is* holy unto the LORD." (Lev. 27:30)

As the Israelites were instructed to bring a tithe of everything from the land, the Levites were also instructed to bring a tenth of this tithe to the Lord. Examining the original Hebrew regarding Jacob's vow of a tithe, it is interesting to note that this word is written twice. In other words, the original translation states, "all that you shall give me I will surely give the tithe tithe to You." This indicates that Jacob vows to give a tenth of the tenth of all God promised to give him. In proper understanding, this is consistent with what Abraham gave as a tithe (a part of the best part) and what the Levitical tithe would be to the Lord (the unblemished, spotless tithe of the tithe).

While Jacob's vow to tithe was conditional, Abraham's (Abram's) tithe came only after the blessing was given. This infers that if God did not bless Abraham or give to Jacob first, there would be no offer of a tithe. It is also important to note that God did not say, "I will bless you" or "I will give you", and out of that blessing or giving, you will give Me a tithe." It is also interesting to note that this tithe is given after a blessing or promise, not out of a need or requirement to bring a tithe and/or to obtain a blessing or promise. In other words, Jacob does not tithe on what he doesn't have, he says he will tithe from all that God will give him (the land). Jacob doesn't tithe in order to satisfy a condition that would cause God to bless him.

As Jacob never received the gift of the promised land (leaving the condition for his tithe unfulfilled), there is no record of him keeping his vow to tithe to the Lord. The Levitical tithe, however, became the fulfillment of Jacob's vow to God as the Israelites prepared and entered into the promised land. Because Jacob himself never entered into this promised land, God instituted "the law" so that this vow would be fulfilled by his seed.

It is generally well understood that Christians are no longer bound to keep the Mosaic Law. Jesus didn't come to abolish the law, but to fulfill it. As He fulfilled the law, He fulfilled the vow that Jacob made to God, so that those that are in Christ are no longer required to continue fulfilling this vow (law) made by Jacob. However, as mentioned earlier, it is taught that because both Abram (Abraham) and Jacob tithed before the Mosaic Law, if one invokes the law of first mention this commandment should continue through the new covenant. The inconsistency, however, is that if we were to hold to this argument we would need to go back to the first intention of the tithe in each of these cases. ***Jacob's tithe, although established by his free will, became the requirement of the law so as to honor what Jacob had vowed to do if God kept His promise to give him (and his seed) the land.*** While one might argue that this is reason for Jacob's tithe to continue we know as Christians we are no longer under the law, but under grace (through faith in Christ). In addition, if it were to continue it would only be of things from the land (livestock and grain) and not of money.

If one were to look at circumcision through the law of first mention, one could argue that circumcision is required today because it was required by God before the Mosaic law. However, it is well established by Paul in his letters of the New Testament that circumcision is not required (more on that later). And again, we see Abel's blood offering of a "firstling" (Genesis 4:4) was acceptable and pleasing to the Lord, yet we know that we are no longer required (nor is it desirable to the Lord) for us to continue to bring a blood sacrifice of livestock before him. So again, we can see that this argument of first mention to establish tithing as a requirement in either case is not valid.

Tithing and the Law

We have learned that prior to Jacob's vow Abraham's tithe was given freely. It was not a requirement of God, and it was not done to receive anything from God but rather was given after a blessing was received. However, as a result of Jacob's vow, the Mosaic Law was established, and tithing became a requirement of God's people. This was necessary so that Jacob's vow would be fulfilled by his seed.

The Levitical Tithe

Here we read of the establishment of the Levitical tithe:

> "A tithe of everything from the land, whether grain from the soil or fruit from the trees, belongs to the Lord; it is holy to the Lord. If a man redeems any of his tithe, he must add a fifth of the value to it. The entire tithe of the herd and flock—every tenth animal that passes under the shepherd's rod—will be holy to the Lord. He must not pick out the good from the bad or make any substitution. If he does make a

> substitution, both the animal and its substitute become holy and cannot be redeemed." These are the commands the Lord gave Moses on Mount Sinai for the Israelites. (Lev. 27:30–34 NIV)

This is one of many passages that point to the fact that tithing has become part of the law. Here is where the commandment to tithe comes forth. This tithe, however, has a completely different directive than what was previously discussed in the Abramic tithe. Remember that before this time, the tithe given by Abram was a free-will gift, and Jacob's pledge to tithe was conditional upon God giving the land to him and his seed.

In addition, it is important to examine the directive of this Levitical tithe, to whom it was to be given and what was to be included in the tithe.

Who was to collect the tithe?

We read God's instruction on who was to collect the tithe:

> The Lord said to Aaron, "You will have no inheritance in their land, nor will you have any share among them; I am your share and your inheritance among the Israelites. "I give to the Levites all the tithes in Israel as their inheritance in return for the work they do while serving at the Tent of Meeting. From now on the Israelites must not go near the Tent of Meeting, or they will bear the consequences of their sin and will die. It is the Levites who are to do the work at the Tent of Meeting and bear the responsibility for offenses against it. This is a lasting ordinance for the generations to come. They will receive no inheritance

> among the Israelites. Instead, I give to the Levites as their inheritance the tithes that the Israelites present as an offering to the Lord. That is why I said concerning them: 'They will have no inheritance among the Israelites.'" (Num. 18:20–24 NIV)

Here, we see that the tithe was given only to and through the Levites. It was unlawful for anyone else to receive or command the tithe. Since there is no longer a Levitical priesthood (Jesus established a new priesthood (Heb. 7:12), there is no longer one to receive the tithe as the law prescribes. Because of this fact, today most Jews believe it's a sin to tithe.

Some would argue that as followers of Christ, we are the new Levitical priesthood (1 Pet. 2:9 says we are a "royal priesthood"), and so in this reasoning it would follow that pastors should receive the tithe. However, in reality, this also creates the new challenge: if indeed Christians are the new Levitical priesthood, then all Christians would be eligible to receive the tithe, not just those in church leadership such as pastors, priests, apostles, etc. So who would bring the tithe forward? However, we are not of the Levitical line, but rather, through Jesus, we are from the Lion of the tribe of Judah and are born anew in the line of Melchizedek with Jesus as our High Priest. Teaching that Christians are the new Levitical priesthood teaches a "replacement theology," in which it is taught that Christians have replaced the Jewish people as God's chosen people (which is a false teaching). In other words, neither argument stands under the examination of God's Word.

Where Was the Tithe to Be Taken?

We read in Deuteronomy, "Then to the place the Lord your God will choose as a dwelling for his Name—there you are to bring everything I command you: your burnt offerings and sacrifices, your tithes and special gifts, and all the choice possessions you have vowed to the Lord" (Deut. 12:11, NIV).

Here, we see the instructions on where the tithe is to be taken. Specifically it was to be taken to the dwelling place for His name. It is argued that today this dwelling place is the church (where congregations of Christians gather). However, God does not dwell in a building or place but rather in the hearts of those who receive Jesus:

> The old temple is destroyed: "Jesus left the temple and was walking away when his disciples came up to him to call his attention to its buildings. 'Do you see all these things?' he asked. 'I tell you the truth, not one stone here will be left on another; everyone will be thrown down'" (Matt. 24:1–2, NIV).

> The new temple established in Christ is every follower of Him: "What agreement is there between the temple of God and idols? For we are the temple of the living God. As God has said: 'I will live with them and walk among them, and I will be their God, and they will be my people'" (2 Cor. 6:16, NIV).

> "Don't you know that you yourselves are God's temple and that God's Spirit lives in you?" (1 Cor. 3:16, NIV).

This clearly shows that there is now no "building" or "temple/storehouse" because God has chosen to make His dwelling among us (John 1:14). Therefore, there is no established place to bring the tithe.

What Was to Be Tithed?

While Abraham's free-will tithe included only spoils of war, in the Mosaic law, the tithe was very specific as were the instructions on how it was to be brought forward:

> A tithe of everything from the land, whether grain from the soil or fruit from the trees, belongs to the Lord; it is holy to the Lord. If a man redeems any of his tithe, he must add a fifth of the value to it. The entire tithe of the herd and flock—every tenth animal that passes under the shepherd's rod—will be holy to the Lord. He must not pick out the good from the bad or make any substitution. If he does make a substitution, both the animal and its substitute become holy and cannot be redeemed." These are the commands the Lord gave Moses on Mount Sinai for the Israelites. (Lev. 27:30–34, NIV)

Note that, here, it instructs only things from the land and livestock are subject to the tithe. Also, it is only every tenth of the herd and flock that passes under the rod, not the first to go under. One was not supposed to pick and choose. This also indicates that if the flock or herd only consists of nine, there is no tithe offering.

The Levitical tithe (from the law) only and always was dealing with "everything from the land." It was never required to tithe from money or income. There was never a requirement for a "tradesman" (i.e., tent maker, carpenter, etc.) who sold product for money to bring a tenth of the income they received to the storehouse. The only time money was given to the Levites/priests in the form of a tithe was when the person making the offering of herd or flock wanted to redeem the offering (buy it back), they were to pay according to the temple shekel ("If it is one of the unclean animals, he may buy it back at its set value, adding a fifth of the value to it. If he does not redeem it, it is to be sold at its set value" (Lev. 27: 27, NIV).

Is Money to Be Included in the Tithe?

As we see from the above passage, money was only involved if the giver of the tithe was to redeem the tithe, and then they were to add one-fifth to the value. The only other time money was mentioned with regard to the tithe was in Deuteronomy:

> Be sure to set aside a tenth of all that your fields produce each year. Eat the tithe of your grain, new vine and oil, and the firstborn of your herds and flocks in the presence of the Lord your God at the place he will choose as a dwelling for his Name, so that you may learn to revere the Lord your God always. But if that place is too distant and you have been blessed by the Lord your God and cannot carry your tithe (because the place where the Lord will choose to put his Name is so far away), then exchange your tithe for silver, and take the silver with you and go to the place the Lord your God will choose. Use the silver to buy whatever you like: cattle, sheep, wine or other fermented drink, or anything you wish. Then you and your household shall eat there in the presence of the Lord your God and rejoice. And do not neglect the Levites living in your towns, for they have no allotment or inheritance of their own. At the end of every three years, bring all the tithes of that year's produce and store it in your towns, so that the Levites (who have no allotment or inheritance of their own) and the aliens, the fatherless

> and the widows who live in your towns may come and eat and be satisfied, and so that the Lord your God may bless you in all the work of your hands. (Deut. 14:22–29 NIV)

Here, we see that money was only used if the distance was too far to bring the tithe (things from the land) to the place of the Lord. And then the tithe was to be converted back to "something from the land" to be given as the offering (by buying "whatever you like"). Then you were to consume it yourself before the Lord and not neglect the Levites, aliens, widows, and orphans.

One can search all other scriptures regarding tithe, tithes, and tithing or offering a tenth and find that in regard to the Levitical tithe, it never indicates that money is required or asked for as part of the tithe (accept as listed in the above passages) but rather always refers to a tithe of something from the land (Lev. 27:30–32; Num. 18:21, 24, 26, 28; Deut. 12:6, 11, 17, 14:23–25, 28, 26:12; 2 Chron. 31:5–6, 12; Neh. 10:37–38, 12:44, 13:5,12; Amos 4:4; Mal. 3:8,10, Exod. 16:36, 29:40; Lev. 5:11, 6:20, 14:21; Num. 5:15, 15:4, 28:5, 13; Eze. 45:11).

Money vs the Tithe

Certainly, money was brought to the temple. However, money was not part of the tithe, nor was there any instruction to bring one-tenth of the financial income to the temple or to the Levites.

Here is an example of how God's commandment was to bring money:

> And Jehovah spoke to Moses saying, When you count the sons of Israel, of those who are to be counted, then they shall each man give a ransom for his soul to

> Jehovah when you number them, so that there may be no plague among them when you number them. They shall give this, every one that passes among those who are counted, half a shekel after the shekel of the sanctuary (a shekel is twenty gerahs); a half shekel shall be the offering of Jehovah. Everyone that passes among those who are numbered, from twenty years old and above, shall give an offering to Jehovah. The rich shall not give more, and the poor shall not give less, than half a shekel, when they give an offering to Jehovah to make an atonement for your souls. And you shall take the atonement silver of the sons of Israel, and shall appoint it for the service of the tabernacle of the congregation, so that it may be a memorial to the sons of Israel before Jehovah, to make an atonement for your souls. (Exod. 30:11–16)

One can see here that the bringing of the shekel was to bring atonement for the souls and was used for the service of the tabernacle of the congregation. As Jesus has become the atonement for our souls, this type of offering is no longer required. In fact, if one were to try to atone for one's soul through this offering, it would insult the atoning act of Jesus's sacrifice on the cross, suggesting that Christ's blood is not sufficient. While this money was used for the service of the tabernacle, today, there would be no atonement money (because of Jesus).

God's Instruction to Bring Money (Riches) for the Tabernacle

> And Moses spoke to all the congregation of the sons of Israel saying, "This is the thing which Jehovah commanded. He said; Take from among you an offering to Jehovah. Whoever is of a willing heart, let

> him bring it, an offering of Jehovah: gold, and silver, and bronze, and blue, and purple, and scarlet, and bleached linen, and goats' hair, and rams' skins dyed red, and badgers' skins, and acacia-wood, and oil for the light, and spices for anointing oil, and for the sweet incense, and onyx stones, and stones to be set for the ephod and for the breast-pocket. And they received all the offerings from Moses, the offering which the sons of Israel had brought for the work of the service of the sanctuary, to make it. And they still brought to him free offerings every morning. (Exod. 35:4–9, 36:3)

As a law of first mention, God's first instruction to bring money, riches, etc., to the tabernacle was to be from a willing heart and of free will. This word *offering* comes from the Hebrew word *t'rumah*, which is also (and more accurately) defined as "gift."

This is established again in the book of Ezra:

> And some of the chief of the fathers, when they came to the house of Jehovah at Jerusalem, offered freely for the house of God to set it up in its place. They gave according to their ability to the treasure of the work, sixty-one thousand drachmas of gold, and five thousand minas of silver, and one hundred priest's garments. And I said to them, You are holy to Jehovah, and the vessels are holy. And the silver and the gold are a free-will offering to Jehovah, the God of your fathers. (Ezra 2:68–69, 8:28)

Paul, in the New Testament letters, also confirms and establishes this type of free-will giving from the heart when he says: "Each one, as he purposes in his heart, let him give; not of grief, or of necessity, for God loves a cheerful giver" (2 Cor. 9:7).

We can see a true pattern of the heart of God as He

delights in His people giving riches, money, etc., freely from the heart, not out of a requirement of law. It is also clear that it is given out of abundance, not out of lack, for giving was out of their ability to give. This is an important point, which will be elaborated on later.

Malachi, Jesus and the Tithe

My journey to investigate the validity of tithing began when I heard someone say that tithing was illegal for a Christian (more on that at the end of this book). As someone who, at the time, strove to be a tither, I dismissed this statement at first. I had read Malachi 3:8–11 many times and had even spoken to and taught others about this scripture. However, the Lord kept bringing this statement back into my mind. After some time, I finally determined I would investigate the claims this person had made. So I asked the Lord to show me His truth.

As I dug into Malachi, it changed my thinking, brought a joy to my spirit, and deepened my love for God in ways beyond explanation. The following is an in-depth discovery of what the Lord revealed to me as I asked Him to show me His truth.

God has revealed much detail throughout the book of Malachi. For this discussion we will look at key passages that will allow us to maintain the context and tone of what is written. While there is additional detail in other passages in Malachi, the passages used here capture the heart of the message of the Lord in this book. It is important to remember that the tithe spoken about in Malachi is clearly describing the tithe as it relates to the Mosaic law. It is not a tithe as understood in the tithe of Abraham or Jacob. As we explore this tithe in Malachi, remember that this tithe was not one of free will, but rather it was required of God for the Israelites to fulfill the statutes set forth in the Mosaic law.

Blessings, Curses, and the Tithe

One of the most commonly used scriptures used to compel Christians to tithe is from Malachi 3:8–11(NIV):

> "Will a man rob God? Yet you rob me. "But you ask, 'How do we rob you?' "In tithes and offerings. You are under a curse—the whole nation of you—because you are robbing me. Bring the whole tithe into the storehouse, that there may be food in my house. Test me in this," says the Lord Almighty, "and see if I will not throw open the floodgates of heaven and pour out so much blessing that you will not have room enough for it. I will prevent pests from devouring your crops, and the vines in your fields will not cast their fruit," says the Lord Almighty.

This has become, in my opinion, one of the most misused and misinterpreted passages in the Bible and has been used to create a fear in the Christian so that they will give one-tenth of everything they have, including wages, to God through the church.

To gain a more accurate understanding of this passage, it is critical to look at this scripture in the complete context of the whole book of Malachi as well as examine the true meaning of the words used in this passage. To accomplish this, I was directed back to the *Strong's Concordance*, which looks at the complete definition. In addition, it is important to remember that all the prophets speak of Jesus as was confirmed when Philip found Nathanael. He told him, "We have found the one Moses wrote about in the Law, and about whom the prophets also wrote—Jesus of Nazareth, the son of Joseph" (John 1:45, NIV).

Since this is the truth, we must also look to see how the prophet Malachi's writings point to Jesus as well.

Malachi: A Closer Look

The Word of the Lord, as captured in the book of Malachi, rebuked the priests for bringing defiled offerings to God. The rebuke was not, as is often suggested, because the storehouse had no food; it had plenty. The real issue was that the offerings were defiled by the corrupt motives of the priests. In addition, the translation of the specific words is important. For example, "robbing" God is more accurately translated as "defrauding" God, and to bring the "whole" tithe is better translated "unblemished," speaking of a condition rather than an amount brought into the storehouse. This is confirmed by the writer in Hebrews 9:1-4: "How much more will the blood of Christ, who through the eternal Spirit offered himself without blemish to God, purify our conscience from dead works to serve the living God" (these dead works being the works of the law). You will find as you read through the entire book of Malachi that the Word of the Lord was not only directed to the priests as a rebuke for bringing defiled offerings to God but was so beautifully pointing to Christ, the unblemished sacrifice. The underlying reason for the rebuke given through Malachi was because of their heart on the matter of bringing the tithe. It was not a matter of not having any "food" in the storehouse (the Jews were indeed bringing their tithe), but rather that the offerings were defiled, tainted, and brought with impure hearts and motives. One must keep this in mind as the passage in Malachi 3 is read.

Malachi and Jesus

The book of Malachi opens with God reminding Israel of how much he loves and has loved His people throughout the years (Mal 1:1-5). Knowing this, let's look first at how the Lord's word through Malachi points to Jesus. As described earlier in this book, God will always keep His covenants. God confirms his faithfulness in keeping His covenant that He made with Levi the High Priest, even in the midst of their falling away, when He speaks in Malachi 2:

> And you shall know that I have sent this command to you, to be My covenant with Levi, says Jehovah of Hosts. My covenant with him was life and peace, and I gave them to him for fear; and he feared Me, and he is awed before My name. The Law of Truth was in his mouth, and iniquity was not found in his lips. He walked with Me in peace and uprightness, and turned away many from iniquity. (Mal.2:4–6)

This is important because the covenant with Levi ties to the covenant of Abraham which is the promise of Jesus through Abraham's seed as written about in Galatians 3:16. Malachi continues to prophesy about the coming of Jesus in Chapter 3:

> "Behold, I will send my messenger, and he shall prepare the way before me" (Mal. 3:1a, KJV).

It is readily and widely accepted that this verse is referring to John the Baptist (Mark 1:3) who was the voice in the desert, crying, "Prepare ye the way of the Lord."

Continuing on, we read:

> "And the Lord, whom ye seek, shall suddenly come to his temple, even the messenger of the covenant, whom ye delight in: behold, he shall come, saith the Lord of hosts. But who may abide the day of his coming? And who shall stand when he appeareth? for he is like a refiner's fire, and like fullers' soap: And he shall sit as a refiner and purifier of silver: and he shall purify

> the sons of Levi, and purge them as gold and silver, that they may offer unto the Lord an offering in righteousness. (Mal. 3:1b–3, KJV)

This passage is rich in proclaiming the coming of Jesus. God says he will suddenly come to His temple. He will be the purifier that they may offer unto the Lord an offering in righteousness. Jesus says: "For I say unto you, that except your righteousness shall exceed the righteousness of the scribes and Pharisees, ye shall in no case enter into the kingdom of heaven" (Matt. 5:20). While the Pharisees were keeping to the "letter" of the law, they were not righteous before God (see also Rom. 4:2). A righteousness exceeding the Pharisees can only be established through faith in Christ.

This is again emphasized when Paul writes we now have a righteousness apart from the law:

> Now we know that whatever the law says, it says to those who are under the law, so that every mouth may be silenced and the whole world held accountable to God. Therefore no one will be declared righteous in his sight by observing the law; rather, through the law we become conscious of sin. But now a righteousness from God, apart from the law, has been made known, to which the Law and the Prophets testify. This righteousness from God comes through faith in Jesus Christ to all who believe. There is no difference, for all have sinned and fall short of the glory of God, and are justified freely by his grace through the redemption that came by Christ Jesus. (Rom. 3:19–24, NIV)

While many have used this scripture to emphasize that we all have sinned and fall short of the glory of God, it is important to note here that this is not the intention of this scripture. The intention is to emphasize that this righteousness that is through faith in Jesus is available to all, since all have sinned and are unable to fulfill the requirement of the law, even the Pharisees. But the righteousness that is greater than that of the Pharisees is available to all through Jesus. Paul goes on to write that "it was not through law that Abraham and his offspring received the promise that he would be heir of the world, but through the righteousness that comes by faith. For if those who live by law are heirs faith has no value and the promise is worthless, because law brings wrath. And where there is no law there is no transgression" (Rom. 4:13–15, NIV).

Also in the Malachi 3:2 passage is the word *abide*. According to Strong's Concordance (H3557) this word holds several definitions, including "to keep in, to measure, to contain, receive." It also means "to continue in a particular condition, attitude, or relationship, to pay the price or penalty of, to suffer for." As one reads *abide* with the Hebrew understanding "contain or measure," one can see how it relates to verse 3:10 when God says He will pour out a blessing that there shall not be room enough to receive (contain or measure). This begins to establish that the outpouring is referring to Jesus, who is the only one who can abide/contain the full measure of God.

As one reads *abide* with the Hebrew understanding "to pay the price or penalty of this verse would read," who can pay the price or penalty (of sin) on the day of His coming and who can stand when He appears?" The obvious answer is that no one can pay the price or penalty nor stand before the Lord in righteousness when He appears. But Jesus alone is worthy to pay the price and take up the scroll (see Rev. 5:2–5). As we relate this to Malachi 3:10 (as we will discuss in a moment), we discover that Jesus is the unblemished offering that allowed God to open up the windows of heaven and pour out a blessing no man could contain.

In addition, the word *abide* is also translated “receive”. In John 3:32–33, John the Baptist confirms this translation when he says,

> and what He has seen and heard, that He testifies, and no one receives His testimony. He who has received His testimony has set his seal to this, that God is true. (Joh 3:32-33)

The Amplified Bible says it this way:

> It is to what He has [actually] seen and heard that He bears testimony, and yet no one accepts His testimony [no one receives His evidence as true]. Whoever receives His testimony has set his seal of approval to this: God is true. [That man has definitely certified, acknowledged, declared once and for all, and is himself assured that it is divine truth that God cannot lie]. (John3:32–33,amp)

As Malachi writes “who may abide (receive) the day of his coming” John writes that no one receives His testimony, but for those that do receive His testimony agree that God is true.

In Malachi 3:2, it is written “And who shall stand when he appeareth?” This word *“stand”* means to “raise up,” “to endure or undergo without harm or damage or without giving way.” Here, again, we understand that when God is asking “who can stand when He appears,” He is asking for one who is worthy to “pay the price and suffer for, to undergo without harm or damage or without giving way.” Again, we know that there is none worthy with the exception of Jesus Christ (Rev. 5:4–5). Here, God was establishing that what is impossible with man is possible with God Himself (Mark 10:27).

The word *purge* in Malachi 3:3 ("and he shall purify the sons of Levi, and purge them as gold and silver") means to "purify and cleanse". Here, God is showing us how He himself will purify the Levites, the priests who have been impure and had not been keeping God's law. He will purify by bringing Jesus as the pure, clean offering. "Then shall the offering of Judah and Jerusalem be pleasant unto the Lord, as in the days of old, and as in former years" (Mal. 3:4 KJV). This confirms that the offering (of Jesus) will be pleasing to God. Jesus is the "lion of the tribe of Judah" (Hosea 5:14) and Jerusalem is the Holy City. God states that the offering of Jesus, who is both of Judah and Jerusalem, will be pleasant unto Him.

Continuing with Malachi, it is written,

> "And I will come near to you to judgment and I will be a swift witness against the sorcerers, and against the adulterers, and against false swearers, and against those that oppress the hireling in his wages, the widow, and the fatherless, and that turn aside the stranger from his right, and fear not me, saith the Lord of hosts. For I am the Lord, I change not; therefore ye sons of Jacob are not consumed. (Mal. 3:5–6 KJV)

Both John the Baptist and Jesus preached the kingdom of God is "near" or "at hand." This is the same message in Malachi where the Lord says, "I will come near to you." This is, of course, referring to Jesus being among us and establishing God's kingdom on earth.

The Lord does not change. Even if we do not keep covenant, God will keep His covenant. Remember, God Himself made the blood covenant with Himself to bless Abraham (Gen. 15:17) and provided the ram for Abraham

(Gen. 22:13) when the "ultimate" sacrifice was called for of Isaac his son. God provided Jesus as the spotless sacrificial lamb (John 1:29, 36). Even when we are not faithful, God is faithful (2 Tim. 2:13).

Malachi writes in chapter 3:7,

> "Even from the days of your fathers ye are gone away from mine ordinances, and have not kept them. Return unto me, and I will return unto you, saith the Lord of hosts. But ye said, Wherein shall we return?" (Mal. 3:7 KJV)

The word *return* means to "turn back" or "repent". Compare this to the message of repentance which both John the Baptist and Jesus preached, calling for a reversal and different thinking.

Then the question is asked "How shall we return?" The instruction is to repent, turn back, and think differently. "Return unto me" also means to lie down/rest. In returning God is inviting us to lie down and rest with Him, and He will lie down and rest with us. This is important to grasp as God's Word speaks to us in Hebrews, saying, "Therefore, a promise being left to enter into His rest, let us fear lest any of you should seem to come short of it" (Heb. 4:1). (More on this in the section "Fear and Unrest".)

We understand that the temple (storehouse) on earth is a model for the real temple in Heaven. Malachi 1:7 points to the priests offering defiled and polluted bread on His altar. Remember that Jesus is described as the 'bread of life'. He is the undefiled bread that God was ultimately looking to be brought to His altar. Malachi 3:10b states, "That there may be meat in my house." Here, God is challenging the priests to bring the unblemished (undefiled) tithe into the temple, that there may be "something torn" (bread, meat or flesh) in His house. While *meat* means the flesh of animals used for food, it also means the edible part of anything, as a fruit or nut. (Houghton Mifflin Company, 2005) In Nehemiah 10:39, it describes the offering as "bread," new wine, and oil. Since the Old Testament is a model of things to come (Heb. 8:5), it shows us again how Jesus was the ultimate fulfillment of the law and of the required tithe/offering. Jesus is the bread of life, His flesh was torn for us, His blood is the new wine of the new covenant, and the oil is the oil/anointing of Holy Spirit (1 Cor. 11:23–29, Acts 2:33–39).

Jesus confirms this in the book of John:

> Then Jesus said to them, Truly, truly, I say to you, Moses did not give you that bread from Heaven, but My Father gives you the true bread from Heaven. For the bread of God is He who comes down from Heaven and gives life to the world. Then they said to him, Lord, evermore give us this bread. And Jesus said to them, I am the bread of life. He who comes to Me shall never hunger, and he who believes on Me shall never thirst. I am the Living Bread which came down from Heaven. If anyone eats of this Bread, he shall live forever. And truly the bread that I will give is My flesh, which I will give for the life of the world. (John 6:32–35, 51).

While these verses clearly point to Jesus, we will also bring together some additional verses to confirm this later in this section. But first, let's investigate what Malachi was speaking regarding the tithe.

Malachi and the Tithe

To better understand what the Lord was saying through Malachi it is important to understand the context of the entire book and to whom Malachi was speaking. While the burden of the word of the Lord is addressed to Israel, it becomes evident in the beginning that it is addressing the priests of Israel more directly.

In the first chapter of Malachi we find the Lord asks of the priests, "Where is My honor?" and "Where is my fear?" The priests are bringing a defiled offering to the altar.

> "A son honors his father, and a servant his master. If then I am a father, where is My honor? And if I am a master, where is My fear?" says Jehovah of Hosts to you, "O priests who despise My name. And you say, 'In what way have we despised Your name?' You offer defiled bread upon My altar; and you say, 'In what way have we defiled You?' In your saying, 'The table of Jehovah, it is a thing to be despised'" (Mal. 1:6–7)

The word *defiled* means "desecrated, polluted, or stained" (Strong's Concordance H1351). This is expounded on in verses 8 to 12 when the offerings are described. The priests were required to bring the spotless and unblemished sacrifice to the altar, but because their hearts were hardened toward God, they were simply and begrudgingly going through the motions of the law. They were holding back the best for themselves while bringing a blemished offering to the Lord. There was no honoring of God in their offering and they no longer had the fear of the Lord. Malachi writes, "And if you offer the blind for sacrifice, is it not evil? And if you offer the lame and the sick, is it not evil? The table of Jehovah, it is polluted; and its fruit, His food, is to be despised" (Mal. 1:8, 12).

God continues in His rebuke of the priests for bringing a polluted and defiled offering. He is not pleased with an offering that is brought out of the wrong heart and intention.

> You also said, Behold, what a weariness it is! And you have puffed at it, says Jehovah of Hosts. And you bring plunder, and the lame, and the sick, and you bring the food offering. Should I accept it from your hand, says Jehovah? But cursed be a deceiver; and there is in his flock a male, yet he vows it, but sacrifices to Jehovah a blemished one. For I am a great king, says Jehovah of Hosts, and My name is feared among the nations. (Mal. 1:13–14)

In this passage, the word *cursed*, means "to execrate, to bitterly curse" (Strong's Concordance H779). This word is used as an action. This is important to remember when we look later at Malachi 3. We also see the word *deceiver*, which means "to defraud." This too will be important to remember as we read Malachi 3.

When reading these verses, it is very clear the issue wasn't that the priests were not bringing the sacrifice. The indication here was that they were bringing the sacrifice, even the correct "amount" of the sacrifice (tithe). The issue was that they were bringing a blemished offering that was polluted by their actions and the motivation of their hearts. Malachi 2 begins with confirmation that this rebuke is for the priests as he identifies them directly by title: "And now, O priests, this command is for you. If you will not hear, and if you will not set it on your heart to give glory to My name, says Jehovah of Hosts, then I will send a curse upon you, and I will curse your blessings. And indeed I have cursed it, because you do not set it on your heart" (Mal. 2:1–2).

Here, we also see the word *curse* when God says He will

"send a curse." This is a different word from *curse* as seen in 1:14. This word *curse* is an object or noun (an execration) and is different from the action form of the word used before as was written "I will curse." To explain this difference better one might consider the analogy of the word *fly*. If one would say, "To fly with a fly" we would understand that one would be in the act of flying with an insect (fly). We will discuss the importance of this a little later.

We have discussed God's faithfulness in keeping His covenant with Levi and how the remaining sections of Malachi 2 and the beginning of Malachi 3 begin to point to God's plan for Jesus to enter into this world. With that in mind we move ahead to Malachi 3:7-8.

> From the days of your fathers, you have turned aside from My statutes, and have not kept them. Return to Me, and I will return to you, says Jehovah of Hosts. But you say. In what way shall we return? Will a man rob God? Yet you have robbed Me. But you say, In what have we robbed You? In the tithe and the offering! (Mal 3:7-8)

Remember that the word "*return*" means to "turn back or repent". This is the message that was prominent in the ministries of both John the Baptist and Jesus. After the question "how shall we return (repent)," it is asked, "Will a man rob God? Yet you have robbed me. But you say, Wherein have we robbed You? In tithes and offerings" (Mal. 3:8). The word *rob* means "to defraud". Remember verse 1:14, the word *deceiver* is also "to defraud". This root word *rob* is repeated three times in this verse. *Webster*'s definition of *rob* is, "2. To deprive of, or withhold from, unjustly or injuriously: to defraud." (Webster's Collegiate Dictionary, 1948) Relate this to the earlier verses where God has come against the priests for bringing a polluted and blemished offering. By doing so, they were defrauding God. This is different than stealing as they were trying to deceive and defraud God with these impure offerings.

So with this understanding, a more accurate translation would be, "Will a man defraud God? Yet ye have defrauded me. But you say, where and how have we defrauded You?" God's answer is, "In tithes and offerings." God is reestablishing here that the priests have defrauded God through their tithes and offerings. In this context, "robbing God" is not stealing from Him as in taking something from, but rather bringing a defrauded offering and thus trying to deceive God. This again is a more consistent translation within the entire context of Malachi.

Next is the verse that is most often preached to place the fear of a curse upon Christians who do not bring their tithe: "You *are* cursed with a curse: for you have robbed me, even this whole nation" (Mal. 3:9). Note here that the word *are* is italicized. This means that this word was not in the original translation but was added by the translators. This is very important to understand, because it changes the entire meaning of this statement. Let's look at the meaning of this phrase from the original translation if we take the word *are* out and then examine the word *curse* in this passage. The meaning of the first use of the word *cursed* is "to execrate (to curse) (Strong's Concordance H779)." As the same use of this word is used earlier in Malachi 1, we see that this is an action word, for it is the act of execrating. The second use of the word *curse* is a different form of the word also as in Malachi 1, as this curse is an object or noun (an execration, curse) (Strong's Concordance H3994). To grasp this difference remember the analogy of "flying with a fly" discussed earlier in this section. They were "cursing with a curse."

So more properly translated, this verse says that "you curse with a curse, for you have defrauded me, even the whole nation."

Also in this sentence it is written "even the whole nation". In the original KJV the word "even" is also in italicized which means it was added by the translators. With this in mind it emphasizes that the priests were not only robbing (defrauding) God but were defrauding the whole nation in the sight of God. In other words, God is saying that the priests were cursing (as an act) with a curse (noun) offering and were defrauding God and the nation. This fits with the context of the rest of Malachi, in particular how the Lord was rebuking the priests for bringing a polluted (defiled) offering and that they have robbed (deprived, withheld, defrauded) God. When the priests brought the defiled offering, they were cursing God with a cursed offering. And this action also represented the entire nation of Israel (see also Num. 18:28–32). It does not mean that the people "are cursed with a curse" the Lord has put on them. Even as God stated earlier that He has cursed the priests because of the offering, the meaning of these words in this passage do not support the interpretation that suggests God is cursing His people if they don't tithe. Reading further the Lord says, "Bring ye the whole tithe into the storehouse" (Mal. 3:10a). In some translations, the word *all* is used instead of *whole*. Both words come from the Hebrew word kole, which means "properly the whole" (Strong's Concordance H3605). *Kole* also comes from the Hebrew word *kalal* (Strong's Concordance H3634), which means "complete: – (make) perfect". One of *Webster*'s definitions for *all* is "the whole of, referring to quality. (Webster's Collegiate Dictionary, 1948) The definition for the word *"whole"* is: 1. Being uninjured or without signs of injury; of a wound, healed; more widely sound and healthy, or restored to soundness and health. 2. Not broken or defective;

unimpaired; undamaged; intact." A synonym for the word *whole* is *perfect* (Webster's Collegiate Dictionary, 1948)

So with this understanding and placing this verse in context, bringing the "whole" tithe is not talking about an amount but rather is describing the condition of the tithe. It is to be unblemished, undamaged, and intact; not broken or defective. This is in direct contrast to what the priests were presenting as a blemished and polluted offering to the Lord.

This definition of the word *whole* or *all* is also confirmed in Mark: "And to love him with all the heart, and with all the understanding, and with all the soul, and with all the strength, and to love his neighbor as himself, is more than all whole burnt offerings and sacrifices" (Mark 12:33 KJV). In this verse, the phrase "all whole burnt offerings and sacrifices" shows both an amount and a condition. *All* is anything that is brought forth. *Whole is* the condition of the burnt offerings and sacrifices. So, again, Malachi was speaking to the condition of the tithe that was to be brought forward, not the amount. Remember, it was never a lack of amount of the tithe offering that was the issue but rather the quality that was brought forth and the heart with which it was presented (as it was brought forth out of a profaned and contemptible spirit (v 1:12)). God said that He will not accept this offering (v 1:10). Again, it was not about the amount, but it was about the heart.

This understanding of the word *whole* or *all* fits more accurately within these texts as God, again, was rebuking the priests for bringing a defiled, blind, broken and imperfect offering, not the whole or the greatest possible. God is not instructing the priests to bring the amount of the tithe, as it was established that the amount of the tithe was not what was in question. Rather, God was rebuking and instructing to bring the "whole, unblemished, uninjured, perfect" tithe with a pure heart.

Malachi, Jesus and the Tithe...bringing it all together

Then God places the challenge to the priests: "And prove me now herewith, saith the Lord of hosts, if I will not open you the windows of heaven, and pour you out a blessing, that there shall not be room enough to receive it." (Mal. 3:10c).

When the previous verses are properly understood, one can now see that God is again saying that when the whole unblemished tithe offering is brought to the temple with a pure heart, we can be sure that the windows of heaven would be open and He would pour out a blessing so great there shall not be room enough to receive it. This pure offering was Jesus, and God fulfilled His own requirement. God Himself made a way to pour out this blessing that is so great that no one can contain it. This is the promised blessing that God made to Abraham: "Behold! I, even I, establish My covenant with you, and with your seed after you (this seed being Jesus)" (Gen. 9:9). John writes, "For He whom God has sent speaks the Words of God, for God does not give the Spirit by measure. The Father loves the Son and has given all things into His hand" (John 3:34-35) confirming that Spirit is without measure (uncontainable). Jesus has given us that same Spirit. He shows us that God Himself has provided the pure, undefiled, unblemished "meat" to the temple. (John 6:32-35,51)

When properly understood, one can see that God, in the form of Jesus, fulfilled His own requirement even in the midst of disobedience and rebellion, making a way for God Himself to pour out this blessing that is so great that no one can contain it. This is the promised blessing that God made to

Abraham: "Behold! I, even I, establish My covenant with you, and with your seed after you [this seed being Jesus]" (Gen. 9:9).

As Jesus walked among us, He surely walked in the fullness of the blessing of God. As He walked among us, He was declaring the fulfillment of Malachi as He suddenly came near to us, preaching the good news of the kingdom, healing the sick, casting out demons, raising the dead, and setting the captives free.

The uncontainable blessing that Jesus walked in was confirmed by John when he wrote, "And there are also many things, whatever Jesus did, which, if they should be written singly, I suppose the world itself could not contain the books that would be written. Amen." (John 21:25). It is reaffirmed in Hebrews, as it is written: "For when God made His promise to Abraham, because He could swear by no greater, He swore by Himself, saying, 'Surely in blessing I will bless you, and in multiplying I will multiply you.' And so, after he had patiently endured, he obtained the promise" (Heb. 6:13–15).

Jesus declared that this blessing would be poured out in an uncontainable way to His followers as He spoke, "Truly, truly, I say to you, He who believes on Me, the works that I do he shall do also, and greater works than these he shall do, because I go to My Father" (John 14:12). If, as spoken of by John, the works that Jesus did could not be contained in the books, how much greater the immeasurable outpouring of blessing that is poured out upon all flesh and is upon all who believe! This is the outpouring of Holy Spirit and everything that comes with Him. And this uncontainable blessing is still uncontainable today!

We know that God made a way for the outpouring of His Holy Spirit upon all flesh, as it is written:

> But this is that which was spoken by the prophet Joel: "And it shall be in the last days, says God, I will pour out of My Spirit upon all flesh. And your sons and your daughters shall prophesy, and your young men shall see visions, and your old men shall dream dreams. And in those days I will pour out My Spirit upon My slaves and My slave women, and they shall prophesy. And I will give wonders in the heaven above, and miracles on the earth below, blood and fire and vapor of smoke. (Acts 2:16–19)

Then the Lord says, "And I will rebuke the devourer for your sakes, and he shall not destroy the fruits of your ground; neither shall your vine cast her fruit before the time in the field, saith the Lord of hosts" (Mal. 3:11). Jesus defeated Satan (the devourer) on the cross, and now, all authority in heaven and on earth has been given to Him. So once again, God Himself provided the required undefiled sacrifice that was required for Him to not only pour out His blessing on humanity but also to rebuke Satan the devourer.

Because of the misunderstanding of this passage in Malachi 3, the church has set an entire doctrine regarding tithing. What is taught in the church is that Christians are required (by God) to bring a tithe (one-tenth) of their income into God's house or to certain people/ministries. Then in response God would pour out a blessing so great they would not able to contain it. This suggests that God's blessing can somehow be purchased and ignores the work that Jesus has completed on the cross.

In addition, popular teaching suggests that the blessing will be financial. But God was not talking about nor limiting Himself to that at all! While a blessing may be financial, there are blessings so much greater that come from our

Father. In Christ, He has blessed us with every spiritual blessing, and His promises are yes and amen. Blessings of health, of favor, of family, of relationships, of peace, and of prosperity are just some of the blessings that the Lord gives us through Christ.

Financial blessings can always be contained. They are finite in their impact and can't buy health, peace, or other spiritual blessings. If the currently accepted teaching of the church were accurate, one has to believe that even throughout history, there had to be at least one person who brought their entire tithe of income into some storehouse (temple or church). Yet there is no recording that there has been an outpouring of blessing upon any individual, particularly a financial blessing, that could not be contained. In this passage, God is even saying, "Prove me on this," so God would not lie or even exaggerate on this. So since God cannot lie, our understanding must be inaccurate if we are to think that when we perform this act of tithing, God should pour out this type of blessing (financial or other). Again, the *only* time the windows of heaven were opened and a blessing was poured out so great "that there shall not be room enough to receive it (Mal 3:10 KJV)" was through Jesus. By His sacrifice, "the veil of the temple was torn in two" (Matt. 27:51), putting an end to the law for those who believe, making us heirs and coheirs with Him in the kingdom of God (Gal. 4:7). As Christians we may receive and move in this uncontainable blessing of God.

So at the risk of being redundant, it is important to understand that the prophet Malachi is speaking the Word of the Lord that is declaring the coming of Jesus and how God will bring the unblemished offering to the temple. This will fulfill the command and make a way for God to pour out such a great blessing on all people that no one can contain it. This is how much God loves us!

What Should We Conclude Then from Malachi?

After examining Malachi in complete context, with an understanding of the law (particularly tithing), we see the heart and meaning of this Word of the Lord spoken through Malachi. God was speaking and rebuking the priests for defrauding Him by bringing Him their blemished tithes and offerings. While the Priests represented the nation of Israel, this Word was brought to the priests, not the people. It was not a question of the amount of tithe that was brought; the people were bringing their tithe into the storehouse. The priests were even bringing their tithe to the altar. However, the condition of the hearts of the priests was wrong before the Lord. This was evident in their bringing blemished offerings as they tried to deceive God. God was not pleased, but in His infinite love and mercy, God had a plan.

An entire doctrine has been developed which pivots around a few words i.e., "robbing God," "you are cursed with a curse," "bring the whole tithe," and to "open up the windows of heaven" from God. By not understanding the true meanings of these words and phrases, this doctrine has caused the uninformed Christian to follow a teaching that is not the heart of God. In an attempt to support this incorrect doctrine of tithing, many other scriptures have been brought forward out of context and misinterpreted. These scriptures will be discussed in later chapters of this book.

Remember, Jesus said that all the prophets and Moses spoke of Him. Malachi was no exception. The Lord spoke prophetically through Malachi of how He (God) would prove Himself that when the pure "whole" complete and unblemished tithe/offering was brought to the temple; the curse would be taken away and God would then open the windows of heaven and pour out His blessing upon all flesh that was so great no man could contain it. This unblemished offering was Jesus who came from the Father; the spotless, unblemished sacrificial Lamb. Through this offering, the Lord opened the gates and windows, the Holy Spirit was poured out upon all flesh, and the kingdom of heaven was established on earth.

In addition, the tithe written in Malachi was never a tithe of money (as is now taught in the church). This is understood in the text of Malachi as he was talking about "meat" and not money. And it is also understood in the context and understanding of what a "biblical tithe" was to be through the Mosaic law. Again, if one were to extend teaching of the tithe to include the Abramic tithe, then it should also be understood that this type of tithe was not required of God, and the first tithe was given of free will, as Abram purposed in his heart. And it was only of the spoils of war.

So from an in-depth study of Malachi, we can clearly see that the common teaching promoting tithing based on Malachi 3:8–11 is not accurate. It has been taken out of context and has been used to establish a doctrine that is not consistent with the original intention of God's Word. This has created a misunderstanding of who God is, what He asks of us, and discounts the fullness of what Jesus has done for us through the cross. After examination, we can see that the scripture in Malachi has nothing to do with a requirement of giving money or a tithe but, rather, is a beautiful prophetic revelation of Jesus Christ.

Curses from God?

A friend said to me, "I could never understand why the only curse that made it through the cross was the curse if I didn't tithe." Truly I say that Jesus took *all* curses to the cross, even the supposed curse from not tithing (even as we have learned in the previously that this so called "curse" was not actually a curse from God, but rather the priests were cursing with a cursed offering). However, as we have spoken about "blessing" in the previous section, it is important also to examine the "curse" in some detail. The opposite of *bless* is *curse*. When teaching that tithing is a requirement for Christians, it proclaims that to open up your blessing from God, it is required to bring a tithe. However, if one fails to bring a tithe, God will place a curse on you. Even if a church or teacher doesn't emphasize this particular aspect of the consequences of not tithing, it is an assumed and understood part of the teaching because it must always reference the passage in Malachi 3:8–10. For those that tithe or teach tithing, there is always this underlying hope and fear of blessing and curse. If a teacher would try to eliminate this portion of the aspect of tithing, they would simply be eliminating part of God's Word. To speak that tithing is a requirement and to say that God would not curse if you don't tithe but only bless when you do tithe requires picking and choosing parts of the Bible. In other words, tithing cannot be taught without including both blessing and curse.

However, this is the farthest thing from our Father's heart! In fact, God will never place a curse on His children that are in Christ. Any good father would not curse his own children, and we have a loving Father in heaven who loves us more perfectly. I say it again emphatically: God will never curse

His child. Those who are not "in Christ" are already under a curse. Christ has come to set us free from the curse of the law.

But, you may say, God either placed or allowed a curse to be placed on His people. That is true in the scriptures of the Old Testament. However, these were only in times when the people were disobedient to the law. It was their disobedience that brought the curse, and the curse was in place because of and through the law itself. So in other words, the law has a cause and effect. Keep the law and you will be blessed, but disobey the law and you will be cursed. It was the people (by their own actions and disobedience) who were causing the curse to come upon themselves. But we know that no one would be able to be completely obedient and fulfill the whole law. Paul writes, "There is none righteous, no not one" (Rom. 3:10 KJV). So, much like the law of gravity (what goes up must come down), if you do not keep the law, then the result will be a curse.

So being under the law causes one to be subjected to its blessings and curses:

> And the rest of the people, the priests, the Levites, the gatekeepers, the singers, the temple-slaves, and all those who had separated from the people of the lands to the Law of God, their wives, their sons, and their daughters (everyone who had knowledge, and who had understanding), were holding fast to their brothers, their honored ones. And they entered into a curse and into an oath, to walk in God's Law which was given by Moses the servant of God, and to be careful to do all the commandments of Jehovah our Lord, and His judgments and His statutes. (Neh. 10:28–29)

Christ has set us free from the law, and so we can't break

a law that does not exist any longer, for it is written "For the law brings wrath, but where there is no law there is no transgression"(Rom. 4:15 ESV).

So we find now that we are no longer under the law and therefore no longer subject to its curse (or blessing) because there is no transgression. This is true, of course, unless we place ourselves back under the law.

God's Word states that He will curse those who curse Abraham (Num. 12:3). However, it does not say that He will curse His children. Keep in mind that before Christ the people of Israel were considered servants of God and now those in Christ are considered children and co-heirs with Him. These following verses confirm God's love for his children. We read that He does not curse His children and that through Christ He has taken away the curse.

> For what father of you, if the son asks for bread, will he give him a stone? Or if he asks for a fish, will he give him a snake for a fish? Or if he shall ask for an egg, will he give him a scorpion? If you then, being evil, know how to give good gifts to your children, how much more shall your heavenly Father give the Holy Spirit to those who ask Him? (Luk 11:11-13)

> Christ redeemed us from the curse of the law by becoming a curse for us, for it is written: "Cursed is everyone who is hung on a tree." He redeemed us in order that the blessing given to Abraham might come to the Gentiles through Christ Jesus. This blessing was not given out of response to a tithe, but rather the promise was given through faith so that by faith we might receive the promise of the Spirit. (Gal. 3:13–14 NIV)

In the grace of God, through the blood of Jesus, there is absolutely no curse placed by God upon his children.

However, it is possible for someone to place themselves under the spirit of a curse. Even though Christ has redeemed us from the law and taken away the curse, Christians can place themselves back under the curse of the law by trying to fulfill even part of the law in order to gain a right standing (righteousness) before God. This is what happens when tithing becomes the means to receive God's blessing rather than receiving God's blessing that is in Christ. We must also remember that there is power of death and life in the tongue (Prov 18:21). When one speaks over themselves that they are a tither, the power of their statement places them back under the law.

Remember, Satan is the deceiver. Just as he used words to deceive Eve and tried to use words to deceive Jesus, I believe he uses the same ploy today in the church, saying, "Doesn't God's Word say that you must tithe to get your blessing? Won't God curse you if you don't tithe?" By this, Satan places fear in the hearts of the believers. But "God has not given us a spirit of fear, but of power and of love and of a sound mind" (2Ti 1:7). Don't be deceived and allow yourself to be overtaken by a spirit of fear because you don't tithe.

Consider this: What if every time instructions on tithing were spoken and/or received, it actually caused a curse to be placed over people's lives, because no one is able to fully keep the ordinances of the Mosaic Law all the time? When one leads themselves or another into the "bondage" of tithing, they are tying back into the curse of the law. Even though Jesus has freed us from the curse of the law, one can place themselves back under a curse either by actions, thinking, or alignment with wrong teaching or understanding. When under the curse of the law, there are many undesirable consequences. The worst consequence is falling from grace (see Gal 5:4).

Tithing in the New Testament?

Teachers will often quote passages in the New Testament that might seem to confirm the requirement of tithing and reasons why it should continue today, even when the rest of the law has been overcome by Jesus. Here, we will look at some of these teachings in the context they were given to discover the true meaning of these New Testament references to tithing.

Jesus and Melchizedek

It is often taught that the book of Hebrews confirms that the tithe should continue as it recounts the event of Abraham tithing to Melchizedek. Since Jesus is in the line of Melchizedek, it is argued that we too should continue to tithe as Abraham did. However, as we examine these passages, we can see that the writer is referencing Melchizedek in order to establish Jesus, not to establish the principle of tithing. To be clear, Jesus is being established as a High Priest in the order of Melchizedek and is greater than the priests who are in the line of Aaron (the Levites). Let's examine these passages inHebrews.

> When God made his promise to Abraham, since there was no one greater for him to swear by, he swore by himself, saying, "I will surely bless you and give you many descendants." And so after waiting patiently, Abraham received what was promised. People swear by someone greater than themselves, and the oath

> confirms what is said and puts an end to all argument. Because God wanted to make the unchanging nature of his purpose very clear to the heirs of what was promised, he confirmed it with an oath. God did this so that, by two unchangeable things in which it is impossible for God to lie, we who have fled to take hold of the hope offered to us may be greatly encouraged. We have this hope as an anchor for the soul, firm and secure. It enters the inner sanctuary behind the curtain, where Jesus, who went before us, has entered on our behalf. He has become a high priest forever, in the order of Melchizedek. (Heb. 6:13–20 NIV)

In these passages leading up to the discussion of Melchizedek, the writer is recalling the promise God made to Abraham. This promise was unchanging in nature, and to underscore that it would not change, God confirmed His promise with an oath in which He swore upon Himself. Therefore, this oath is not dependent upon any man to keep but upon God alone.

As we read further, the writer describes how this unchangeable oath is established through Jesus, who is a priest in the line of Melchizedek.

> This Melchizedek was king of Salem and priest of God Most High. He met Abraham returning from the defeat of the kings and blessed him, and Abraham gave him a tenth of everything. First, his name means "king of righteousness"; then also, "king of Salem" means "king of peace." Without father or mother, without genealogy, without beginning of days or end of life, like the Son of God he remains a priest forever. Just think how great he was: Even the patriarch Abraham gave him a tenth of the plunder! Now the law requires

the descendants of Levi who become priests to collect a tenth from the people—that is, their brothers—even though their brothers are descended from Abraham. This man, however, did not trace his descent from Levi, yet he collected a tenth from Abraham and blessed him who had the promises. And without doubt the lesser person is blessed by the greater. In the one case, the tenth is collected by men who die; but in the other case, by him who is declared to be living. One might even say that Levi, who collects the tenth, paid the tenth through Abraham, because when Melchizedek met Abraham, Levi was still in the body of his ancestor. If perfection could have been attained through the Levitical priesthood (for on the basis of it the law was given to the people), why was there still need for another priest to come—one in the order of Melchizedek, not in the order of Aaron? For when there is a change of the priesthood, there must also be a change of the law. He of whom these things are said belonged to a different tribe, and no one from that tribe has ever served at the altar. For it is clear that our Lord descended from Judah, and in regard to that tribe Moses said nothing about priests. And what we have said is even more clear if another priest like Melchizedek appears, one who has become a priest not on the basis of a regulation as to his ancestry but on the basis of the power of an indestructible life. For it is declared: "You are a priest forever, in the order of Melchizedek." The former regulation is set aside because it was weak and useless (for the law made nothing perfect), and a better hope is introduced, by which we draw near to God. And it was not without an oath! Others became priests without any oath, but he became a priest with an oath when God said to him: "The Lord has sworn and will not change his mind:

> "You are a priest forever." Because of this oath, Jesus has become the guarantee of a better covenant. Now there have been many of those priests, since death prevented them from continuing in office; but because Jesus lives forever, he has a permanent priesthood. Therefore he is able to save completely those who come to God through him, because he always lives to intercede for them. Such a high priest meets our need—one who is holy, blameless, pure, set apart from sinners, exalted above the heavens. Unlike the other high priests, he does not need to offer sacrifices day after day, first for his own sins, and then for the sins of the people. He sacrificed for their sins once for all when he offered himself. For the law appoints as high priests men who are weak; but the oath, which came after the law, appointed the Son, who has been made perfect forever. (Heb. 7:1–28, NIV)

Here, the writer establishes that Melchizedek is greater than any priest who was in the line of Levi. While the priests in the line of Levi came after Melchizedek, this establishes not only that Melchizedek was greater but also that there was weakness in the Levitical priesthood since these priests would see death, but Melchizedek was without "end of life." Because of this, the writer explains that there was need for another to come after the line of Levitical priests to establish the everlasting priesthood that is without death. Not only did Jesus come as the promised one in the order of Melchizedek, but this passage points out that Jesus was not in the line of Levi but rather in the line of Judah. Since all the regulations established by God through Moses were to be carried out only by those descendants of the tribe of Levi, Jesus would not have been qualified because of his lineage. However, God qualified

Him through His promise and through the power of an indestructible life. And in doing so, there was created a new line of priests through Jesus, who is our High Priest. And with this, the new order of priests caused the old regulation (which includes tithing) to be set aside.

We read further in Hebrews:

> The point of what we are saying is this: We do have such a high priest, who sat down at the right hand of the throne of the Majesty in heaven, and who serves in the sanctuary, the true tabernacle set up by the Lord, not by man. Every high priest is appointed to offer both gifts and sacrifices, and so it was necessary for this one also to have something to offer. If he were on earth, he would not be a priest, for there are already men who offer the gifts prescribed by the law. They serve at a sanctuary that is a copy and shadow of what is in heaven. This is why Moses was warned when he was about to build the tabernacle: "See to it that you make everything according to the pattern shown you on the mountain." But the ministry Jesus has received is as superior to theirs as the covenant of which he is mediator is superior to the old one, and it is founded on better promises. For if there had been nothing wrong with that first covenant, no place would have been sought for another. But God found fault with the people and said: "The time is coming, declares the Lord, when I will make a new covenant with the house of Israel and with the house of Judah. It will not be like the covenant I made with their forefathers when I took them by the hand to lead them out of Egypt, because they did not remain faithful to my covenant, and I turned away from them, declares the Lord. This is the covenant I will make with the house of Israel after that time, declares the Lord. I will put my laws in their minds and write them on their hearts. I will be their God, and they will be my people. No longer will

> a man teach his neighbor, or a man his brother, saying, 'Know the Lord,' because they will all know me, from the least of them to the greatest. For I will forgive their wickedness and will remember their sins no more." By calling this covenant "new," he has made the first one obsolete; and what is obsolete and aging will soon disappear. (Heb. 8:1–13, NIV)

Here, again, the writer is emphasizing the fact that the covenant established through Moses and the Levitical priesthood was weak, and therefore, in its weakness, God called forth a new mediator of the new covenant who had no weakness. The covenant established in Jesus is superior to the covenant of Moses, and this new covenant has made the old covenant obsolete. As God confirms this new covenant, it also states that it will not be like the covenant made with the forefathers when He led them out of Egypt (the covenant with Moses through the law). This confirms that this new covenant is replacing the Mosaic covenant. While the Mosaic covenant and law is still in place (it is waxing away), its purpose is still to show that no one can fulfill the law by their own actions and points us to Jesus as the only way to the Father.

Clearly, this section of Hebrews establishes the weakness of the "old regulation," and that, in fact, the old regulation (specifically the tithe that is discussed in this passage) is set aside. God has established a new covenant through Jesus Christ, which is guaranteed. To make it clear, this passage claims that tithing (and keeping any other part of the law) is not only not required but lays insult against the blood of Jesus. We are covered by a new covenant that is established in Christ and is by grace through faith (Eph. 2:8–9).

This passage in Hebrews is often misused today to teach that the Levitical priesthood is represented by the church pastors. This is because of a lack of understanding. Some also teach that those called as apostles today are representing the high priests of the Old Testament. This is why, in the tithing teaching, the people are to bring their tithes and first fruit offerings to the church/pastors, and the pastors are to give their first fruit offering/tithe to the apostles. However, this teaching is directly opposed to these scriptures in Hebrews, where it declares the Levitical priesthood is set aside and that Christ is not the line of Levi but of the line of Judah. Christ, therefore, is not allowed to receive the tithe (according to Mosaic Law), and to do so would be breaking the law. If we are in the line of Christ (which we are), then we are in the line of Judah, and so it follows that it is illegal for any of Christ's followers to receive the Levitical tithe as well. Research also shows that the traditional Jews currently do not tithe. In fact, tithing is a sin to the Jew since God's Word says specifically that the tithe can only be brought to the Levitical priesthood. Since there is currently no Levitical priesthood established today in the Jewish synagogues, tithing is not allowed. (askelm/tithing, 2015)

In addition, even if one would still argue that we should bring a tithe to Jesus as He is in the line of Melchizedek, then it should be the same type as Abraham brought, as this is our example in this case. But as discussed earlier, Abram's tithe was of his own free will. He was blessed first, and then he brought the tithe; his tithe was only of the spoils of war, not of any of Abraham's own possessions. And even after this, Abraham gave the rest away to the king of Sodom and kept none for himself. Furthermore, if we are to give a tithe to those who represent Christ (in the line of Melchizedek), we would bring our tithes to anyone who is a Christ follower as we are all a royal priesthood (1 Pet. 2:9). This would include bringing a tithe to ourselves. Hebrews 8:1-13 states that we are in a new line of priests, in the line of Judah, if we indeed follow Jesus and not the Mosaic Law. Clearly, this argument of pastors being the modern-day Levites does not hold weight.

Hebrews teaches specifically that God has made a new covenant with His people. This is the fulfillment of what was spoken in Jeremiah:

> Behold, the days come, says Jehovah, that I will cut a new covenant with the house of Israel, and with the house of Judah, not according to the covenant that I cut with their fathers in the day I took them by the hand to bring them out of the land of Egypt; which covenant of Mine they broke, although I was a husband to them, says Jehovah; but this shall be the covenant that I will cut with the house of Israel: After those days, says Jehovah, I will put My Law in their inward parts, and write it in their hearts; and I will be their God, and they shall be My people. (Jer. 31:31–33)

Consider this, as Hebrews instructs, "Let us not be carried away by divers and strange teachings: for it is good that the heart be established by grace; not by meats, wherein they that occupied themselves were not profited" (Heb. 13:9). In this particular instance the writer references eating (or not eating) certain foods. The spirit of the instruction, however, is to not be carried away with "strange" teachings but rather be established in grace. This word *strange* is also translated as *alien. Alien* is defined as "adverse; hostile; opposed (usually followed by to or from): ideas alien to modern thinking." (Random House, Inc, 2015) This "modern" thinking that Paul speaks about is that of grace rather than law. In this context, the writer is instructing to not be carried away by diverse and alien, adverse, hostile doctrines and articles either allowed or forbidden in Jewish law that are opposed to grace itself but rather be established in that grace.

Jesus Talks about Tithing

It is readily pointed out by those who support tithing that Jesus himself spoke about the importance of tithing. In this thinking, it is concluded that since Jesus spoke about the importance of tithing, it should continue to the modern day even though the remaining portion of the law is set aside. We read in Matthew, "Woe to you, teachers of the law and Pharisees, you hypocrites! You give a tenth of your spices-mint, dill and cumin. But you have neglected the more important matters of the law—justice, mercy and faithfulness. You should have practiced the latter, without neglecting the former" (Matt. 23:23 NIV).

In this passage, Jesus is speaking to the Pharisees and correcting them for their misuse of the "heart" of the law. Consider this in the same light as Malachi, where the Word of the Lord was directed toward the priests. Here, as in Malachi, it was not a matter of amount of the tithe that they were bringing, as they were bringing one-tenth of the spices. It was a matter of their heart, as they were neglecting the more important matters of God's law (to love one another).

When Jesus addresses the tithe, it is important to understand what He was saying. The tithe was only of mint, dill, and cumin (things from the land) and not a tithe of income. This is consistent with what the "tithe" actually was to the Jews. Both Jesus and the Pharisees understood the meaning of the tithe. But to underscore this, Jesus stated the tithe was only of mint, dill, and cumin. Remember that Jesus was talking to the Pharisees (not the Gentiles or even His Jewish followers), who he frequently was rebuking for their wrong heart. In addition, this passage does not indicate that tithing should continue, but rather it points to the weakness and inability of anyone to keep the law, even if they were performing the "act of the law" as subscribed.

This is also underscored in Luke.

> And He spoke this parable to certain ones who trusted in themselves, that they were righteous, and despised others: Two men went up into the temple to pray; the one a Pharisee, and the other a tax-collector. The Pharisee stood and prayed within himself in this way: God, I thank You that I am not as other men are, extortioners, unjust, adulterers, or even like this tax-collector. I fast twice on the Sabbath, I give tithes of all that I possess. And standing afar off, the tax-collector would not even lift up his eyes to Heaven, but struck on his breast, saying, God be merciful to me a sinner! I tell you, this man went down to his house justified rather than the other. For everyone who exalts himself shall be abased, and he who humbles himself shall be exalted. (Luke 18:9–14)

We see here again that tithing will not gain a right standing before God; but rather a heart of repentance will.

Where Jesus Does Not Talk about Tithing

While Jesus mentions tithing in the above passages, it is interesting and important to be aware of when Jesus does not speak of tithing. After His resurrection Jesus spent forty days with His disciples and expounded on the kingdom of God. After He had given them both revelation of God's Word and the charge to go into the world and teach all nations, they went about proclaiming the kingdom of God. There is no record that they ever spoke of any instruction of the requirement of tithing, and they never spoke instruction to follow the law. On the contrary, there was agreement that the Gentiles were not to be burdened with the law (see "The Jerusalem Council" section later in this book). Instead, they spoke of righteousness apart from the law. If tithing was such an important piece for Christians to gain God's favor and/or blessing, surely there would have been some mention of this in the post resurrection scriptures.

In addition, Jesus taught us to pray, "Your Kingdom come, your will be done on earth as it is in heaven." Through Christ, His kingdom is here. And we are to walk in that kingdom here on earth the same way that it is in heaven. There is no mention of tithing in heaven. Tithing is not a heavenly principle nor is it an eternal principle. It is not performed in the heavenly temple since Jesus entered that temple through His blood and put an end to tithing and sacrifices for all time. The book of Revelation gives us a true picture of heaven, which includes worship but is absent of tithing. If we are truly to represent heaven's kingdom here on earth, it will be void of tithing but fully glorifying God and Jesus.

Mercy, Not Sacrifice

Jesus rebuked the Pharisees on more than one occasion. In Matthew 9:13 and 12:7 He spoke to them saying, "But go and learn what this is, I will have mercy and not sacrifice." Jesus was referring to what was spoken in Hosea: "For I desired mercy and not sacrifice, and the knowledge of God more than burnt offerings" (Hosea 6:6). As we break down the meaning in Hosea as Jesus instructed, we find from Strong's Concordance that the word *desire* is from the Hebrew word *châphêts* (H2654), which means properly, to incline to; by implication (literally but rarely) to bend; figuratively to be pleased with, desire:–X any at all, (have, take) delight, desire, favor, like, move, be (well) pleased, have pleasure, will, would.

The word *not* is from *lo* (H3808): a primitive particle; *not* (the simple or abstract negation); by implication no; often used with other particles:–X before, + or else, ere, + except, ig [-norant], much, less, nay, neither, never, no ([-ne], -r, [-thing]), (X as though…, [can-], for) not (out of), of nought, otherwise, out of, + surely, + as truly as, + of a truth, + verily, for want, + whether, without.

What I suggest God (and Jesus) is saying here is that He desires, delights in, has pleasure, and is pleased with mercy without sacrifice. In other words, God delights in giving us His mercy without the requirement of a sacrifice. So God brought the everlasting sacrifice in the form of Jesus so that there would no longer be the requirement of a sacrifice for God to show us His mercy.

God also desires for us to know Him more than He wants us to bring a burnt offering. And God's heart is for us to follow His example, which is to give mercy (forgive) to others without the need for them to bring anything as an offering to us.

In Matthew 23:23 as Jesus was speaking to the Pharisees about tithing on mint, dill, and cumin he was correcting them for neglecting justice, mercy, and faithfulness. In this his words were consistent with God's heart, which is to have mercy without sacrifice. Because of Jesus's obedient sacrifice, once for all, God now extends that mercy upon all who believe, as it is written: "But now a righteousness of God has been revealed apart from Law, being witnessed by the Law and the Prophets; even the righteousness of God through the faith of Jesus Christ, toward all and upon all those who believe" (Rom 3:21–22). In Hebrews, the writer addresses this completely:

> Therefore when He comes into the world, He says, "Sacrifice and offering You did not desire, but You have prepared a body for Me. In burnt offerings and sacrifices for sin You have had no pleasure. Then I said, Lo, I come (in the volume of the Book it is written of Me) to do Your will, O God." Above, when He said, "Sacrifice and offering, and burnt offerings and offering for sin You did not desire, neither did You have pleasure in them" (which are offered according to the Law), then He said, "Lo, I come to do Your will, O God." He takes away the first so that He may establish the second. By this will we are sanctified through the offering of the body of Jesus Christ once for all. And indeed every priest stands daily ministering and offering often the same sacrifices, which can never take away sins. But this Man, after He had offered one sacrifice for sins forever, sat down on the right of God, from then on expecting until His enemies are made His footstool. For by one offering He has perfected forever those who are sanctified. The Holy Spirit also is a witness to us; for after He had said before, "This is the covenant that I will make with them after those days, says the Lord; I will put My Laws into their hearts, and in their minds, I will write them," also He adds, "their sins and their iniquities I will remember no more." Now where remission of these is, there is no more offering for sin. (Heb. 10:5–18)

This passage again points to God's desire to bring mercy without sacrifice as, through Jesus, there is no more need for a sin offering.

In addition, as we examine these passages through other translations we see an additional picture of God's heart:

> For I desire and delight in [steadfast] loyalty [faithfulness in the covenant relationship], rather than sacrifice, And in the knowledge of God more than burnt offerings. (Hosea 6:6 Amp)

And again:

> I want your loyalty, not your sacrifices. I want you to know me, not to give me your burnt offerings. (Hosea 6:6 GW)

As we read these translations, we discover that God desires for us to know Him and to be in relationship with Him more than he wants us to bring offerings and sacrifices. It was out of God's love and compassion that He brought the ultimate sacrifice as He had Jesus go to the cross, extending His mercy to all, (which is upon all who believe). It was Jesus who was loyal, being loyal to the death, so that we may come to the fullness of the knowledge of God. He doesn't want us to simply "go through the motions" of being a God / Christ follower. His desire is for us to know His heart. It has been said that Jesus did not come to establish a religion, but to restore a relationship. This relationship is with our Creator, God, and Father. He established this new covenant relationship through the blood of Jesus. In doing so, He has put away the requirements of the law, including the requirement of tithing.

So, be encouraged to listen to what Jesus is asking: to learn what it means that God desires mercy and not sacrifice, and the knowledge of God more than burnt offerings. Be drawn into an amazing relationship that God wants to have with you. He is the one worthy of our loyalty.

The Temple Tax

It is often taught that the tithe is like "God's tax," the portion that we owe God for what he gives us. However, Jesus even addresses this misconception:

> After Jesus and his disciples arrived in Capernaum, the collectors of the two-drachma tax came to Peter and asked, "Doesn't your teacher pay the temple tax?" "Yes, he does," he replied. When Peter came into the house, Jesus was the first to speak. "What do you think, Simon?" he asked. "From whom do the kings of the earth collect duty and taxes—from their own sons or from others?" "From others," Peter answered. "Then the sons are exempt," Jesus said to him. "But so that we may not offend them, go to the lake and throw out your line. Take the first fish you catch; open its mouth and you will find a four-drachma coin. Take it and give it to them for my tax and yours." (Matt. 17:24–27, NIV)

Looking at this passage closely, one sees that Jesus is not instructing on the need to pay the tax, but rather he instructed Peter to pay this so that they were not offended. In the question "From whom do the kings of the earth collect duty and taxes—from their own sons or from others?" it calls for a thought-out response, of which Peter answered: "From others." Jesus confirms that his answer is correct as He responds, "Then the sons are exempt."

As we receive Christ as our Savior, we are born again in new life and are now seen by God as sons (and daughters), Kings and priests, ambassadors of Christ. Therefore, by Christ's own words, we (as sons) are exempt from this tax. Also note that, even though Peter paid this tax, he did not pay it with his own money or Jesus's money but retrieved it from the fish. He did not ask Peter to pay for all the disciples (and there is no indication that they paid the tax or not) but just for

Jesus and Peter.

Although it is understood that Jesus and His disciples had money (income), there is no record that Jesus required they give a tithe of this money to the temple. There is also no indication that Jesus ever paid a "true" tithe. In reality, because Joseph was a tent maker, he did not bring a tithe because the tithe was not money and he did not raise crops or livestock. Of course, Joseph likely paid the temple tax, but Jesus addresses this in the above passage stating the Sons of God are exempt.

To be clear, this passage is not speaking about the tithe but rather the temple tax. So to use this passage as support of the requirement of tithing is not supported in the scriptures.

The Rich Young Ruler

The Bible shares the account of an interaction between Jesus and a rich young ruler. This account is also spoken of in Matthew 19:16–30 and Luke 18:18–30. Here we will look at Mark's account of this.

> And when He had gone out into the way, one came running up and kneeled to Him, and asked Him, Good Master, what shall I do that I may inherit eternal life? And Jesus said to him, Why do you call Me good? No one is good except one, God. You know the commandments: Do not commit adultery, do not kill, do not steal, do not bear false witness, do not defraud, honor your father and your mother. And he answered and said to Him, Teacher, all these I have observed from my youth. Then Jesus, beholding him, loved him and said to him, One thing you lack. Go, sell whatever you have and give it to the poor, and you shall have treasure in Heaven. And come, take up the cross and

> follow Me. And he was sad at that saying and went away grieved, for he had great possessions. And Jesus looked around and said to His disciples, How hardly those having riches will enter into the kingdom of God! And the disciples were astonished at His words. But Jesus answering again said to them, Children, how hard it is for those who trust in riches to enter into the kingdom of God! It is easier for a camel to go through the eye of a needle than for a rich one to enter into the kingdom of God. And they were astonished beyond measure, saying to themselves, And who can be saved? And Jesus looking on them said, "With men it is impossible, but not with God; for with God all things are possible". Then Peter began to say to Him, Lo, we have left all and have followed You. And Jesus answered and said, Truly I say to you, There is no man that has left house or brothers or sisters or father or mother or wife or children or lands for my sake and the gospel's sake, but he shall receive a hundredfold now in this time, houses and brothers and sisters and mothers and children and lands with persecutions, and in the world to come, eternal life. But many that are first shall be last; and the last shall be first. (Mark 10:17–31)

Some have used this teaching by Jesus to suggest that if you choose not to give ten percent of your income, you should follow this example and give it all to Jesus. While it is true that we are to "lay aside" (leave) everything and follow Him, Jesus is using this example to teach that even if you think you have kept all the commandments, there will still be something that would hinder you from entering into eternal life. In this case, the young man kept all God's commandments, yet it became evident that his heart was divided when he was asked to give up his money and follow

Jesus. No one can enter the kingdom of God if you are trying to do this through your own works. Again, as earlier described, it is a matter of the heart and not a matter of doing. "With men it is impossible, but not with God; for with God all things are possible."

Again, this teaching by Jesus was more focused on the fact that we cannot "earn" our way into heaven (and kingdom blessing) by what we do or even by what we give. This passage was really showing that no matter what we try, even if we give it all, our works and efforts are not good enough to get us into right standing and favor with God. The blessing comes only as we return to God with all our hearts, not by doing certain acts. "But seek first the kingdom of God and His righteousness; and all these things shall be added to you" (Matt. 6:33).

Jesus knew the young ruler's heart. Imagine if the young ruler agreed to go sell all he had and gave it to the poor to follow Him. This would establish that eternal life could be obtained by works and would make grace unnecessary (Rom. 11:6). Jesus knew the young man's heart and was able to speak to the thing that he had placed greater worth and trust in above God. As Jesus declares "It is easier for a camel to go through the eye of a needle than for a rich one to enter into the kingdom of God", He is showing that it is impossible for any man (even through great wealth) to enter the kingdom of God on their own. But then He says, "With men it is impossible, but not with God". Here the mystery is revealed: in Christ alone may we enter into eternal life.

It is also encouraging to know that as we place all our trust in the Lord there is a reward both in heaven and on earth. This reward of "receiving a hundredfold" is not through giving of any money or tithe. It is received as we lay down our lives and follow Christ.

The Jerusalem Council

As Paul "ran his race," he continually came up against those who were teaching that new Christians were to also follow circumcision and the Law.

> And certain ones who came down from Judea taught the brothers, saying, unless you are circumcised according to the custom of Moses, you cannot be saved. Therefore dissension and not a little disputation occurring by Paul and Barnabas, they appointed Paul and Barnabas and certain others of them to go up to Jerusalem to the apostles and elders about this question. And indeed being set forward by the church, they passed through Phoenicia and Samaria, declaring the conversion of the nations. And they caused great joy to all the brothers. And arriving in Jerusalem, they were received by the church, and by the apostles and elders. And they declared all things that God had done with them. But some of those from the sect of the Pharisees, having believed, rose up, saying, It was necessary to circumcise them and to command them to keep the Law of Moses. And the apostles and elders were assembled to see about this matter. And after much disputing, Peter rose up and said to them, Men, brothers, you recognize that from ancient days God chose among us that through my mouth the nations should hear the Word of the gospel, and believe. And God, who knows the hearts, bore them witness, giving them the Holy Spirit even as to us. And He put no difference between us and them, purifying their hearts by faith. Now therefore why do you tempt God by putting a yoke on the neck of the disciples, a yoke which neither our fathers nor we were able to bear?

But we believe that through the grace of the Lord Jesus Christ we shall be saved, according to which manner they also believed. And all the multitude kept silent and listened to Barnabas and Paul declaring what miracles and wonders God had worked among the nations through them. And after they were silent, James answered, saying, Men, brothers, listen to me. Even as Simon has declared how God at the first visited the nations to take out of them a people for His name. And the words of the Prophets agree to this; as it is written, "After this I will return and will build again the tabernacle of David which has fallen down; and I will build again its ruins, and I will set it up, so those men who are left might seek after the Lord, and all the nations on whom My name has been called, says the Lord, who does all these things." All His works are known to God from eternity. Therefore my judgment is that we do not trouble those who have turned to God from among the nations, but that we write to them that they should abstain from pollutions of idols, and from fornication, and from things strangled, and from blood. For Moses from ages past has those in every city proclaiming him, being read in the synagogues every Sabbath day. Then it pleased the apostles and elders, with the whole church, to send chosen men from them to Antioch with Paul and Barnabas; Judas, whose last name was Barsabas; and Silas, chief men among the brothers. And they wrote these things by their hand: The apostles and elders and brothers send greeting to the brothers, from the nations in Antioch and Syria and Cilicia. Because we have heard that certain ones who went out from us have troubled you with words, unsettling your souls, saying, Be circumcised and keep the law! (to whom we gave no such command); it seemed good to us, being

> assembled with one accord, to send chosen men to you with our beloved Barnabas and Paul, men who have given up their lives for the name of our Lord Jesus Christ. Therefore we have sent Judas and Silas, who will also announce to you the same things by word. For it seemed good to the Holy Spirit and to us to lay on you no greater burden than these necessary things: that you abstain from meats offered to idols, and from blood, and from things strangled, and from fornication; from which, if you keep yourselves, you shall do well. Be prospered. Then indeed they being let go, they came to Antioch. And gathering the multitude, they delivered the letter. And when they had read it, they rejoiced at the comfort. And Judas and Silas, also being prophets themselves, exhorted the brothers with many words and confirmed them. (Acts 15:1–32)

This interaction is also spoken about in Paul's letter to the Galatians:

> Then through fourteen years, I went up again to Jerusalem with Barnabas, and took Titus with me also. And I went up by revelation. And I put before them the gospel which I proclaim in the nations, but privately to those seeming to be pillars, lest I run, or I ran, into vanity. (But not even Titus, the one with me, a Greek, was compelled to be circumcised.) But because of those false brothers stealing in, who stole in to spy out our liberty which we have in Christ Jesus; they desiring to enslave us; to whom not even for an hour did we yield in subjection, that the truth of the gospel might continue with you. But from those who seemed to be something (what kind they were then does not matter to me; God does not accept the face of man), for those seeming important conferred nothing

> to me. But on the contrary, seeing that I have been entrusted with the gospel of the uncircumcision, as Peter to the circumcision; for He working in Peter to the apostleship of the circumcision also worked in me to the nations. And knowing the grace given to me, James, and Cephas, and John, who seemed to be pillars, gave right hands of fellowship to Barnabas and me, that we go to the nations, but they to the circumcision. Only they asked that we remember the poor, which very thing I was eager to do. (Gal. 2:1–10)

This account alone should be enough to convince the inquirer that circumcision, tithing, or any other part of the law is not required by followers of Christ to gain any right standing with God in His kingdom. This account not only addresses circumcision but the whole of the Law of Moses as well. As Paul met with other apostles and leaders in Jerusalem, he shared the Gospel that Jesus revealed to him. They agreed this good news set believers free from the requirement of the law, and it was confirmed by the Jerusalem Council. They added nothing to it nor took anything away. They only asked that we remember the poor and to abstain from meats offered to idols, from blood, from things strangled and from fornication. There is no greater burden laid upon Christ followers. This includes the burden of tithing.

However, the pressure to be circumcised and follow Jewish regulations is such a strong deceptive argument that even Peter was at one time deceived, as we read this account in Galatians:

> But when Peter came to Antioch, I opposed him to his face, because he was to be blamed. For before some came from James, he ate with the nations. But when they came, he withdrew and separated himself, fearing those of the circumcision. And the rest of the Jews also

> dissembled with him, so as even Barnabas was led away with their dissembling. But when I saw that they did not walk uprightly with the truth of the gospel, I said to Peter before all, If you, being a Jew, live as a Gentile, and not as the Jews, why do you compel the nations to Judaize? We Jews by nature, and not sinners of the nations, knowing that a man is not justified by works of the Law, but through faith in Jesus Christ; even we believed in Jesus Christ, that we might be justified by the faith in Christ, and not by works of the Law. For all flesh will not be justified by works of law. But if, while we seek to be justified in Christ, we also were found to be sinners, is Christ therefore a minister of sin? Let it not be said! For if I build again the things which I destroyed, I confirm myself as a transgressor. For through the Law I died to the law that I might live to God. I have been crucified with Christ, and I live; yet no longer I, but Christ lives in me. And that life I now live in the flesh, I live by faith toward the Son of God, who loved me and gave Himself on my behalf. I do not set aside the grace of God, for if righteousness is through law, then Christ died without cause. (Gal. 2:11–21)

If Peter, who was with Jesus, could be deceived and persuaded to go back to following the Jewish Law, even those today who know and love the Lord Jesus could be susceptible to this deceptive argument. Jesus warned of these deceptions when he said, "For false Christs and false prophets will arise and show great signs and wonders; so much so that, if it were possible, they would deceive even the elect" (Matt. 24:24). Jesus again warns, "Beware of the leaven of the Pharisees, which is hypocrisy" (Luk 12:1). Paul also instructed us as well as he wrote, "Do not be carried about with different and strange doctrines, for it is good for the heart to be established with grace" (Heb. 13:9a).

Jesus met Paul on the road to Damascus and gave him the revelation of who He was. As a devout Pharisee, Paul knew the Torah and the Law very well. When Jesus revealed Himself, Paul knew better than anyone the depth of what this meant. Jesus had fulfilled the Law and made a way to God by grace through faith alone for those that believed in Christ. This is the message he preached unswervingly to all he encountered. As he met opposition he began to question what he had received. When he took this message to the Jerusalem Council they fully confirmed what God had done through Christ, setting aside the Law and putting no burden on those that believe in Christ. This includes the burden of tithing.

Is There Tithing Under Grace?

It is important to understand that all acts of 'works of the flesh' have been placed under the law so that all things could be redeemed and fulfilled by Christ. Acts of "works", in essence, are doing something that would try to please God or would try to obtain a better position or blessing from God. God wants us free and Christ has come to set us free from the law of sin and death. The only way we can truly be free from depending on our works is to fully rely on Jesus' blood to set us free.

Consider this. The first recorded offerings that were brought before the Lord were from Cain and Abel. Cain's offering was brought first, which was of the harvest of the field. The Lord was not pleased with this offering as it was brought through a curse, since the ground was cursed when Adam fell into sin (see "Offerings Brought Under a Curse" page 170). Abel's offering was of the firstlings of the flock and of fat. These were pleasing to the Lord. These were also a shadow and indication of Jesus to come, being the first born of Mary and the first born of the dead. Both of these offerings were freely given and without solicitation from God.

If one would apply the "law of first mention", considering the first-time offerings, one could argue that this is the model God is pleased with, and that we should at least continue to bring offerings of firstlings and fat before the Lord. Since this pleasing act was long before the law, some could argue (as is done with the tithe given by Abram to Melchezidek) that this act should continue because it preceded the law.

However, we know that both offerings of firstlings and fat and offerings of harvest of grains became a requirement to bring to the lord under Mosaic law. There is no argument that these offerings should continue past the Mosaic law simply because they occurred long before the law was established.

In a similar way the free will tithe given by Abram to the Lord (Melchezidek) was also brought under the law so that it, too, would become submissive to the law and be subjected to both the fulfillment by Christ and the redemption through Grace. Again, we must look at this subject in complete context to properly understand it.

In Genesis 14:18-20 we see the account where Melchezidek met Abram after a victorious battle, brought bread and wine, and blessed Abram. Abram then gave freely a tithe of the spoils of war. Later it was then recorded that tithes were to be part of the Mosaic law. Just like the offerings of Cain and Abel were brought under the law, so was the giving of a tithe. To better understand this, we must go to the Book of Hebrews where this is discussed.

We have already established earlier in this book that the account given by the writer of Hebrews was to establish Jesus as high priest, not to establish the requirement of a tithe (as many often suggest). It is important to read all of this in proper context as well. This has been explained in greater detail in the section "Jesus and Melchezidek ". In addition, it bears examining this passage more closely again to understand that even Abram's tithe was brought under the law:

> "For this Melchizedek, king of Salem, priest of the Most High God, who met Abraham returning from the slaughter of the kings and blessed him, to

> whom also Abraham gave a tenth part of all, first being translated "king of righteousness," and then also king of Salem, meaning "king of peace," without father, without mother, without genealogy, having neither beginning of days nor end of life, but made like the Son of God, remains a priest continually. Now consider how great this man was, to whom even the patriarch Abraham gave a tenth of the spoils. And indeed those who are of the sons of Levi, who receive the priesthood, have a commandment to receive tithes from the people according to the law, that is, from their brethren, though they have come from the loins of Abraham; but he whose genealogy is not derived from them received tithes from Abraham and blessed him who had the promises. Now beyond all contradiction the lesser is blessed by the better. Here mortal men receive tithes, but there he receives them, of whom it is witnessed that he lives. Even Levi, who receives tithes, paid tithes through Abraham, so to speak, for he was still in the loins of his father when Melchizedek met him. Therefore, if perfection were through the Levitical priesthood (for under it the people received the law), what further need was there that another priest should rise according to the order of Melchizedek, and not be called according to the order of Aaron? For the priesthood being changed, of necessity there is also a change of the law." (Heb. 7:1-12 NKJV)

The additional key understanding is that, while Abram paid a tithe to Melchezidek it indicates that Levi also paid tithes to him as well, as he was in his father's loins. This indicates that the tithe of Abram is also subject to the Mosaic law because the Levitical tithe is under that law. In other words, since the Levitical tithe was under the law and Levi gave tithes to Melchezidek (through Abram while he was in his 'loins') once the law was established Abram's tithe became subject to the law. So, in the very next line (which many leave out) we read that if perfection of these tithes (tithes that went to Melchezidek) were perfected by the law, then there would be no need for another to come in the line of Melchezidek (meaning there would be no need for Jesus).

Some claim that this act of Levi bringing their tithe to Melchezidek through the loins of Abram is a model that should be followed today, suggesting that tithing in this manner brings blessing and redemption to our offspring and future generations. This suggests that tithing is the paramount act that brings this blessing and redemption rather than the blood of Jesus. As we will discuss later, this is a dangerous assumption and, according to Galatians 5 places one dangerously close to "making the blood of Jesus as naught" and "falling from grace". Also, when citing the passage of Levi bringing a tithe to Melchezidek through Abram there is failure to read the next line, which states that this tithe does not bring perfection, therefore there was need for another to come in the line of Melchezidek. As this other one (Jesus) came, He alone brought perfection (and completion) to this and any other tithe offering.

Knowing that Melchezidek was without father or mother, without beginning or end of days, and was priest of the Most-High God, it is sometimes suggested that this encounter was with Jesus. It is important to note, however, that Melchezidek was priest, but was not "high priest". In addition, if Melchezidek was Jesus, He would be coming in the "line of Himself" not in the line of another: the line of Melchezidek. So, while this encounter was probably not with Jesus directly it is important to note that there was no record of an earthly temple at that time. Because Melchezidek as priest must have ministered before the Lord, he must have had access to the heavenly temple. Having access to the heavenly temple he would have seen the original and true temple as Moses did and known the pattern of tithes and offerings that would be required at that time. As Melchezidek brought bread and wine to Abram (another model of Jesus, as He is our bread and wine of the new covenant), he received Abram's tithe. While it is not recorded what Melchezidek did with that tithe, it is reasonable that he brought it before the Lord as priest (knowing he had access to the heavenly temple) and presented it there before the Lord. While Melchizedek was priest he would continually minister before the Lord. However, because he was not "high priest", according to the earthly model established on earth, he would not have had access to the "Holiest of Holies". This was only accessible by the High Priest, and never without a blood sacrifice. We'll talk more about this in the section "The Ultimate Tithe" but know for now that this place in the heavenly temple was reserved only for Jesus, our High Priest.

This first act of bringing a free will gift of a tithe was then later repeated by Jesus as he freely went to the cross and fulfilled the word spoken in Malachi 3:11 where God challenged the priests to bring the whole unblemished spotless tithe to the temple storehouse. As Jesus was the pure unblemished spotless lamb and came freely as the offering and tithe, He fulfilled the requirement of the tithe (both Levitical and Abramic) and the offering, setting us free from all the law and all the curse. As stated in Hebrews, because the Abramic free will tithe was brought under the law, we have been set free from any kind of tithe.

By placing this in context we can now see that even though these offerings and tithes were brought before the Lord prior to the law, God intentionally brought both of these acts under the law so that all things would be subject to the law. In this, then, all things would be fulfilled and redeemed by Christ so that we could be free from all the law. This restores us, then, to the original intention of a relationship that God has chosen for us. One that is of love, born out of faith, with a freewill, choosing to serve, love, honor, and obey the rule of love as shown by our Father and His Son. Whom the Son has set free is free indeed!

In addition, as was discussed in the chapter "Jesus and Melchizedek", to suggest that Pastors (or Apostles) have taken the place of the Levites for receiving tithes teaches replacement theology and is not Biblically sound. In the same manner, if one suggests that we are to bring tithes to Melchizedek as Abram did, we would technically need to bring them directly to Jesus, as He is the one who came in the line of Melchizedek. To suggest that the Pastors or Apostles are standing on behalf of Jesus discounts the fact that all who are in Christ are in the line of Melchizedek and therefore all could receive tithes (if tithing was correct). It would seem this teaching is embraced primarily to justify tithing and is not based on sound doctrine. When fully considered one can see that bringing a tithe under grace, whether it be to the Levites as part of the law, or to Melchizedek (Jesus) as part of the instruction to follow the Abramic tithe, is not Biblically justified.

Honoring God

Some church leaders that previously embraced, upheld, and championed tithing based on Malachi 3 have been confronted with the truth that we are no longer obligated to bring a tithe based on these scriptures. With this realization there has been a shift in their teaching. As some preachers / teachers acknowledge that, as Christians, we are no longer required to bring our tithe to gain a blessing and / or to prevent a curse, the new teaching proclaims that our tithe is critical (if not required) if we are to honor God. This new teaching is based on the suggestion that Abram's tithe was one of honoring God through Melchezidek. It is not my intention to disclaim Abram bringing honor through this tithe. However, it has been stated that "the tithe is an earthly token and honor to gain access to a heavenly covenant", declaring that, in addition to honoring God, it is the way for believers to align with the Abrahamic covenant and its promises. Teaching that paying our tithes is important to show honor to God also instructs that if we don't pay our tithes we are not bringing honor to God, implying that we don't honor God in our hearts. It also instructs that we aren't able to gain access to the blessings of Abraham unless we tithe.

This teaching shifts the fear from being one of preventing a curse or gaining a blessing (as was taught from Malachi) to the fear of not honoring God. It creates fear in the heart of the believer and the result is, again, that the tithe is paid out of fear. In hearing this teaching the individual is exposed to the accusation of not honoring God if they don't pay their tithe and it has the potential of shaming the person into giving (the tithe) from a wrong motivation and understanding.

With this new reasoning to promote tithing, one would have to ask the question, if tithing was always about honoring God why was it ever about Malachi (and the curses and blessings)? Innocently, this new teaching could have simply grown out of a love for God and desire to show him that love. However, in the least, this seems like an attempt for leaders and teachers to justify tithing to get money for the church. At worse, it is a continued manipulation of the people, keeping them in the bondage of giving through fear and shaming them into trying to honor God through tithing. In any case, it prevents people from seeing and experiencing the fullness of what Christ has done and what grace offers.

The only acceptable way to honor God is to honor Jesus and the blood He shed for us; to honor the sacrifice that established a new covenant with God. In trying to re-establish the old covenant with its rules and regulations we dishonor Jesus and what He accomplished. Paul writes:

> If I rebuild something that I've torn down, I admit that I was wrong to tear it down. When I tried to obey the laws in the Scriptures, those laws killed me. As a result, I live in a relationship with God. I have been crucified with Christ. I no longer live, but Christ lives in me. The life I now live I live by believing in God's Son, who loved me and took the punishment for my sins. I don't reject God's kindness. If we receive God's approval by obeying the laws in the Scriptures, then Christ's death was pointless. (Gal. 2:19-21 GW)

We have learned from many other Biblical passages that we enter into the Abrahamic covenant not by works, but through faith. This covenant is sealed by the blood of Jesus, not by the act of tithing. Specifically, Paul writes "And if you are Christ's, then you are Abraham's seed, and heirs according to the promise." (Galatians 3:29 NKJV) Any attempt to gain access to this promised covenant by any means other than Jesus fails. Likewise, any attempt to gain access by honoring God with earthly belongings falls short. We are called to honor God with our body, a living sacrifice, holy and acceptable to Him. (Romans 12:1) When we do this, as we receive Christ and submit our life to Him, He will direct our steps and show us what to do with our earthly possessions. These will be acceptable to him as they come out of our honoring Jesus, submitting to Holy Spirit, and being obedient to His call.

This includes honoring what Jesus' complete work on the cross has provided. It includes honoring the commandments that Jesus gave to us: to "love the Lord your God with all your heart, with all your soul, with all your mind, and with all your strength" and to "love your neighbor as yourself" (Mark 12:30 NKJV). It is to disciple all nations, teaching them of God's love and declaring the good news of God's Kingdom here on earth as it is in Heaven (Matthew 18-20 and Mark 15-18).

Of course there are many tangible ways to honor God through Jesus. One of these ways is to give financially. This is a tangible way to show God's love to others. Giving to those in need shows God's love and is a testimony of Jesus' love. By giving to a church it helps establish God's Kingdom and provides a place for believers to gather, to be equipped and to be sent out into the world. This financial support comes through simple giving as "one purposes in their heart" as led by Holy Spirit.

Please don't misunderstand this message. It is not intended to suggest we don't give, but rather that we give generously with a joyful heart. We are called to love others as Christ commanded and demonstrated. Spreading the gospel both as a personal witness and by sharing resources with others who are able to "go out" and minister is a vital part of establishing God's Kingdom here on earth.

Our giving may be a percentage of income or just a simple amount. However, don't be tied to a system that creates guilt and fear. Honor God by honoring Jesus. As we focus on the wonderful things God has done through Jesus, be inspired and spurred on to give generously as you are able.

Paul writes:

> I can give witness about them that they really want to serve God. But how they are trying to do it is not based on what they know. They didn't know how God makes people right with himself. They tried to get right with God in their own way. They didn't do it in God's way. Christ has completed the law. So now everyone who believes can be right with God. (Romans 10:2-4)

Remember, honoring God and being in right standing with Him is not by means of a tithe, it is by receiving Jesus as Lord and Savior. As Christ followers we do well, then, to walk obediently in faith, honor Jesus and all He has done for us, love God and love people.

Mature Christians

I listened to a well-known pastor and teacher that had come to understand that tithing is no longer required based on the Malachi 3 teaching (as was previously taught). However, the new instruction claims that as one "matures" as a Christian, they will receive this revelation of the importance of tithing. The foundation for this premise is Hebrews 5:

> And having been perfected, He became the author of eternal salvation to all who obey Him, called by God as High Priest "according to the order of Melchizedek, of whom we have much to say, and hard to explain, since you have become dull of hearing. For though by this time you ought to be teachers, you need someone to teach you again the first principles of the oracles of God; and you have come to need milk and not solid food. For everyone who partakes only of milk is unskilled in the word of righteousness, for he is a babe. But solid food belongs to those who are of full age, that is, those who by reason of use have their senses exercised to discern both good and evil. (Heb 5:9-14 NKJV)

Understanding the definition of the word "oracle" is helpful. It means "a divine communication or revelation". In siting this scripture the teaching incorrectly surmises that this is referring to a revelation of tithing and the importance of Abram's tithe (to Melchizedek) to honor Jesus. While the teaching urges tithing as a sign of the mature Christian, it also claims that those that don't have this revelation are immature. Once again, however, it is important to look at these scriptures in the proper context.

As was described in earlier sections, we understand that the writer of Hebrews is not attempting to establish tithing but rather is establishing Jesus. The "meat" that the writer is referring to is not about a revelation of Melchezidek but rather a revelation of Jesus and His establishing a new and greater covenant; one that is not of the law but is by faith. The writer is declaring the qualifications that Jesus met as our new High Priest so we may receive Him fully in this position. But the people had become "dull in their hearing".

As in many letters written by Paul, his battle was to keep

people from going back to the bondage of the Mosaic Law. He was continually instructing them not to be "bewitched" and to remain in the faith and teaching of grace that he had originally instructed of them; a grace that is only found in Jesus. This is why the writer said that "for though by this time you ought to be teachers, you need someone to teach you again the first principles of the oracles of God. For everyone who partakes only of milk is unskilled in the word of righteousness, for he is a babe". Being "unskilled in the word of righteousness" means to be found trying to earn righteousness through "works" of the law rather than through faith. The first principles of the oracles of God are Jesus and the new covenant that He established; that "we are saved by grace through faith, not by works, so that no man can boast."

So, again, the "meat" is not about Melchizedek, but about what Jesus has done for us and the grace we receive through faith. To suggest that only mature believers understand the revelation of tithing brings shame and guilt on any Christian that does not currently tithe and accuses them of being weak and immature in their faith. Under this teaching, new or young Christians may feel pressured to tithe to show a sign of their maturity. And to suggest that as one moves into Christian maturity one should tithe, spurs the Christian on to "works" based model to achieve blessing and away from faith. This situation is not aligned with grace and brings a false understanding of God's heart. Those that find themselves aligning with this teaching on tithing may become "puffed up" as they would see themselves as more spiritually mature in Christ than others, honoring Jesus more than those who don't tithe. They may also believe they are better than those that don't tithe, bringing a false belief that they should expect a greater blessing. Truly, blessing is found only in

Christ.

In addition, this teaching refers to Genesis 14:20 as it defines the word "tithe" as Ma'aser in Hebrew language. This word Ma'aser, is accurately defined as "a tenth; especially a tithe". However, it is taught that when you break the word down, if you remove the "M" it leaves the word "aser". It is then taught that "aser" means "rich", declaring that there is "richness" or "wealth" in the tithe. The implication is that when you tithe, you gain riches. However, to declare the word "aser" means "rich" is not accurate. In looking at Strong's Concordance, the word "aser" or "asar" in combination with Ma' means "ten". Nowhere in the definition of this word is it defined as "rich". If you search the word "rich," you will find it in a later passage, Genesis 14:23(KJV), when Abram declares "I will not take anything that is thine, lest thou shouldest say, I have made Abram rich". Here the word "rich" is from the Hebrew word "ashar" and is not the same as the above word "asar". This clearly is a misunderstanding or misuse of these words in this teaching. So, to declare that riches are found in the tithe is not biblically supported.

As expressed in this teaching, tithing (and thus riches) is grasped by those mature enough to receive and understand the revelation. This suggestion is not only condescending and belittling, it is not founded in the spirit of grace itself. Once again, it brings guilt to those that are not tithing and accuses non-tithers of an immaturity in Christian faith. It brings a false hope for those tithing to receive a greater blessing from God, a blessing that God Himself provided for through Christ alone for all who believe.

One might argue that this belittling "tactic" was used by Paul when he first spoke about immature and mature Christians in Heb 5:9-14. While it may be true, it is important to understand what Paul was spurring people towards. As in many of Paul's letters, he was battling against people turning away from a righteousness by faith (Romans 1:17) back to a righteousness of the law, which relies on works. His words were meant to urge them on to the fullness of Christ, not to guilt them into doing works like tithing.

Maturing as a Christian is about learning to stand in the fullness of what Christ has done, empowered by the grace that God extended, moving in the freedom that Christ has provided, completely trusting in our Heavenly Father. This is the meat that the writer is talking about. So take this "meat" of instruction and hold fast to the sound words Paul has spoken (2 Timothy 1:13) and do not be entrapped in teachings that bring us back into bondage.

The Warning

Giving and tithing; what's the difference and why does it matter? When reflecting again on this topic it is good to remember that God's mercy will triumph over judgment (James 2:13). However, there are specific warnings in God's Word that should cause concern for one who would dishonor the grace afforded through the blood of Christ. As a reminder, the intention of this book is to bring God's love and freedom, not condemnation and judgement. However, if someone is heading for a cliff, love would cause us to call out and bring a warning of the impending danger. In a similar manner, it is with love that these warnings from God's Word are brought forth. There are several warnings that we must not ignore. The author of Hebrews writes,

> "Of how much worse punishment, do you suppose, will he be thought worthy of punishment, the one who has trampled the Son of God, and who has counted the blood of the covenant with which he was sanctified an unholy thing, and has insulted the Spirit of grace?" (Heb. 10:29).

The Judgment Throne

It is written that "it's appointed to men once to die, but after this the judgment, so Christ was once offered to bear the sins of many. And to those who look for Him He shall appear the second time without sin to salvation" (Heb. 9:27–28).

One day, we will all stand before the Lord. If He were to ask, "What have you done that would make you worthy to deserve and receive my blessing?" How will you answer? If the answer is, "I obeyed your requirement and paid my tithe regularly," will God be pleased? Or will you say, "I trusted in the complete finished work of Jesus on the cross and rely solely on him for my blessing."

God will not share His glory or the glory of His Son with any man. We may enter in to His glory through Jesus, but there is no place to share credit for that glory. If you say that you paid your tithe and did your best to deserve the blessing, you are saying that Jesus's sacrifice was not sufficient. Therefore, I believe, you are at risk of God saying, "Your works are as filthy rags, you are a debtor to the whole law and you have fallen from grace."

Again I pose this question: what if tithing, which is intended to honor God, is actually a strategy of the enemy whereby it dishonors God because it cheapens and brings insult to the blood of Jesus, making the blood of Jesus for naught? The devil's strategy has always been to deceive. He revealed this strategy in the garden of Eden as we discussed Genesis 3:1-5 in the chapter "Confusion in the Church".

Falling from Grace

It is a frightful thing to think of falling out of the grace of God that is through Jesus Christ. Yet there is one instance that Paul says this happens. In fact, this is the only way that Paul says we can fall from grace (apart from unbelief).

> Stand fast therefore in the liberty with which Christ has made us free, and do not again be held with the yoke of bondage. Behold, I, Paul, say to you that if you are circumcised, Christ shall profit you nothing. For I testify again to every man that is circumcised, that he is a debtor to do all the Law, you who are

> justified by Law are deprived of all effect from Christ; you fell from grace; for we through the Spirit wait for the hope of righteousness out of faith. For in Christ Jesus neither circumcision nor uncircumcision has any strength, but faith working through love. You were running well. Who hindered you that you do not obey the truth? This persuasion is not from Him who calls you. A little leaven leavens all the lump. I have confidence in you in the Lord that you will think nothing else, but that he troubling you shall bear the judgment, whoever he may be. And I, brothers, if I yet proclaim circumcision, why am I still persecuted? Then the offense of the Cross has ceased. I wish that those causing you to doubt will cut themselves off. For, brothers, you were called to liberty. Only does not use the liberty for an opening to the flesh, but by love serve one another. (Gal. 5:1–13)

While Paul speaks here of circumcision, he is describing a position of becoming held again by the yoke of bondage of the law. Very directly, Paul states that if you are circumcised to gain right standing with God, you must also fulfill the entire law. In a similar way, if you were to try to gain right standing by any act of the law, including tithing, one must fulfill the entire law, and Christ will be of no value to you. You are deprived of all the effect from Christ and have fallen from Grace. Paul also indicates that this is such an infectious way of thinking that when one accepts even a little bit of this teaching, it becomes incorporated into everything, as "a little leaven leavens all the lump."

This warning should cause the Christian to place great consideration to anything that would take the place of the complete work that Christ has finished through His life, death, and resurrection. To fall back into the thinking that performance, works, and works of the law will redeem us says that Christ's blood is not sufficient and somehow places the effort back on us (either in part or in whole) and this insults God.

Offerings Brought through a Curse

God is not pleased with offerings brought through a curse. This statement took me by surprise, yet during worship one day, I believe Holy Spirit impressed that upon my heart then immediately reminded me of Cain and Abel.

> Adam made love to his wife Eve, and she became pregnant and gave birth to Cain. She said, "With the help of the Lord I have brought forth a man." Later she gave birth to his brother Abel. Now Abel kept flocks, and Cain worked the soil. In the course of time Cain brought some of the fruits of the soil as an offering to the Lord. And Abel also brought an offering of fat portions from some of the firstborn of his flock. The Lord looked with favor on Abel and his offering, but on Cain and his offering he did not look with favor. So Cain was very angry, and his face was downcast. Then the Lord said to Cain, "Why are you angry? Why is your face downcast? If you do what is right, will you not be accepted? But if you do not do what is right, sin is crouching at your door; it desires to have you, but you must rule over it." (Gen 4:1–7, NIV)

Knowing that under the Mosaic Law offerings of both livestock and things grown from the land were acceptable offerings to the Lord, I asked the Lord why Cain's offering was not acceptable to Him at that time. Some have speculated that it was because Cain brought the offering with an impure heart, but there is no indication whatsoever of this in this passage. Then the Lord took me to Genesis 3:17: "And to

Adam he [God] said, 'Because you have listened to the voice of your wife and have eaten of the tree of which I commanded you, "You shall not eat of it," cursed is the ground because of you; in pain you shall eat of it all the days of your life.'"

The ground had become cursed because of Adam's sin. Therefore, when Cain brought an offering from the land, it was an offering brought through a curse. So I asked the Lord, "What changed?" As my wife and I discussed this, He directed her to Genesis 8, which is the account of Noah and the flood. We read the account after the flood:

> And Noah built an altar to Jehovah. And he took of every clean animal, and of every clean bird, and offered burnt offerings on the altar. And Jehovah smelled a sweet odor. And Jehovah said in His heart, I will never again curse the ground for man's sake, because the imagination of man's heart is evil from his youth. And I will not again smite every living thing as I have done. (Gen 8:20–21)

The curse that was upon the ground was lifted, and God vowed that He would never curse the ground again. So now, as Moses comes, offerings from the land are now acceptable to the Lord once again because they are no longer coming through a curse (even when the hearts of the people aren't perfect and pure). Jesus changed everything. As Jesus fulfilled the law, we know that He made a way for us to come to the Father apart from the law, and we bring him a "living sacrifice, which is holy and acceptable to God" (Rom. 12:1). However, there is a curse of the law which Christ has redeemed us from (Gal. 3:13). Therefore, any sacrifice that is now brought through the law (including a tithe) is brought through the curse, and God is not pleased with this.

So again, as we read with Cain and Abel God urges us to do what is right; but if you don't, sin is ready to attack you.

That sin will want to control you, but you must control it.

The Consequence of Bringing a "Strange/Profane Fire"

The Scripture tells us,

> Nadab and Abihu, the sons of Aaron, each took his censer and put fire in it, and put incense on it, and offered strange fire before Jehovah, which He had not commanded them. And there went out fire from Jehovah and devoured them, and they died before Jehovah. Then Moses said to Aaron, It is that which Jehovah spoke, saying, I will be sanctified in them that come near me, and before all the people I will be glorified. And Aaron held his peace. (Lev. 10:1–3)

Before this incident occurred, Aaron and Moses brought an offering to the Lord as per His (God's) instruction. The glory of the Lord then appeared to all the people (Lev. 9: 23). Perhaps in their desire to have more of God's glory and presence, they decided to bring a fire in a similar way as Aaron and Moses did. God did not instruct them to, and they were consumed.

Jesus brought the ultimate and final offering that was acceptable to the Lord through His fulfillment of the law on the cross. In this final act, no other offering would be required or even be acceptable to the Lord.

One day, in worship and prayer, I felt the Lord would say, "In My mercy and love, I have kept the fullness of my presence from you so that you would not be consumed in your bringing of an unholy fire, the offering of a tithe, which grieves and makes the blood of My Son for naught. Repent, therefore, and turn away from your empty offerings that are imperfect in My sight. Step in to the fullness that is in Christ.

He paid it all." (Prophetic word received July 8, 2014.)

Fear of Unrest

The writer of Hebrews gives us a great insight to the rest that is found in Christ. But he also gives us an unusual warning, which is to fear that we seem to come short of it.

> Therefore, holy brothers, called to be partakers of the heavenly calling, consider the Apostle and High Priest of our profession, Christ Jesus, who was faithful to Him who appointed Him, as Moses also was faithful in all his house. For He was counted worthy of more glory than Moses, because he who has built the house has more honor than the house; for every house is built by someone, but He who built all things is God. And Moses truly was faithful in all his house, as a servant, for a testimony of those things which were to be spoken afterward. But Christ was faithful as a Son over his own house; whose house we are, if we hold fast the confidence and the rejoicing of the hope firm to the end. Therefore, as the Holy Spirit says, "Today if you will hear His voice, do not harden your hearts, as in the provocation, in the day of temptation in the wilderness, when your fathers tempted Me, proved Me, and saw My works forty years. Therefore I was grieved with that generation and said, "They always err in their heart, and they have not known My ways." So I swore in My wrath, They shall not enter into My rest." Take heed, brothers, lest there be in any of you an evil heart of unbelief, in departing from the living God. But exhort one another daily, while it is called today, lest any of you be hardened through the deceitfulness of sin. For we are made partakers of Christ, if we hold the beginning of our confidence

> steadfast to the end, while it is said, "Today if you will hear His voice, harden not your hearts, as in the provocation." For some, when they had heard, did provoke; however, not all who came out of Egypt by Moses. But with whom was He grieved forty years? Was it not with those who had sinned, whose carcasses fell in the wilderness? And to whom did He swear that they should not enter into His rest, but to those who did not believe? So we see that they could not enter in because of unbelief. (Heb. 3:1–19)

This thought continues into the next chapter of Hebrews:

> Therefore, a promise being left to enter into His rest, let us fear lest any of you should seem to come short of it. For also we have had the gospel preached, as well as them. But the Word preached did not profit them, not being mixed with faith in those who heard it. For we who have believed do enter into the rest, as He said, "I have sworn in My wrath that they should not enter into My rest;" although the works were finished from the foundation of the world. For He spoke in a certain place of the seventh day in this way: "And God rested the seventh day from all His works." And in this place again, "They shall not enter into My rest." Since then it remains that some must enter into it, and since they to whom it was first preached did not enter in because of unbelief, He again marks out a certain day, saying in David, "Today," (after so long a time). Even as it is said, "Today, if you will hear His voice, harden not your hearts." For if Joshua had given them rest, then He would not afterward have spoken of another day. So then there remains a rest to the people of God. For he who has entered into his rest, he also has ceased from his own works, as God did from His. Therefore let us labor to enter into that rest, lest anyone fall after

> the same example of unbelief. For the Word of God is living and powerful and sharper than any two-edged sword, piercing even to the dividing apart of soul and spirit, and of the joints and marrow, and is a discerner of the thoughts and intents of the heart. Neither is there any creature that is not manifest in His sight, but all things are naked and opened to the eyes of Him with whom we have to do. Since then we have a great High Priest who has passed into the heavens, Jesus the Son of God, let us hold fast our profession. For we do not have a high priest who cannot be touched with the feelings of our infirmities, but was in all points tempted just as we are, yet without sin. Therefore let us come boldly to the throne of Grace, that we may obtain mercy and find grace to help in time of need. (Heb. 4:1–16)

Here, the writer is relating back to the days when God brought the Israelites out of Egypt through Moses. As they were shown the promised land they turned away in fear and unbelief that God would provide the way for them to possess the land (Num. 13, 14).

In those days, it was a lack of faith (or disobedience to faith) that caused them not to enter into the rest that God had for them. Today, there continues to be a "fear" lest any should seem to come short of it. However, we can enter into this rest through faith in Christ. In reality, it depends upon the faith of Jesus who has already entered into that rest. Jesus declares that "from now on the Son of Man shall sit at the right hand of the power of God" (Luke 22:69). This sitting down is not only a position of power but also a position of rest at God's right hand. By having faith in what Jesus has done we are able to enter in to this rest.

The question then becomes, "Do we have faith to enter

into God's rest by trusting in the finished work of Jesus Christ, to enter boldly to the throne of grace established through his sacrifice?" Or do we have doubt, fear, and unbelief so as to cause us to think we need to bring our own tithe to try to appease God, to enter into His blessing, and to keep from being cursed by Him? In the old covenant, it was only the high priest who dared enter into the throne room and only if he brought the proper offering, lest he be killed in the presence of a Holy God. Now, through Christ, we bring no offering to enter in, but stand only on and behind the offering of Jesus Christ. Any offering other than this is not sufficient and, in fact, would disrespect the blood of Jesus. And through this faith of the finished work of Christ, we also entered into this rest. In entering this rest we have been seated with Christ in heavenly places (Eph 2:6) in the same position of both power and rest.

You may have heard it said, "Do your best and God will do the rest." If your best is good enough to get the job done sufficiently, is there even any room for God in your efforts? Do you even have to rely on or get God involved? Who gets the glory? Even if your effort comes first before God, who gets or shares in the glory? Are you relying on your own effort and how far will you go until you ask God to enter in? No man shall share in God's glory, only Jesus Christ. So who gets (or shares) the glory in the tithe? Doesn't the tithe say, "I must do my part (10 percent) so God can do His part?" So instead of saying, "Do your best and God will do the rest," I hear God saying, "I (God) have given My best, now enter into My rest." Don't be confused with rest suggesting no action or work but rather a position of confidence and acknowledgment that Christ has made the way for us to do all things through Him who gives us strength (Phil. 4:13).

Buying God's Blessing

It is taught by some that in bringing your tithe, offering, or first fruit offering to God (through the pastor, prophet, or apostle), He (God) will impart a special blessing upon the giver. Some have even taught that our giving to an apostle gives the apostle permission and the ability then to release the spiritual gifting of that apostle to the giver. In other words, the release is conditional upon the bringing of a tithe, offering, or first fruit to the spiritual authority.

However, this does not line up with God's Word as described in the book of Acts:

> Then laid they their hands on them, and they received the Holy Ghost. And when Simon saw that through laying on of the apostles' hands the Holy Ghost was given, he offered them money, Saying, Give me also this power, that on whomsoever I lay hands, he may receive the Holy Ghost. But Peter said unto him, Thy money perish with thee, because thou hast thought that the gift of God may be purchased with money. Thou hast neither part nor lot in this matter: for thy heart is not right in the sight of God. Repent therefore of this thy wickedness, and pray God, if perhaps the thought of thine heart may be forgiven thee. For I perceive that thou art in the gall of bitterness, and in the bond of iniquity. Then answered Simon, and said, Pray ye to the Lord for me, that none of these things which ye have spoken come upon me. (Acts 8:17–24)

This should be a warning to those who would seek to buy what God has freely given through Christ. It should also be a warning to those who would teach that somehow these gifts could be purchased by bringing a tithe or offering.

We cannot "buy" God's gifts. In addition, if our hearts are positioned to think that we can, should, or want to purchase such a "gift," there is rebuke and warning from the Scripture.

Worse Than an Infidel

Tithing is often rooted in (or at least is accompanied by) fear. The fear is that one must give to avoid the curse of God. It has also been taught by some that one can "give their way out of poverty." In other words, as it is taught, if you want to get out of poverty, you must give, even when you don't have the resources to give, trusting that God will honor your giving and fulfill your need. This has motivated many (including myself at one time) to give their tithe out of what they don't have rather than out of what they do have. People may be in debt, not be able to pay for food or gas, or even provide adequately for their family or relatives. But instead of caring for these things they pay the church a tithe. This, I believe, not only breaks God's heart but Scripture also carries a warning: "But if anyone does not provide for his own, and especially his family, he has denied the faith and is worse than an infidel" (1 Tim. 5:8). Irresponsible giving can also result in others turning from God. When children have to "go without" life's necessities in order to pay the church as a way to appease God, they see God as judgmental and condemning rather than the loving Father He is. Many have turned away from God in these circumstances.

Tithing and Mammon (Money)

One could argue that tithing has become an idol. Many tithe expecting to either receive the blessing or prevent the curse. Even if we are tithing out of "obedience," we have placed something in front of God and the work of Jesus Christ, which is our work of bringing a tithe. When we rely on anything but the complete and finished work of Christ, we have made it an idol (put something before God).

Tithing is focused on giving ten percent of income to receive a financial blessing (and avoid a curse). It not only keeps one focused on money, but it causes one to miss the fullness of the blessing that God provides by grace through faith of Jesus. To become so focused on money brings one dangerously close to Jesus's warning:

> "No servant can serve two masters. For either he will hate the one and love the other, or else he will hold to the one and despise the other. You cannot serve God and mammon. And being money- lovers, all the Pharisees also heard all these things. And they derided Him" (Luke 16:13–14).

And in Matthew, Jesus says,

> No one can serve two masters. For either he will hate the one and love the other, or else he will hold to the one and despise the other. You cannot serve God and mammon. Therefore I say to you, do not be anxious for your life, what you shall eat, or what you shall drink; nor for your body, what you shall put on. Is not life more than food? And the body more than clothing? Behold the birds of the air; for they sow not, nor do they reap, nor gather into barns. Yet your heavenly Father feeds them; are you not much better than they are? Which of you by being anxious can add one cubit to his stature? And why are you anxious about clothing? Consider the lilies of the field, how they grow. They do not toil, nor do they spin, but I say to you that even Solomon in his glory was not arrayed like one of these. Therefore if God so clothes the grass

> of the field, which today is, and tomorrow is thrown into the oven, will He not much rather clothe you, little-faiths? Therefore do not be anxious, saying, what shall we eat? Or, what shall we drink? Or, with what shall we be clothed? For the nations seek after all these things. For your heavenly Father knows that you have need of all these things. But seek first the kingdom of God and His righteousness; and all these things shall be added to you. Therefore do not be anxious about tomorrow; for tomorrow shall be anxious for its own things. Sufficient to the day is the evil of it. (Matt. 6:24–34)

As discussed earlier, by ascribing to the requirement of tithing, it can cause one to place more emphasis on getting money by giving ten percent rather than being content with what God has given. God wants us all to prosper. And there is nothing wrong with having money. However, each one's prosperity is different. Being wealthy and having money can be a blessing from God. Remember, though, that it is not money but, rather the *love* of money that is the root of all evil. So striving for money can bring us close to what Jesus warned about in the scripture above. It is good to be content in all situations, as Paul writes:

> I'm not saying this because I'm in any need. I've learned to be content in whatever situation I'm in. I know how to live in poverty or prosperity. No matter what the situation, I've learned the secret of how to live when I'm full or when I'm hungry, when I have too much or when I have too little. I can do everything through Christ who strengthens me. (Philippians 4:11-13 GW)

A friend shared this thought with me: "If the problem is money, and the solution is money, be careful that it's not the spirit of Mammon that's involved." In other words, if we are always trying to give money to get more money, then there's a good chance that we are tying into the worldly system of money (Mammon) rather than operating out of God's Kingdom. Giving money is not the issue…we do well to be inclined to give generously. However, to give in order to get more money ties us to the wrong "kingdom" and wrong thinking. "Seek first the kingdom of God and His righteousness, and all these things shall be added to you." (Matthew 6:33)

Replacement Theology

Replacement theology, also known as supersessionism, has long been a part of many church doctrines and beliefs. In part, Replacement Theology suggests that Christians have replaced the Jews in God's eyes, as Christians are no longer bound to the Mosaic Law. In addition, it suggests that pastors, priests, apostles, etc. have replaced the Levitical priests to tend to the things of the church and receive the tithes, offerings, and firstfruit offerings. While this section is not intended to engage the greater debate of this topic, it bears separate mention as it relates to the discussion about tithing.

The earlier section "Who was to collect the tithe" discussed the Biblical instruction of how tithes and offerings were put in place not only to be a continual sacrifice to the Lord, but also to provide provision to the Levitical Priesthood while they tended the altar and the things of the Lord. All the other tribes of Israel were given an inheritance by the Lord in the form of land. But those of the tribe of Levi were not given a land inheritance. The Lord had said that He was their inheritance among the children of Israel (Numbers 18:20).

As we examine the book of Nehemiah, we discover that as the temple was left unattended, the Levites had gone back to their fields. During this time tithes and offerings, the portions for the Levites, had not been given to them (Nehemiah 13:10). However, these tithes and offerings were restored when Nehemiah rebuilt the temple and began consecrating “holy things” for the Levites (Nehemiah 12:47 and Nehemiah 13:10-13).

It is reasonable to concluded that the Israelites understood that bringing a tithe, offering, or firstfruit offering to anyone outside the Levitical priesthood would be a sin against the Lord, as it went directly against His instruction. Likewise, today the Jewish people do not bring a tithe, offering, or firstfruit offering into the temple because there is no Levitical Priesthood established to receive these things. There may likely come a time, when the full temple is restored in Jerusalem, that the Jews will re-establish the Levitical Priesthood and begin the practice of tithes, offerings and firstfruit offerings again, just as they did in the days of Nehemiah. But be sure, these tithes, etc. will follow the instructions of the Torah and include only things from the land and livestock. The only time that money will be used will be to redeem a tithe or when it is too far to bring the tithe to the temple (see the chapter “The Tithe Defined”).

For many years there have been those in the Christian church that believe Christians have taken the place of the Jewish people and that Christian pastors, priests, apostles, etc. have taken the position of the Levites and High Priests. This thinking is part of a teaching called “Replacement Theology”. However, this replacement theology of placing pastors, priests, apostles, etc. in a position to function as the "new" Levitical priesthood goes against Paul's teaching and God's heart. To ascribe to this thinking that Christians have replaced the Jewish people dishonors both God and Jew. This teaching is used to justify tithing based on Malachi 3 and, whether knowingly or unknowingly, manipulates Christians to bring a tithe to the church.

To suggest that the Jewish people have been replaced by Christians in God's eyes is not only dangerous, but goes against both Biblical and historical evidence. Throughout history it can be seen that the Jewish people are among those that have been highly persecuted. This is particularly troublesome when the persecution comes through the Christian church. Martin Luther, the great reformer, brought a new freedom to the church as he received the revelation and understanding that we are saved by grace through faith, not by works. Yet his words regarding the Jews have influenced and been used to persecute the Jewish people. In his writing *On the Jews and Their Lies* Martin Luther writes:

> There is no other explanation for this than the one cited earlier from Moses – namely, that God has struck [the Jews] with 'madness and blindness and confusion of mind' [Deuteronomy 28:28]. So we are even at fault in not avenging all this innocent blood of our Lord and of the Christians which they shed for three hundred years after the destruction of Jerusalem, and the blood of the children they have shed since then (which still shines forth from their eyes and their skin). We are at fault in not slaying them.

We also find that

> "The prevailing view among historians is that Luther's anti-Jewish rhetoric contributed significantly to the development of antisemitism in Germany, and in the 1930s and 1940s provided an ideal foundation for the Nazi Party's attack on Jews. While it is important to note that these are not the views of Lutherans today, one cannot ignore the influence that this view had on the history of the Jewish people. (wikipedia, 2009)

While this view is no longer held by the Lutheran church or most Protestant churches, this writing along with others have fueled many in antisemitism. Today there are nations that rise up with the intention of persecuting and/or eliminating God's people. While these nations may no longer cite works like Martin Luther, their own religion and beliefs direct them into this persecution and antisemitism. However, in the midst of all these trials, one can see that God has not forgotten His people. Isaiah prophetically wrote, "Who has ever heard of such things? Who has ever seen things like this? Can a country be born in a day or a nation be brought forth in a moment? Yet no sooner is Zion in labor than she gives birth to her children (Isaiah 66:8 NIV)". There is no doubt his prophecy from years ago came to pass in a moment as the nation of Israel was born out of the tragedies that were World War II. God has and will continue to preserve the Jewish people even in the midst of their flaws. God loves His people and continues to have a plan for them. Paul writes, "I say then, has God cast away His people? Certainly not! Rom 11:1 NKJV)" and "Again I ask: Did they stumble so as to fall beyond recovery? Not at all! Rather, because of their transgression, salvation has come to the Gentiles to make Israel envious. But if their transgression means riches for the world, and their loss means riches for the Gentiles, how much greater riches will their full inclusion bring! I do not want you to be ignorant of this mystery, brothers and sisters, so that you may not be conceited: Israel has experienced a hardening in part until the full number of the Gentiles has come in, and in this way all Israel will be saved. (Rom 11:11,25 NIV)."

The point is that God has not forgotten the Jewish people. nor has He replaced the Jewish people with Christians in His eyes. Replacement theology is born out of Christian antisemitism. Antisemitism of any form is not of God and should not have a place in Christianity. Merrill Bolender writes:

> Malcom Hedding writes in his article, *Standing with Israel Today:*
>
> > Replacement theology is nowhere to be found in the Bible. Those who hold to it do so merely based on a presupposition and nothing more. However, its destructive impact is all too clear. From a theological perspective, the Replacement doctrine can only exist if one can prove that the Abrahamic Covenant has been abolished. (Bolender, 2011)

While many would proclaim they are not anti-Semitic, actions speak louder than words. Any action that would imply or proclaim that the Jewish people have been replaced by Christians is anti-Semitic, whether it's done knowingly or unknowingly. In the section "Jesus and Melchezidek" it was discussed in detail how the writer of the book of Hebrews was not writing about Melchezidek in order to establish the tithe, but rather was establishing Jesus as a High Priest in the line of Melchezidek. Being in this line, Jesus was not able to receive tithes, offerings, and firstfruit offerings according to the established Mosaic Law. However, because Jesus was in a higher order than the Levitical order, He brought a more excellent sacrifice before the Lord: the sacrifice of His body and blood. This sacrifice satisfied and fulfilled the requirements of the Mosaic Law once and for all. By establishing this new covenant we are no longer required to fulfill the requirements of the Mosaic Law. So, to suggest that we are still required to bring a tithe, offering, or firstfruit offering to the Lord is not Biblically sound. In addition, to suggest that tithes, offerings and firstfruit offerings should be brought to pastors, priests, or apostles negates the fact that no Christians stands in the line of the Levitical tribe. If we are indeed in Christ, we follow in His lineage, which is of the tribe of Judah. We are also made as kings and priests in the line of Melchezidek as He is established as a High Priest in the order of Melchezidek (Hebrews 7:1-28).

To follow the thinking of replacement theology is not only Biblically unsound, it can become another "Slippery Slope" and path to follow. The spirit that gives birth to this thinking is subtle and cunning. However, as is the case with many inaccurate teachings, once they have entered into the church, it steers the Christian away from the heart of God and the call of the Church. There are many in the church today who love and support Israel and the Jewish people. Yet teaching and practicing the doctrine of tithing proclaims this replacement theology, teaching that Christians have replaced the Levitical tribe. To come against God's people in such a way does not reflect God's heart. God also has a warning for those who come against the nation of Abraham, Isaac and Jacob as it is written, "I will bless those who bless you, and whoever curses you I will curse; and all peoples on earth will be blessed through you. (Gen 12:3)." Believing that Christians have replaced the Jews or

Levites in one sense could be seen as a curse towards God's people and may open one up to a curse from God.

As Christians grow in the understanding that Replacement Theology is not Biblically founded it is important to reject any doctrine that would suggest or lead to this theology. Therefore it is important to turn away from any teaching that proclaims Christians, particularly Christian pastors, priests, or apostles, are the modern-day Levites. It also requires rejecting the principle of tithing, since the only way to declare that tithing is acceptable is to suggest that Christians have replaced the Jews.

The Heart of the Giver

"God is love" (1 John 4:8). Out of His love flows giving. Giving of and from God is from the beginning of time. Here, we read of God's heart in giving.

> And God created man in His image; in the image of God He created him. He created them male and female. And God blessed them. And God said to them, Be fruitful, and multiply and fill the earth, and subdue it. And have dominion over the fish of the sea and over the fowl of the heavens, and all animals that move upon the earth. And God said, Behold! I have given you every herb seeding seed which is upon the face of all the earth, and every tree in which is the fruit of a tree seeding seed; to you it shall be for food. And to every beast of the earth and to every fowl of the heavens, and to every creeper on the earth which has in it a living soul every green plant is for food; and it was so. (Gen. 1:27–30)

God (and Jesus) gives "not as the world gives" (John 14:27). The world gives with a condition or expectation of getting something in return for the gift. God's love is unconditional. This first blessing was unconditional from God as He created mankind. As we remember the law of first mention (when something is first mentioned in the Bible, it gives more weight and shows God's heart and/or intention in the matter), we see here God's intention was to both love and give unconditionally. This is also expressed in the following verses:

> "For all the land which you see I [God] will give to

> you and to your seed forever" (Gen. 13:15).
>
> "For God so loved the world that He gave His only-begotten Son, that whoever believes in Him should not perish but have everlasting life" (John 3:16).

This gift of everlasting life is given "toward all, and upon all who believe" (Rom. 3:22). In other words, God gave this gift unconditionally. All we must do is receive and believe in Him. And it is available to all. With this gift, by grace through faith, we are born again as God's own children:

> But as many as received Him, He gave to them authority to become the children of God, to those who believe on His name, who were born, not of bloods, nor of the will of the flesh, nor of the will of man, but were born of God. And the Word became flesh, and tabernacled among us. And we beheld His glory, the glory as of the only begotten of the Father, full of grace and of truth. (John 1:12–14)

God's giving is unconditional. It is poured out of His love, and it pleases His heart to give good things to His children. This is evident in the following passages:

> "If you then, being evil, know how to give good gifts to your children, how much more shall your Father in Heaven give good things to those who ask Him?" (Matt. 7:11)
>
> "Every good gift and every perfect gift is from above, and cometh down from the Father of lights, with whom is no variableness, neither shadow of turning" (James 1:17KJV).
>
> "But Peter said, Silver and gold have I none, but what I have I give you. In the name of Jesus Christ of Nazareth, rise up and walk!" (Acts 3:6).

> "What then shall we say to these things? If God is for us, who can be against us? Truly He who did not spare His own Son, but delivered Him up for us all, how shall He not with Him also freely give us all things?" (Rom. 8:31–32).

> "The blessing of the Lord, it maketh rich, and he addeth no sorrow with it" (Prov. 10:22 KVJ).

> "A faithful man shall abound with blessings" (Prov. 28:20a KJV).

> "Saying with a loud voice, Worthy is the Lamb that was slain to receive power, and riches, and wisdom, and strength, and honour, and glory, and blessing" (Rev. 5:12).

> "For You; O Lord, will bless the righteous; with favor You will surround him as with a shield" (Ps. 5:12 NKJV).

Throughout these passages it is very evident that God loves to give good things to His people and children.

Redeemed by God

What does it mean to be redeemed, justified or brought into right standing with God?

Ever since the fall of mankind through Adam's sin God's plan was to restore the relationship that He had with man in the garden. This was a relationship where Adam and Eve walked and talked with God, and was in full fellowship with their Father. It was an intimate, close, and inseparable relationship marked by a deep love. Christ, the second Adam, restored that relationship once again as he died on the cross. As God raised him from the grave he made a way for us to be received into God's kingdom once again. Through Christ we are brought into the right standing and back into the right relationship that God intended from the beginning. In this relationship we are now invited to walk, talk and fellowship with God. He provides for all our needs as He did for Adam before "the fall", and as He did for Jesus. They did not have to "work to earn" this blessing from God. They were blessed because that is God's heart and nature, because of the love He had for them. And He has that same love for us.

Walk, therefore, confidently and with a clear conscience that God has established this relationship through Christ and longs deeply for us to come, "taste, and see that the Lord is good." In Christ, He loves us unconditionally. He blesses us unconditionally. And He gives unconditionally. Not because of who we are or what we've done, but because of Jesus.

The moment you receive Jesus as Lord and Savior you are redeemed. You are established to return to the original place God intended for you to be.

God's Peace

Much has been written about God's peace, the shalom of God. This word *shalom* can be found in *Strong's Concordance* H7965 with the meaning: (from H7999) safe, that is, (figuratively) well, happy, friendly; also (abstractly) welfare, that is, health, prosperity, peace: – X do, familiar, X fare, favour, + friend, X greet, (good) health, (X perfect, such as be at) peace (-able, -ably), prosper (-ity, -ous), rest, safe (-ly), salute, welfare, (X all is, be) well, X wholly.

Some describe it as "nothing missing, nothing broken, everything whole, and that which is bound to chaos is broken." It is important to note that included with shalom is "prosperity," which, means "a successful, flourishing, or thriving condition, especially in financial respects; good fortune." (Douglas Harper Historian) As you discover the fullness of God's peace and what He has already done for His children through Christ, you will certainly live in and with a "Peace that passes all understanding" in whatever situation or condition arises.

Jesus embodies God's Peace. In reality, in the beginning, God (Jesus, Peace) walked with Adam and Eve in the Garden of Eden as John described:

> In the beginning was the Word, and the Word was with God, and the Word was God. He was in the beginning with God. All things came into being through Him, and without Him not even one thing came into being that has come into being. In Him was life, and the life was the light of men. And the light shines in the darkness, and the darkness did not overtake it. (John 1:1–5)

But when sin came into the world, Jesus (Peace) was removed from the earth and no longer walked among men. So from that time, Peace (Jesus) did not freely move on the earth. But when Christ was born, the angels declared, "Peace on Earth" (Luke 2:14), which was declaring "Peace" (Jesus) has returned to the earth once again.

This peace does not mean an absence of war, as Jesus said, "Do you suppose that I have come to give peace on earth? I tell you, no, but rather division" (Luke 12:51). This peace is a supernatural peace, a peace that passes understanding (Phil. 4:7) that has made a way for mankind to be brought back again to unity with God. This word 'peace' in the New Testament also declares prosperity, as does "shalom" peace from the Old Testament (Strong's Concordance H7965). As shown in Strong's Concordance it comes from the Greek word *eirēnē* (G1515), "probably from a primary verb *eirō* (to *join*); *peace* (literally or figuratively); by implication *prosperity:* –one, peace, quietness, rest, + set at one again".

Jesus has given us His peace, whereas we can be set at one again with God and live in shalom, prosperity, nothing missing, nothing broken, everything whole, and that which was bound to chaos is broken; to live in a "successful, flourishing, or thriving condition, especially in financial respects, and good fortune."

Jesus gives us this peace out of His love for us, not expecting anything in return. It is a free gift, as He says: "Peace I leave with you, My peace I give to you. Not as the world gives do I give to you. Let not your heart be troubled, neither let it be afraid" (John 14:27).

This peace, in a sense, is the fulfillment of the parable of the Prodigal Son in that we (mankind) had taken what God had given us as an inheritance (dominion over the earth [Gen. 1:28]) and squandered it away. But while we were still afar, God "ran" to us by sending us His only Son Jesus. And as He meets us on this road of life, He welcomes us back into His family, not as a slave or worker but as His child. And His peace becomes ours again.

One cannot "earn" or "purchase" this peace but can only receive it by faith (the faith of Christ). If peace (which includes prosperity) is freely given, we should not expect to be required to purchase it through the tithe.

> But we know that whatever things the Law says, it says to those who are under the Law; so that every mouth may be stopped and all the world may be under judgment before God, because by the works of the Law none of all flesh will be justified in His sight; for through the Law is the knowledge of sin. But now a righteousness of God has been revealed apart from Law, being witnessed by the Law and the Prophets; even the righteousness of God through the faith of

> Jesus Christ, toward all and upon all those who believe. For there is no difference, for all have sinned and come short of the glory of God, being justified freely by His grace through the redemption that is in Christ Jesus; whom God has set forth to be a propitiation through faith in His blood, to declare His righteousness through the passing by of the sins that had taken place before, in the forbearance of God; for the display of His righteousness at this time, for Him to be just and, forgiving the one being of the faith of Jesus. (Rom. 3:19–26)

Note here that our right standing before God is not dependent upon our faith, although we must believe that Jesus Christ is Lord and God has raised him from the dead. Rather it is dependent upon the "faith of Jesus," which is complete. He is the author and finisher of our faith (Heb. 12:2).

So as we place our complete trust in Jesus, His peace (as defined above) moves and works in us. Our directive is to enter into His rest in assurance of what Christ has done for us. This rest is not simply to believe, but it must be coupled with faith: "And who did God say would never enter his place of rest? Weren't they the ones that disobeyed him? We see that those people did not enter the place of rest because they did not have faith" (Heb. 3:18–19, ASV).

> Therefore, a promise being left to enter into His rest, let us fear lest any of you should seem to come short of it. For also we have had the gospel preached, as well as them. But the Word preached did not profit them, not being mixed with faith in those who heard it. For we who have believed do enter into the rest, as He said, "I have sworn in My wrath that they should not enter into My rest;" although the works were finished from the

> foundation of the world. For He spoke in a certain place of the seventh day in this way: "And God rested the seventh day from all His works." And in this place again, "They shall not enter into My rest." Since then it remains that some must enter into it, and since they to whom it was first preached did not enter in because of unbelief, He again marks out a certain day, saying in David, "Today," (after so long a time). Even as it is said, "Today, if you will hear His voice, harden not your hearts." For if Joshua had given them rest, then He would not afterward have spoken of another day. So then there remains a rest to the people of God. For he who has entered into his rest, he also has ceased from his own works, as God did from His. Therefore let us labor to enter into that rest, lest anyone fall after the same example of unbelief. (Heb 4:1-11)

A certain 'peace' accompanies a state of rest. As we enter this rest offered by God, we experience an abounding peace. In this peaceful rest we have confidence to come before God not by our works, but through the blood of Jesus. This "rest" is not necessarily a place of inactivity but rather a position or posture of confidence of who we are by what Christ has accomplished for us.

> Therefore, brothers, having boldness to enter into the Holy of Holies by the blood of Jesus, by a new and living way which He has consecrated for us through the veil, that is to say, His flesh; and having a High Priest over the house of God, let us draw near with a true heart in full assurance of faith, having our hearts sprinkled from an evil conscience and our bodies having been washed with pure water. Let us hold fast the profession of our faith without wavering (for He is faithful who promised). (Heb. 10:19–23)

The writer is encouraging us to enter into God's presence with boldness and full confidence. And in his presence, there is fullness of rest. In Ephesians we read, "Therefore take to yourselves the whole armor of God that you may be able to withstand in the evil day, and having done all, to stand. Therefore stand…" (Eph. 6:13–14). This word stand means "to abide, to be established in." It is a position of confidence and full assurance.

As we will read in the next section, God's blessing and promise given through Moses (to be spoken by the priests) included "the Lord will give you His Peace." This word is fulfilled when God sent His son Jesus to earth and is completed as Jesus gives us His peace. Now we can lay hold of this peace when we couple our belief with faith in Him.

The Aaronic Blessing

As stated earlier, Jesus confirmed what Moses and the prophets wrote about Him. With this understanding, let us look at how God instructed Moses and Aaron to bless the people using what is referred to as the Aaronic blessing, or priestly blessing, in Numbers 6:24–26.

There are many different translations of this blessing. One that is often used is,

> The Lord bless you and keep you; the Lord make his face to shine upon you and be gracious to you; the Lord lift up his countenance upon you and give you peace. (ESV)

Another translation says it this way:

> May the Lord bless you and keep you. May the Lord make his face to shine upon you, and be gracious to you. May the Lord lift up his countenance upon you,

> and give you peace. (ERV)

In this translation, by using the word *may*, it leads one to the sense that this blessing is expressing possibility, opportunity, or perhaps contingency. Here, the recipient may be left with hope that God will bless them, but may not be certain of its coming or it may be conditional.

Still, another translation says it this way:

> The Lord will bless you and watch over you. The Lord will smile on you and be kind to you.
> The Lord will look on you with favor and give you peace. (GW)

In this translation, by using the word *will*, it leads one to the sense that God is about to or going to bless. Here, the recipient may be left with the understanding that God will bless them but expecting that it will be happening sometime in the future. This translation is perhaps a more accurate translation.

So as God instructed Moses to have Aaron speak this blessing over His people, it kept them looking forward to what was truly to come, perhaps conditional, perhaps with an expectation. With the understanding that this blessing was actually pointing to Jesus, one can now receive this blessing in the fullness that it was intended and promised:

> Through, with, and in Christ,
> The Lord has blessed you and continues to bless you.
> The Lord has kept you and continues to keep you.
> The Lord has made His face to shine upon you, and He continues to shine His face upon you.
> The Lord has been gracious to you, and He continues to be gracious to you.
> The Lord has lifted up His countenance (approval and

> favor) upon you, and He has given and continues to give you His peace (shalom, nothing missing, nothing broken, everything whole, and that which was bound to chaos is broken, His prosperity). (Author's translation)

Again as stated before, if peace (which includes prosperity) is freely given, we should not expect to be required to purchase it through the tithe.

Receiving from God

God's love is an unconditional love. It is not performance based, and it is not taken away. "He who did not spare his own Son but gave him up for us all, how will he not also with him graciously give us all things?" (Rom. 8:32 ESV). In God's giving, he does not add a requirement. Jesus does not give as the world gives (expecting something in return) but gives freely as it is written: "But we have not received the spirit of the world, but the Spirit from God, so that we might know the things that are freely given to us by God" (1 Cor. 2:12).

As children of God, we are taught how to live and give this love in return. And we are also taught how to receive from God. You will note that not even once does Jesus suggest that one must bring a tithe to be in a position to receive anything from God. The following are scriptures that speak on how to ask and receive from God.

> Ask and it shall be given to you; seek and you shall find; knock and it shall be opened to you. For each one who asks receives; and he who seeks finds; and to him who knocks, it shall be opened. Or what man is there of you, if his son asks a loaf, will he give him a stone? Or if he asks a fish, will he give him a snake? If you

then, being evil, know how to give good gifts to your children, how much more shall your Father in Heaven give good things to those who ask Him? (Matt. 7:7–11)

Jesus answered and said to them, Truly I say to you, If you have faith and do not doubt, you shall not only do this miracle of the fig tree, but also; if you shall say to this mountain, Be moved and be thrown into the sea; it shall be done. And all things, whatever you shall ask in prayer, believing, you shall receive" (Matt. 21:21–22).

For truly I say to you that whoever shall say to this mountain, Be moved and be cast into the sea, and shall not doubt in his heart, but shall believe that what he said shall occur, he shall have whatever he said. Therefore I say to you, All things, whatever you ask, praying, believe that you shall receive them, and it will be to you. (Mark 11:23–24) Believe Me that I am in the Father and the Father in Me, or else believe Me for the very works themselves. Truly, truly, I say to you, He who believes on Me, the works that I do he shall do also, and greater works than these he shall do, because I go to My Father. And whatever you may ask in My name, that I will do, so that the Father may be glorified in the Son. If you ask anything in My name, I will do it. If you love Me, keep My commandments. And I will pray the Father, and He shall give you another Comforter, so that He may be with you forever, the Spirit of Truth, whom the world cannot receive because it does not see Him nor know Him. But you know Him, for He dwells with you and shall be in you. I will not leave you orphans. I will come to you. (John 14:11–18)

"I am the gate; whoever enters through me will be saved. He will come in and go out, and find pasture.

> The thief comes only to steal and kill and destroy; I have come that they may have life, and have it to the full" (John 10:9–10, NIV)

> All things have been committed to me by my Father. No one knows the Son except the Father, and no one knows the Father except the Son and those to whom the Son chooses to reveal him. "Come to me, all you who are weary and burdened, and I will give you rest. Take my yoke upon you and learn from me, for I am gentle and humble in heart, and you will find rest for your souls. For my yoke is easy and my burden is light. (Matt. 11:27–30, NIV)

> "Christ redeemed us from the curse of the Law, being made a curse for us (for it is written, 'Cursed is everyone having been hanged on a tree'); so that the blessing of Abraham might be to the nations in Jesus Christ, and that we might receive the promise of the Spirit through faith" (Gal. 3:13–14).

> "Heal the sick, cleanse the lepers, raise the dead, cast out demons. You have received freely, freely give" (Matt. 10:8).

> "Truly He who did not spare His own Son, but delivered Him up for us all, how shall He not with Him also freely give us all things?" (Rom. 8:32)

> "But we have not received the spirit of the world, but the Spirit from God, so that we might know the things that are freely given to us by God" (1 Cor. 2:12).

> "And He said to me, It is done. I am the Alpha and Omega, the Beginning and the End. To him who thirsts I will give of the fountain of the Water of Life freely" (Rev. 21:6).

We can easily see that God's heart is revealed in Jesus.

This is a heart to give. And it pleases God's heart for us to simply receive all that He has for us.

Consider our own giving and receiving. If you've ever given a gift only to have it either refused or discounted, you may have had a feeling of rejection or disappointment. If the recipient says, "That's not what I wanted" or "I hate it," you may in turn think, "Well, I'll never give something to them again."

When giving a true gift (not giving something as if we expected a return), we hope that the recipient will accept what we have given. The more "near and dear" to our heart the gift is, the greater hope we have that the recipient will accept it in the light as it was given. In fact, if we give a special gift and the recipient does not receive it, the giver may be turned away with hurt, resignation, or even anger. The same thing can happen if the recipient takes the gift but then complains about it, saying things like, "I don't like that color" or "That's not my style." If the recipient were to say things like, "I'm not worthy" or "I could never live up to this," it discounts the view that the giver has of the recipient and in turn negates the intention of the gift to whom it is given.

Rather when receiving a gift, a simple and heartfelt "Thank you" covers it all. Then if we display the gift or put the gift into use, it not only brings pleasure to the giver but acknowledges the receivers' feelings of both the gift and the giver.

Let us receive the gifts of God with a grateful heart, not discounting or refusing. And certainly, let's not discount the view that God has of us as He gives good gifts to His children. In receiving His gifts it pleases our Father's heart.

God's Plan for Our Provision

God shows His heart for us regarding provision from the time He created us. In Genesis 1: 26–31, we read God "created them male and female, He blessed them, and said be fruitful and multiply." God gave Mankind dominion over the earth and "gave" to Adam everything needed for food. He did not have to work for it or labor over it, but rather it was there for his pleasure and as he needed. However, when Adam sinned, everything changed. From this point, what was given by God for provision without work turned into obtaining provision by the works of our hands.

> And to Adam He said, Because you have listened to the voice of your wife and have eaten of the tree, of which I commanded you, saying, You shall not eat of it! The ground is cursed for your sake. In pain shall you eat of it all the days of your life. It shall also bring forth thorns and thistles to you, and you shall eat the herb of the field. In the sweat of your face you shall eat bread until you return to the ground, for out of it you were taken. For dust you are, and to dust you shall return. (Gen. 3:17–19)

But God's plan was always to restore things back to the original relationship between Himself and man as they were in the garden. This includes His provision for us.

God again speaks His heart for us in Jeremiah. God's people have fallen far away from Him again. God is calling them back to follow Him. Amidst the rebuke of the Lord He pleads with them, saying, "'For I know the plans I have for you,' declares the Lord, 'plans to prosper you and not to harm you, plans to give you hope and a future'" (Jer. 29:11 NIV).

The word used here for *prosper* is *shalom* (Strong's

Concordance H7965), which often is translated as "peace." This shalom peace (which includes prosperity by definition and translation of the word) is the same peace given freely to us by Jesus as described earlier.

The following verses continue to describe God's heart concerning His provision for us.

> I love those who love me; and those who seek me early shall find me. Riches and honor are with me; enduring riches and righteousness. My fruit is better than gold, yea, than fine gold; and what I give is better than choice silver. I lead in the way of righteousness, in the midst of the paths of judgment; I may cause those who love me to inherit riches; and I will fill their treasuries. (Prov. 8:17–21)

I would underscore here that God's plan for giving these things is all done by Him alone…we do nothing.

> Therefore I tell you, do not worry about your life, what you will eat or drink; or about your body, what you will wear. Is not life more important than food, and the body more important than clothes? Look at the birds of the air; they do not sow or reap or store away in barns, and yet your heavenly Father feeds them. Are you not much more valuable than they? Who of you by worrying can add a single hour to his life? "And why do you worry about clothes? See how the lilies of the field grow. They do not labor or spin. Yet I tell you that not even Solomon in all his splendor was dressed like one of these. If that is how God clothes the grass of the field, which is here today and tomorrow is thrown into the fire, will he not much more clothe you, you of little faith? So do not worry, saying, 'What shall we eat?' or 'What shall we drink?' or 'What shall we wear?' For the pagans run after all these things,

> and your heavenly Father knows that you need them. But seek first his kingdom and his righteousness, and all these things will be given to you as well. (Matt. 6:25–33, NIV)

The righteousness we seek is through Christ alone. And Christ has brought God's kingdom to earth for us to share in. So as we seek God's kingdom and His Christ we find all we need will be provided for us. This is reconfirmed as Paul writes about the abundance of provision found in Christ:

> But the free gift shall not be also like the offense. For if by the offense of the one many died, much more the grace of God, and the gift in grace; which is of the one Man, Jesus Christ, abounded to many. And the free gift shall not be as by one having sinned; (for indeed the judgment was of one to condemnation, but the free gift is of many offenses to justification. For if by one man's offense death reigned by one, much more they who receive abundance of grace and the gift of righteousness shall reign in life by One, Jesus Christ.) (Rom. 5:15–17)

> "But my God shall supply all your need according to His riches in glory by Christ Jesus" (Phil. 4:19).

One can readily see that God's plan for our provision is great. It is already established in Christ. It is part of the free gift of salvation for those who believe in Christ and will follow Him. It is not something one must earn or work for, as Christ has already completed the work.

The world's system is for us to toil. But God's system is for provision. Satan manipulates God's system and by doing so manipulates our hope for God's provision. God wants us to operate on His system. He has ordered our steps, and His plan is Jesus. This is how we operate in His system, by daily taking up our cross and following Him. It's based on our relationship with God the Father, Jesus His Son, and Holy Spirit. In this relationship, God freely provides for all our needs, not out of our own efforts or work but out of His love for us.

Please don't misunderstand. This does not mean that we sit around all day and wait for the provision to come to us through the mail or some other entitlement program. God has given us the ability to obtain wealth (Deut. 8:18). As we rest in full confidence of the One who has brought us out of bondage and into freedom, He will give us strategies and wisdom as we ask Him. Use the talents that God has given, step in to whatever opportunities He has set before you, and experience a prosperous life in Him. He will lead us to His provision, whether He leads us to a brook and has ravens fly in our sustenance as He did with Elijah (1Kings 17:6) or He gives us an idea or skill that brings forth millions of dollars. But He always provides for His children that call upon Him. David wrote, "I have never seen the righteous forsaken" (Ps 37:25). Remember, prosperity is so much more than money and riches of this world.

Sowing Seed

There are "principles" that God has set forth in His creation that are accessible to all, whether we are believers or not. These principles are like a law of nature, but we'll call this a principle so as not to be confused again to become entrapped in the law of Moses. This principle is much like the principle, or law, of gravity. With gravity, it is easily and readily understood that "what goes up, must come down." If you jump off a chair, you will hit the ground.

Likewise is the principle of giving or sowing. Farmers are well familiar with this principle. When one sows a seed, one will reap a harvest. However, this principle is not limited to believers in Christ. It is a principle that is available to all who have wisdom to access it. In today's society, one can easily see how nonbelievers have found that giving and charity naturally can lead to more abundance. This is not limited only to the giver but to others as well. Of course, the question becomes who is glorified in the giving and receiving. Is it God through Christ or man and his own efforts? The principle works for all, but not all will reap eternal rewards while accessing this principle.

As a caution, sowing any kind of seed, including a financial seed, to gain God's blessing brings the attention to the sower and away from God. In other words, at the very least, the sower shares in the glory of this blessing with God and Jesus because it was the sower who caused the blessing to flow. At worst this positions the sower as the one who is the key instrument in making the blessing flow from the Father (rather than Christ).

One must also understand the nature of this principle as it relates to the type of seed that is sown. Sowing a seed of corn, for example, into good soil will very likely produce a bountiful harvest. Sowing a seed (or giving) of a cow will certainly not produce the same harvest. In the same manner, sowing a financial seed will not produce the same return.

As we speak of sowing seed, it is important to rightly divide God's Word. Jesus spoke about sowing seed and producing fruit one hundredfold, sixtyfold, and thirtyfold. Many in the church today will use this as an example to compel others to give money to the church. While the principle of sowing may be universal, Jesus was speaking in parables here and explained His meaning clearly to His disciples. Jesus said, "And the parable is this: *The seed is the Word of God*" (Luke 8:11) (emphasis added). Jesus also explains this parable in Mark 4:

> And He said to them, "Do you not know this parable? And how then will you know all parables? The sower sows the Word. And these are those by the wayside, where the Word is sown. And when they hear, Satan comes immediately and takes away the Word that was sown in their hearts. And these are those likewise being sown on stony places; who, when they hear the Word, immediately receive it with gladness. But they have no root in themselves, but are temporary. Afterward when affliction or persecution arises for the Word's sake, they are immediately offended. And these are those being sown among thorns; such as hear the Word, and the cares of this world, and the deceit of riches, and the lust about other things entering in, choke the Word, and it becomes unfruitful. And these are those sown on good ground, who hear the Word and welcome it, and bear fruit, one thirty, one sixty, and one a hundredfold." (Mark 4:13–20)

Again, we see here clearly that the seed sown is the Word of God. It has nothing to do with sowing a financial seed. In addition, the one who receives the seed (the Word) is the one who is producing the fruit, not the one who sows the seed. This is contrary to what is being taught in the church, which is that if you sow a financial seed into good ground (like someone's ministry), you as the sower will produce or receive a return of thirty-, sixty-, or hundredfold. It is clearly the Word that becomes fruitful to the one who receives and welcomes the Word, not to the one who sows it.

Reading further in Mark, Jesus says, "And He said to them, Take heed what you hear. With that measure which you measure, it shall be measured to you. And to you who hear, more shall be given. For he who has, more shall be given to him; and he who has not, from him shall be taken even that which he has" (Mark 4:24–25).

This passage is also used in many teachings to compel one to give to the church and to give abundantly. But it places fear in the giver, for it suggests that if one gives little, what you have may be taken away. However, to get a greater understanding of the meaning of this particular passage, we read from the Amplified Bible:

> If any man has ears to hear, let him be listening and let him perceive and comprehend. And He said to them, Be careful what you are hearing. The measure [of thought and study] you give [to the truth you hear] will be the measure [of virtue and knowledge] that comes back to you—and more [besides] will be given to you who hear. For to him who has will more be given; and from him who has nothing, even what he has will be taken away [by force]. (Mark 4:23–25, AMP)

Here, we see that Jesus (again) is not talking about any instruction on how to give money at all. He is talking about thought and study given to the truth you hear, and virtue and knowledge will come back to you.

So specifically in this passage, one should take great caution in changing what Jesus meant here of sowing a seed as the "Word of God" to sowing a "financial seed" and then indicating that this is Jesus's instruction.

Paul does share instruction on sowing and reaping in 2 Corinthians: "But I say this, He who sows sparingly shall also reap sparingly, and he who sows bountifully shall also reap bountifully" (2 Cor. 9:6). It is, however, important to keep this passage in perspective as well. Perhaps the Amplified Bible does this best:

> Now [remember] this: he who sows sparingly will also reap sparingly, and he who sows generously [that blessings may come to others] will also reap generously [and be blessed]. Let each one give [thoughtfully and with purpose] just as he has decided in his heart, not grudgingly or under compulsion, for God loves a cheerful giver [and delights in the one whose heart is in his gift]. And God is able to make all grace [every favor and earthly blessing] come in abundance to you, so that you may always [under all circumstances, regardless of the need] have complete sufficiency in everything [being completely self-sufficient in Him], and have an abundance for every good work and act of charity. As it is written and forever remains written, "He [the benevolent and generous person] scattered abroad, He gave to the poor, His righteousness endures forever!" Now He who provides seed for the sower and bread for food will provide and multiply your seed for sowing [that is, your resources] and increase the harvest of your righteousness [which shows itself in active goodness, kindness, and love]. You will be enriched in every way so that you may be generous, and this [generosity, administered] through us is producing thanksgiving to God [from those who benefit]. For the ministry of this service (offering) is not only supplying the needs of the saints (God's people), but is also overflowing through many expressions of thanksgiving to God." (2 Corinthians□ 9:6-12 AMP)□□□□□□□□□□

Here we come to understand that the "sowing generously" is to be for the intention "that blessings may come to others". God continually provides the seed so one can continually sow as one purposes in their heart. As we sow generously God supplies more generously. Again, this is not to sow in order to gain more, but to bless others. And while this speaks to the principle of sowing and reaping from a financial perspective, it is important not to mix the parable in Mark with Paul's message. They are two different things.

Pressed and Shaken

It is written: "Give, and it shall be given to you, good measure pressed down and shaken together and running over, they shall give into your bosom. For with the same measure that you measure, it shall be measured to you again" (Luke 6:38).

Many pastors and teachers have used this scripture to motivate people to give money to the church or ministry. In the financial context, this passage clearly suggests that if you give, what you give will be given back to you with good measure, running over, and with the same measure you use, it will be measured back to you. While this scripture appears to be spoken in the same tone as Paul's letter to the Corinthians above, it is important to rightly divide God's Word and examine what Jesus was actually speaking about in this verse.

I recently watched an inspirational movie *When the Game Stands Tall.* This movie was about a football team who held the longest winning streak in high school football at 151 games. One day, in the class room, as the coach was teaching the class, he read the above scripture and then asked the class what it meant to them. I listened closely as they responded.

> One young man says, "That you reap what you sow. You know, like, whatever you do, good or bad, comes back to you."
>
> The coach replies, "Anyone else really think that you give to others and the blessing is returned in equal measure?"

Another responds, "I've always worked hard to do the right thing, and I've always been blessed."

The coach asks, "How's that?"

He responds, "I get to play on the 'streak team.'"

As the classmates chuckle, another classmate (and teammate), Tayshon, interjects, "I hate to burst your bubble, but you're not in line to be starting quarterback on the streak team because you've done the right thing. It's because you're 6'2" and a cannon for an arm."

After some laughter, another classmate asks Tayshon what he believes.

He responds, "Down where I sleep, dealers in Richmond are making mad money. My aunt was an ER nurse working her whole life helping people. Time came for her to get hers, they up and fired her. Six months before they got to pay her retirement. It's dog eat dog, you know, you just got to take what you need. I don't care how good you been, just sittin' around waiting for someone to pay you back, you're going hungry."

The coach asks, "So why does a guy like Luke, who's a doctor, painter, writer, historian, take the time to invent a lie?"

Another classmate, Kam, declares, "It's not a lie."

Tayshon immediately responds to Kam, "You're Pops dies, 'five-0' puts your Mama on trial, when oops, our bad, the shipyard poisoned him. But the damage is already done. All that pressure gives her a stroke, and now she don't got long."

Another classmate interrupts, "Easy, homey, we all know the story."

Tayshon responds to Kam, "So tell me, homey, you really been that bad to deserve all this come your way?"

The next scene takes us to the Kam's house, whose mother had a stroke. He just received word that it's only a matter of time before his mom dies, and his only brother is being shipped to a family out of state. The coach comes to visit, and as they're talking in Kam's room, he pulls out a note that he had written and reads it to the coach. "To Coach Lang, I promise to live the rest of my days by lessons you taught me. Give and it shall be given to you. For whatever measure you use, it will be measured back to you in equal." Then he pauses, looks up, and asks, "Why is this happening to me coach? What did I do? I'm trying. I'm making my perfect effort. It don't matter, it ain't enough. What if Tayshon is right? Maybe God don't see me or He don't care.' Cause I ain't worth His time. It don't make no sense, coach. I'm alone. I have nobody left."

After Kam's mother dies, he withdraws, doesn't go to practices, and won't return his best friend's call. His best friend finds out that they both received scholarships to Oregon for football, so he goes to see Kam to find out why he hasn't returned his calls. Kam says that he's not going to Oregon, but rather he's going as far away from him as he can—he's going to Miami. After an argument, Kam breaks down and says, "You see me, I'm cursed. Everyone I love dies. I can't lose nobody else, man. I got to let you go, man." (Smith, Zelon, & Hayes, 2014)

The sense here was that while Kam worked hard to do the

right things, he believed that somehow, he wasn't doing good enough to keep the bad things from happening, so he needed to get away from the ones he cared about to keep those bad things from happening to them. His giving wasn't good enough to cause good things to come back to him in equal measure. This interaction struck me to the core as I had believed the interpretation of this scripture to give and it will be given back to you, good measure, as you give, so shall it be given to you. I had often put it to the test, and while not subscribing to the tithing principle, I gave freely and experienced many blessings from God. So I was faced with the question and reality that while I thought this was a universal principle, this perceived promise was not being experienced by all Christians. I began to ask God about this. How could this be true when, as this movie brought to light, good things are not given back to those who give in equal measure. The Lord then took me on a deeper investigation of this scripture.

To better understand what Jesus meant it is important to first look at the full context of this scripture.

> But I say to you who hear: Love your enemies, do good to those who hate you, bless those who curse you, and pray for those who despitefully use you. And to him who strikes you on the one cheek, also offer the other. And to him who takes away your garment, do not forbid your tunic also. Give to everyone who asks of you, and from him who takes away your goods, do not ask them again. And as you desire that men should do to you, you do also to them likewise. For if you love those who love you, what thanks do you have? For sinners also love those who love them. And if you do good to those who do good to you, what thanks do you have? For sinners also do the same. And if you lend to those of whom you hope to receive, what thanks do

> you have? For sinners also lend to sinners, to receive as much again. But love your enemies, and do good, and lend, hoping for nothing in return. And your reward shall be great, and you shall be the sons of the Highest. For He is kind to the unthankful and to the evil. Therefore be merciful, even as your Father is merciful. Judge not, and you shall not be judged. Condemn not, and you shall not be condemned. Forgive, and you shall be forgiven. Give, and it shall be given to you, good measure pressed down and shaken together and running over, they shall give into *your bosom*. For with the same measure that you measure, it shall be measured to you again. (Luke 6:20–38; emphasis added)

The first thing to note is Jesus is not talking about money at all. He is talking about love, forgiveness, and mercy. Do good even to those who don't do good to you. Love your enemies. Lend, expecting nothing in return. For God is kind to the unthankful and to the evil. Therefore, be merciful, even as your Father is merciful. Judge not, condemn not, forgive, and give.

Jesus taught us to pray, "Forgive us our trespasses as we forgive those who trespass against us. (Mat 6:12 NIV)" In other words, the measure of forgiveness that we give to others is the same measure of forgiveness we are asking our Father to give to us.

It also struck me that if we are to give to whoever asks and lend without expecting a return, then it would be contradictory to give while expecting that it shall be given back to you, good measure, etc. Jesus tells us that he gives, not as the world gives (John 14:27) but rather gives unconditionally. The world (often) gives with the expectation that there will be a return: "I'll scratch your back, you scratch mine" or "I do this, so you owe me that."

Then I observed where Jesus declared this "return" would be given back to. "They shall give into your bosom." Some translations say, "into your lap." I was stirred to examine the meaning of bosom more deeply. Of course, we know the physical meaning of this word as the chest. But there are other meanings, uses, and inferences for this word as well.

The following uses of the word *bosom* in scripture imply the heart or the inner most being:

> There was a certain rich man who was customarily clothed in purple and fine linen and making merry in luxury every day. And there was a certain beggar named Lazarus, who was laid at his gate, full of sores and desiring to be fed with the crumbs which fell from the rich man's table. But even the dogs came and licked his sores. And it happened that the beggar died and was carried by the angels into *Abraham's bosom*. The rich one also died and was buried. And in hell he lifted up his eyes, being in torments, and saw Abraham afar off, and *Lazarus in his bosom*. And he cried and said, Father Abraham, have mercy on me and send Lazarus so that he may dip the tip of his finger in water and cool my tongue, for I am tormented in this flame. But Abraham said, Son, remember that you in your lifetime received your good things, and likewise Lazarus evil things. But now he is comforted and you are tormented. (Luke 16:19–25; emphasis added; G2859)

> "If I covered my transgressions like Adam, by hiding my iniquity in *my bosom*" (Job 31:33)

> "Do not be hasty in your spirit to be angry; for anger rests *in the bosom* of fools" (Eccles. 7:9)

> Ah, Lord Jehovah! You have made the heavens and the

> earth by Your great power and stretched out arm. Nothing is too great for You. You show loving-kindness to thousands, *and repay the iniquity of the fathers into the bosom of their sons after them*. The great, the mighty God, Jehovah of Hosts, is His name, great in wisdom and mighty in work; for Your eyes are open on all the ways of the sons of men, to give everyone according to his ways and according to the fruit of his doings. (Jer. 32:17–19; emphasis added.)
>
> "Behold, it is written before Me; I will not be silent, except I will repay; yea, I will repay *into their bosom* your iniquities, and the iniquities of your fathers together, says Jehovah, they that burned incense on the mountains, and blasphemed Me on the hills. And I will *measure their former work into their bosom*" (Isa. 65:6–7; emphasis added).

This Isaiah 65:6–7 scripture particularly caught my attention as the Lord declares that He will measure their former work into their bosom, similar to Luke's passage of the measure given "into your bosom." Of course, Jesus, who is the Word made flesh, knew this scripture intimately, considering Isaiah 65:9 speaks of Himself: "And I will bring forth a seed out of Jacob, and out of Judah one who inherits My mountains; and My elect will inherit it, and My servants will dwell there."

It is also interesting when we look at the word bosom in Strong's Concordance (G2859).

From the Greek in the New Testament, *bosom* is defined from the word *kolpos*, which means the *bosom*; by analogy a *bay:* – bosom, creek (as used in Luke 6:38 and Luke 16:19–25).

From the Hebrew in the Old Testament, the word *bosom*

can come from one of two origins. *Khobe*, which means properly a cherisher, that is, the bosom: – bosom (as used in Job 31:33), and *khake*, which means to enclose; the bosom (literally or figuratively): – bosom, bottom, lap, midst, within (as used in Eccles. 7:9, Jer. 32:17–19, and Isa. 65:6–7).

While some translations of Luke 6:38 use the phrase "given into your lap," one can see that the translators had to go back to the Hebrew word to get the translation "lap" rather than using the Greek word which actually means "bosom." Therefore, the more accurate translation for Luke 6:38 is actually the word *bosom*.

If we examine the dictionary definition of *bosom*, we find "4. The breast, conceived of as the center of feelings or emotions. 5. Something linked to the human breast: the bosom of the earth. 6. A state of enclosing intimacy; warm closeness: the bosom of the family. 8. Intimate or confidential. 9. To take to the bosom; embrace; cherish. 10. To hide from view; conceal." (Random House, Inc, 2015)

If we examine the definition of *cherish* (from the Hebrew word *bosom*), we see it is "1. to hold or treat as dear; 2. feel love for 3. To cling fondly or inveterately to. (Random House, Inc, 2015)

With these definitions and the above scripture contexts, it is safe to say that *bosom* also infers the "heart" or depth of a person. From the full context of Luke 6:20–28, it becomes obvious that Jesus is talking about giving mercy, forgiveness, and love, not money. And when you give mercy, forgiveness, and love, "it shall be given to you, good measure pressed down and shaken together and running over, they shall give into your bosom, or your heart, the depth of you." The other interesting part of the Greek meaning of the word *bosom* is "creek." At first, this seemed disconnected. When I inquired of the Lord about this, He reminded me of His word where Jesus declares that “He who believes on Me, as the Scripture has said, ‘Out of his belly shall flow streams of living water’” (John 7:38). The Greek word *belly* also means the “heart.” Included in the meaning for the word *creek* is “a stream or hidden recess”. (Random House, Inc, 2015)

Putting these together, I believe Jesus was saying,

> Give mercy, love, and forgiveness. And as you give these, it shall be given to you good measure pressed down and shaken together and running over, they shall give into your bosom, your heart, the inner most of your being. For with the same measure that you measure, it shall be measured to you again. And out of your belly, heart, inner most being will flow streams of living water. (Author’s Interpretation)

Jesus says, “Do not lay up treasures on earth for yourselves, where moth and rust corrupt, and where thieves break through and steal. But lay up treasures in Heaven for yourselves, where neither moth nor rust corrupt, and where thieves do not break through nor steal. For where your treasure is, there will your heart be also” (Matt. 6:19–21). So, give mercy, love, and forgiveness, and store up treasures in heaven. By this, they will know that we are disciples of Jesus, if we love one another. Do not be caught up in the earthly expectation that as you give money or do good, you will receive money or goods in return. This may happen to some, but there are certainly many who have not experienced this result. Jesus says, “I have spoken these things to you so that you might have peace in Me. In the world you shall have tribulation but be of good cheer. I have overcome the world” (John 16:33). Do not buy into a false truth that suggests when you experience or see trouble, you think you are not good enough or God doesn't care for you. But rather hold on to the eternal truths that Jesus has overcome the world.

Walk in the truth and love of His kingdom here on earth and give not as the world gives but as Jesus has shown us to give. It's about forgiveness…forgive as you have been forgiven. God has forgiven us all our debts as we receive His free gift of salvation through Jesus Christ, including the debt to repay the tithe. This includes not only forgiving others but forgiving ourselves as well. If you continue to live as if you have not been forgiven, you will tend to want to try to repay or make things right (make restitution) by your own efforts. This is what tithing teaches. But if you rest in the righteousness of Christ, which is the finished work of Jesus accomplished on the cross, our forgiveness is full, and we have no debt. Jesus paid the debt in full.

What about Faith without Works?

The book of James clearly says that "faith without works is dead" (James 2:20). This seems to be in contradiction to what Paul writes in Ephesians: "For by grace you are saved through faith, and that not of yourselves, it is the gift of God, not of works, lest anyone should boast" (Eph. 2:8–9). However, with closer examination, one can see that they are speaking of two different types of works.

Paul's letter to the Ephesians is instructing them that they cannot gain a right standing with God (and thus earn His favor) by performing works of the Law. This is well established now as Jesus has fulfilled the Law and made a way for our righteousness through Him by God's Grace through faith alone.

James, however, is speaking about the "royal law," the law of love, not about the Mosaic Law. To understand this it is, once again, important to examine this scripture within the context of which James is writing:

> My brothers, do not have the faith of our Lord Christ, the Lord of glory, with respecter of faces. For if there comes a gold-fingered man in fancy clothing into your assembly, and if there also comes in a poor man in shabby clothing, and if you have respect to him who has the fancy clothing and say to him, You sit here in a good place, and say to the poor, You stand there, or sit here under my footstool; Did you not make a difference among yourselves and became judges with evil thoughts? Listen, my beloved brothers, has not God chosen the poor of this world rich in faith and heirs of the kingdom which He has promised to those who love Him? But you dishonored the poor one. Do not rich men oppress you and draw you before the judgment seats? Do they not blaspheme that worthy Name by which you are called? If you fulfill the royal Law according to the Scripture, "You shall love your neighbor as yourself," you do well. But if you have respect to persons, you commit sin and are convicted by the Law as transgressors. For whoever shall keep the whole Law and yet offend in one point, he is guilty of all. For He who said, "Do not commit adultery," also said, "Do not murder." But if you do not commit adultery, yet if you murder, you have become a transgressor of the Law. So speak and do as those who shall be judged by the Law of liberty. For he who has shown no mercy shall have judgment without mercy, and mercy exults over judgment. My brothers, what profit is it if a man says he has faith and does not have works? Can faith save him? If a brother or sister is naked and destitute of daily food, and if one of you says to them, Go in peace, be warmed and filled, but you do not give them those things which are needful to the body, what good is it? Even so, if it does not have works, faith is dead, being by itself. But someone will

> say, You have faith, and I have works. Show me your faith without your works, and I will show you my faith from my works. You believe that there is one God, you do well; even the demons believe and tremble. But will you know, O vain man, that faith without works is dead? Was not Abraham our father justified by works when he had offered Isaac his son upon the altar? Do you see how faith worked with his works, and from the works faith was made complete? And the Scripture was fulfilled which says, "Abraham believed God, and it was imputed to him for righteousness, and he was called the friend of God." You see then how a man is justified by works, and not by faith only. And in the same way, was not Rahab the harlot also justified by works when she had received the messengers and had sent them out another way? For as the body without the spirit is dead, so faith without works is dead also. (James2:1–26)

James is speaking about acts of love, not works of the Mosaic law. If you see someone in need and simply speak good words or pray for them, yet they go away hungry or cold, it does not show love. Let your love be manifest in the actions that you do, and your faith will be demonstrated. This is as Jesus instructs us to "give to him that asks of you" (Matt. 5:42a).

So let our faith be demonstrated and filled with acts of love and giving. In this way, it will not only come alive, but it will flourish. But do not be caught up in the works of the law, for they lead to death (1 Cor. 15:56).

The Yoke of Jesus

My wife attended a pastor's conference a few years ago. Routinely, when she attends these conferences, she will take extra cash in the event that she has the opportunity to bless someone. One year, she shared the story of her interaction when she went to dinner with a few other pastors. When leaving dinner, they encountered a gentleman who obviously was under some hard times. As this gentleman approached them, they learned of the man's story. He had recently lost his job and was having no luck in finding another. He was desperate and broken as he was trying to find ways to feed his family, so he had resorted to begging on the streets. As the group of pastors witnessed to the man about the love of God and Jesus and then prayed for him, all were inspired to give the man some money. The man was grateful indeed. However, the next interaction grieved my wife. As they were leaving, one of the pastors instructed the man further, saying, "Now get into a church and start tithing." She recalled thinking how this man was doing everything he knew how to simply pay some bills and put food on the table. He had just heard of the love of Jesus but now was faced with a new burden of having to give ten percent of his money to the church. This challenge is faced by innumerable Christians on a daily basis. It is unquestionably a heavy burden to bear for the majority. If it was not, then giving 10 percent of one's income would be done by the majority of Christians. However, in spite of continuous teaching on the Christian's requirement of God to bring a tithe to the church, only a small percentage of people actually fulfill this (seeming) obligation on a regular basis, let alone 100 percent of the time.

Jesus said the greatest commandment is to "love the Lord your God with all your heart, with all your soul, with all your mind and with all your strength. And the second is like this, you shall love your neighbor as yourself" (Mark 12:30–31). Later Jesus says, "A new commandment I give you, love one another" (John 13:34). "If you love me, keep my commandments" (John 14:15). Jesus's commandments were not a list of dos and don'ts as in the Old Testament law of ordinances. They are an action of our hearts: to love.

Jesus says, "Come to Me all you who labor and are heavy laden, and I will give you rest. Take My yoke on you and learn of Me, for I am meek and lowly in heart, and you shall find rest to your souls. For My yoke is easy, and My burden is light" (Matt. 11:28–30).

Peter stood up and said, "Now therefore why do you tempt God by putting a yoke on the neck of the disciples, a yoke which neither our fathers nor we were able to bear? But we believe that through the grace of the Lord Jesus Christ we shall be saved, according to which manner they also believed" (Acts 15:10–11).

Paul states, "Stand fast therefore in the liberty with which Christ has made us free, and do not again be held with the yoke of bondage" (Gal. 5:1).

The yoke of tithing is a yoke that "neither our fathers nor we are able to bear." This requirement of tithing is such a heavy yoke on Christians that it creates stress among Jesus's followers, brings self-condemnation, and leads to doubt of the goodness of God due to our own inabilities to be good enough to obtain His blessing. This yoke of tithing is what has turned many from the church and has kept many others from even entering into a relationship with God. With such stress of not being able to keep a tithing commitment, it is often more "comfortable" for people to flee than it is to stay in an environment where your integrity is out of place or you are reminded of your inadequacy of meeting God's standard. In other words, if one were to believe that they are cursed by God because they are not able to fulfill His requirement to bring a tithe, why should they even bother to be in relationship with a God who has already condemned them.

Jesus invites us to come to Him. He will give rest. As we look at the above passage in greater detail of the Greek words with Strong's Concordance, Jesus says, "Come to me all you who labor [feel fatigued, labored, wearied] and are heavy laden [overburdened with ceremony or spiritual anxiety] and I will give you rest [to repose, to be exempt, remain; by implication to refresh: – take ease, refresh, (give, take) rest]." Jesus is telling us specifically to come to him if we are wearied and overburdened with ceremonial or spiritual anxiety (such as tithing), and He will give us refreshing rest.

Take Jesus's yoke, which is easy and not burdensome. It does not include the requirement of tithing but rather is filled with His love for us. In turn, we respond with love for God and others. Here, we find rest for our souls.

The Leaven of the Pharisees

Jesus warned of the leaven (yeast) of the Pharisees. This is the religious nature, which says we must "do" to please God. This leaven showed up in the early church in the form of those urging the requirement of circumcision. This leaven shows up today in the form of urging the requirement of tithing. Both Jesus and Paul warned about this:

> "For in Christ Jesus neither circumcision nor uncircumcision has any strength, but faith working through love. You were running well. Who hindered you that you do not obey the truth? This persuasion is not from Him who calls you. A little leaven leavens all the lump" (Gal. 5:6–9).
>
> And Jesus said to them, Take heed, and beware the leaven of the Pharisees and of the Sadducees. And they reasoned among themselves, saying, It is because we have taken no loaves. And knowing Jesus said to them, Why do you reason among yourselves because

> you took no loaves, little-faiths? Do you not yet understand, nor remember the five loaves of the five thousand, and how many hand baskets you took up; nor the seven loaves of the four thousand, and how many lunch baskets you took up? How is it that you do not understand that I did not speak to you about loaves, but to beware of the leaven of the Pharisees and of the Sadducees? Then they understood that He did not say to beware of the leaven of bread, but of the doctrine of the Pharisees and Sadducees. (Matt. 16:6–12)

Jesus knew this religious nature or spirit was very powerful and could work its way into His followers' lives. Paul also observed this same challenge. They both warned us and instructed us to beware of this religious nature and to not allow it to enter in to the church.

But Now

"But now" is perhaps one of the most freeing transitional phrases in the Bible (Rom. 3:21). The fall of Adam caused the whole world to be established and rooted in sin. God established the law to show how utterly sinful sin is. And He established a plan for man to come back into a right standing with God (righteousness) that required the fulfillment of the law. The problem is that no man can completely fulfill the law because if one part of the law is broken, then the whole law is broken. Before the Mosaic law was established, there was no law, but sin was still abounding in the earth. And as the law was put in place and increased, sin increased even more. Fulfilling the law was not a matter of doing, but it was a condition of the heart. But it was also established that there was none able to fulfill righteousness through the law. And where there is a law, there is also a judgment that is necessary so as to enforce the law and make guilty all those who do not keep the law. In the absence of the ability for man to fulfill the law, God established a process whereby the judgment under the law could be averted. Once a year, God's people would bring atonement for their sin and offer them to God in the form of tithes, offerings, and first fruit offerings. These tithes and offerings were in the form of livestock and produce from the land and would serve not only to give the Levitical priests provision (so they could tend to and serve the house of the Lord) but to also provide for the required sacrifices necessary to prevent the judgment that was due by not keeping the law. And as stated, no man was able to fulfill the law; none was worthy, no not one. But God had a plan—he always does. So he sent His only begotten son Jesus not to abolish the law but to fulfill the law. And as Jesus fulfilled the law, he made a way to put aside the law and the requirements that were to be performed every year by the sprinkling of blood of ox and goats.

All those that were under the law were also under the judgment that was necessary to establish the law. And if anyone were to try to establish their favor and right standing (righteousness) by fulfilling part of the law, they were required to keep the whole law. *But now*, there is a righteousness that is by faith apart from the law that has been offered to us by God because of His deep and abiding love for us. This righteousness is only available because one man, Jesus, fulfilled the whole law and became the pure, spotless, unblemished sacrifice for sin. The sprinkling of His blood did away with the requirement of the law (which was to bring tithes and offerings so that there would be meat in God's house) to offer a blood sacrifice to avoid judgment under the law. But now this righteousness is established by the faith of

Jesus, by our faith in Him and by His fulfillment of the law. This righteousness is available to all, and it is upon all those who believe (Rom 3:22). So do not be so easily entangled again by the law to try to gain your right standing with God. This brings insult to the blood of Jesus and what God has established for us through His great love.

Released from Tithing, Now What?

It is widely agreed that exercise is an important aspect to living a healthy life. While not a requirement of living, most doctors would agree that there are many benefits to regularly exercising. This includes building and maintaining a healthy heart. WebMD states,

> Exercise may be one of the best moves you can make, even if you have heart disease. Consider just a few of the possible benefits of exercise:
>
> Strengthens your heart
> May improve congestive heart failure symptoms
> Lowers your blood pressure
> Makes you stronger
> Helps you reach (and stay at) a healthy weight
> Helps manage stress
> Boosts your mood and self-esteem
> Improves sleep (webmd, 2015)

While not technically a requirement for those under grace, giving has many of the same benefits. While a life without exercise can lead to becoming sedentary, muscle loss, obesity, and, of course, heart disease, a life with exercise can lead to one reaping the benefits mentioned above. In a similar manner, life without giving can lead to becoming self-focused, bringing an emphasis on worldly possessions, and can eventually lead to a weakened spiritual heart. This is as James wrote that "faith without works is dead" (speaking about works of love in James 2:20). But a life of giving will bring joy to both the giver and receiver, reducing stress, improving sleep, and strengthening and bringing health to the spiritual heart. Just as doctors can recommend a proper exercise program, Holy Spirit will lead us into giving in a way that is best for both the body of Christ and for our own lives. We simply need to ask and follow through. Remember, this is true giving, not out of fear or obligation but because we are able. Bill Johnson says, "The law requires, Grace enables." (Johnson, 2015) So true giving should not cause a stress in life, but rather fulfillment. Out of faith and joy, we gladly give out of what the Father has given us. With this in mind, we realize that one of the greatest challenges for the church is that it takes money to function. At least in the "Western church," there has been such a strong draw toward having worldly possessions, giving to support the Gospel has become less of a priority for many Christians. To compound the challenge, as Christians have decreased in their giving, the church has "ramped up" the pressure to give a tithe. This constant pressure and "fleecing of the flock" has unfortunately turned many away from the church. Many are tired of going to church and hearing that they must give this or that. Some churches even teach that if you don't tithe, you can't be a member of that church.

What is missing with some Christians is they have not grasped the fullness of what Christ has done, or rather what God has done through Christ. In addition, many in Christ are not lead by the Spirit (I say this because for a long time I had been in this number) and so do not listen to the Spirit's direction as to what, where and how to give. I believe that if the Christian would grasp how great, how high, and how wide is the love of God for us through Christ and allow themselves to be led by Holy Spirit, the response would be much like that of the Israelites when God brought them out of Egypt and asked them to bring of their riches to build the temple—there would be more than enough to carry out the work of the church to spread the Gospel and care for the needs or the community.

Through Christ, we are redeemed from the law and come into right standing and relationship with God by grace through faith. We have learned that the correction spoken through Malachi was not so much for the act of tithing (the people were bringing their tithe), but rather it was a condition of their hearts, specifically the hearts of the priests. Jesus spoke about this when referencing Isaiah: "These people draws near to Me with their mouth, and honors Me with their lips, but their heart is far from Me. But in vain they worship Me, teaching for doctrines the commandments of men" (Matt. 15:8-9). And again He said, "Woe to you, scribes and Pharisees, hypocrites! For you are like whitewashed tombs, which indeed appear beautiful outside, but inside they are full of dead men's bones, and of all uncleanness. Even so you also appear righteous to men outwardly, but inside you are full of hypocrisy and iniquity." (Matt 23:27-28)

Paul also referenced this as he spoke in Romans: "For he is not a Jew who is one outwardly, nor is circumcision that outwardly in flesh; but he is a Jew who is one inwardly, and circumcision is of the heart; in spirit and not in letter; whose praise is not from men, but from God" (Rom. 2:28–29).

So, acceptable giving in God's eyes is truly about the heart. If one gives with the intention to somehow please God or gain favor with God, it is as though saying the sacrifice of Jesus and His redemption of us on the cross was not enough. In Galatians we have seen how Paul strongly spoke against this mind-set, and even declared that we have fallen from grace if we do this.

Giving out of love speaks and represents the heart of God. "If I give away all I have, and if I deliver up my body to be burned, but have not love, I gain nothing" (1 Cor. 13:3 ESV). As we become Christlike, our behavior will naturally mimic that of Christ (and God), which is to give from a heart of love So giving, then, becomes an act of who we are, not simply what we do. There is a subtle but distinct difference. Think of it this way, in a loving relationship, a married couple will do things for each other, not so much because we have to but because we want to. As that relationship grows, it becomes second nature to show love by giving of ourselves to each other. As a family, when children are born, it is a natural act to give them food, change diapers, teach them, etc. We lose sleep, sacrifice our own agenda, and do what it takes to take care of them. These are all acts of our love for them. While these are all certainly things that we do, it is a result of who we are being and the love we have.

In the same way, our giving in the body of Christ will naturally grow out of who we are in Him. It doesn't really matter if our giving is ten percent (a tithe) or any other amount. What matters is the heart of the giver. When one realizes the extent that God has reached out to us through Christ to bring us back to relationship with Him, it would be a natural outpouring to respond in kind. In other words, a heart that is filled with the love of God would naturally pour out that love to others and would help in the mission of spreading the good news of Jesus Christ. Giving, as so well spoken by Paul, is a "test" of our love: "I do not speak according to command, but through the eagerness of others, and testing the trueness of your love" (2 Cor. 8:8).

When we are walking in a close relationship with our Heavenly Father, as we ask Him, He will direct us where and how to give. As we respond to His leading, He will give us more so that out of our abundance, we may give abundantly to others.

Paul's Plea to Support the Church

Paul challenged and corrected the early church to not be entrapped in the workings of the law as he wrote: "O foolish Galatians, who bewitched you not to obey the truth, to whom before your eyes Jesus Christ was written among you crucified? This only I would learn from you: Did you receive the Spirit by works of the law, or by hearing of faith? Are you so foolish? Having begun in the Spirit, do you now perfect yourself in the flesh?" (Gal. 3:1–3). He also knew how important it was to give financial support to the church and those in the mission field.

> And, brothers, we make known to you the grace of God which has been given among the churches of Macedonia; that in much testing of trouble, the overflowing of their joy, and the depth of their poverty, abounded to the riches of their generosity. For I testify that according to their ability, and beyond their ability; they gave willingly; with much beseeching, begging us that they might receive of us the grace and the fellowship of the ministry to the saints. And not as we hoped, but first they gave themselves to the Lord, and to us through the will of God, for us to call on Titus, that even as he began before, so he would also complete this grace to you also. But even as you abound in everything, in faith, and in word, and in knowledge, and in all earnestness, and in your love to us; you should abound in this grace also. I do not speak according to command, but through the eagerness of others, and testing the trueness of your love. For you

know the grace of our Lord Jesus Christ, that, thoug. He was rich, for your sakes He became poor, in order that you might be made rich through His poverty. And in this I give my judgment; for this is profitable for you, who began before, not only to do, but also to be willing a year ago. But now also finish the doing of it, so that, as there was a readiness to will, so also the finishing, giving out of what you have. *For if the eagerness is present, it is acceptable according to what one has, and not according to what one does not have.* For it is not that others may have ease, but you trouble; but by equality in the present time; your abundance for their need, that their abundance also may be for your need; so that there may be equality; as it is written, "He gathering much, he had nothing left over; and he gathering little did not have less." But thanks be to God, who put the same earnest care into the heart of Titus for you. For indeed he accepted the entreaty. But being more earnest, of his own accord he went to you. And we have sent with him the brothers whose praise is in the gospel throughout all the churches; and not only so, but also he has been chosen by the churches to travel with us with this gift, which is administered by us to the glory of the Lord Himself, and as a witness of your eager mind; avoiding this, that no man should blame us in this abundance which is administered by us; providing for honest things, not only before the Lord, but also before men. And we have sent with them our brother whom we have often proved earnest in many things, but now much more earnest by the great confidence which I have in you. If anyone inquires of Titus, he is my partner and fellow-worker for you, or of our brothers, they are the messengers of the churches, the glory of Christ. Therefore show them a proof of your love and of our boasting toward you in

> ʰe churches. (2 Cor. 8:1–24 emphasis

ɹere is that Paul was not commanding give or even suggesting that God was ..g the church to give. But rather, he knew that that are mature in love would naturally give, and that giving was a test of their maturity in love. But the giving is out of what we have not out of what we don't have.

The blessing of Abraham not only made a way to receive the abundance of what God has to give, but it is also for us to pour out on others. It is written, "And I will make you a great nation. And I will bless you and make your name great. And you shall be a blessing" (Gen. 12:2). As God blessed Abraham, he made him a blessing. These words *bless* and *blessing* are different words. One is an action and the other is a noun. Remember our analogy of the "flying with a fly". Our ability to give as a Christian is the result of God blessing us and making us a blessing. In other words, God gives to us so that we can be givers to others.

> Charge the rich in this world that they be not high-minded, nor trust in uncertain riches, but in the living God, He offering to us richly all things to enjoy, that they do good, that they be rich in good works, ready to share, to be generous, laying up in store for themselves a good foundation against the time to come, that they may lay hold on eternal life. (1 Tim. 6:17–19)

Kingdom Living, Kingdom Giving

Much has been said about what Christ has done for us. He has established His kingdom here on earth. We enter into that kingdom not by any works of our own but only by His blood. As we receive Christ as our Lord and Savior, we are given the power to be children of the Most High God (John 1:12).

There are many things to be said about being God's children. Not only are we His beloved sons and daughters, but He has placed us in positions of kings, priests, and ambassadors. In his book "*Rediscovering the Kingdom*[7]" (Monroe, 2004) Miles Monroe eloquently describes the mentality of kingdom thinking and kingdom living. This living is different from what we are accustomed to in the United States: We live in democracy in which we vote for things we want and don't want. However, in a kingdom, it is the king who sets policy and protocol. While a good king will listen to his people, it is ultimately the king's position and authority to set things in place. In other words, what the king says is. Of course, history has shown that where unrighteous kings have been in authority, there has been tyranny. But this is not so with our Righteous King.

As kings of our God, we represent the heart of our King. In the same manner, as ambassadors of His kingdom, we represent His kingdom alone. This is critical to understand. An ambassador is not his own person. As an ambassador, we only speak the opinion and heart of the one we represent. We do not give our own opinion on any matter but only the opinion of our king. We lay aside everything we are in order to represent everything He is. As a king, we operate the same way. We learn from our Father, the King of kings, and we go forth in the same manner that He sends us.

As both kings and ambassadors, everything we need is provided for us by our King and through His kingdom. In reality, especially as an ambassador, nothing that we have is ours, but it all belongs to the kingdom. An ambassador is given great wealth and is provided for in abundance, as this is a direct reflection of the kingdom that he represents. In the same manner, our King provides for us in ways that show how great a King He is. As the queen of Sheba saw how great a king Solomon was by observing how he provided for his kingdom and people (1 Kings 10:4–9), so the world should see how great a King we serve by the provision He affords His people. Furthermore, as kings, we have the opportunity to reflect our kingdom (the kingdom of God) as we give and serve others. "Let your light so shine upon all men that they may see your good works and glorify your Father in Heaven" (Matt. 5:16).

Sitting at the King's right hand in His chamber or at His table meant that you had received His prosperity, success, honor, and favor. Christ is seated at the right hand of God the Father, and He has received all these things. And we are seated with Christ in heavenly places. This is an amazing thing and we do well to fully grasp this.

So live with a kingdom mentality and with the confidence of sons and daughters of the Most High God. Give knowing our God provides for all our needs. Let our giving reflect the kingdom we possess as kings, priests, and ambassadors. Let our actions reflect the things that the Father has shown us through Jesus.

The Ultimate Tithe

As we have discovered earlier, the Book of Hebrews is, without doubt, written to establish Jesus; to position Him above all. It has nothing to do with a requirement or expectation for followers to bring a tithe of money. When properly understood, it actually puts an end to tithing from a New Testament perspective the same way that properly understanding Malachi puts an end to the argument for tithing from the Old Testament perspective. As you open your Bible to the first chapter you will see this bears truth. Hebrews 1:1 and forward proclaims Jesus was appointed heir of all things, through whom He also made the world. He is higher than angels and has obtained a more excellent name. Reading on we see that the writer continues to establish Jesus, His throne, and how His enemies will be His footstool. Hebrews 2 starts with "Therefore". Therefore, (because Jesus has been given this position) we must pay attention to what we hear so we don't drift away. God's Word Translation says it this way: "For this reason we must pay closer attention to what we have heard. Then we won't drift away from the truth. After all, the message that angels brought was reliable, and every violation and act of disobedience was properly punished. So how will we escape punishment if we reject the important message that God saves us." (Heb. 2:1-3 GW) It is important to hear this correctly. The foretold "punishment for disobedience" was not because people didn't pay a tithe. It was because the message that God saved us was disobeyed or not believed and followed.

As the writer continues he describes that, even though He was above the angels, Jesus made Himself a little lower than angels for the suffering of death so that He could bring "many sons to glory" and be the "captain of our salvation."

Continuing on to Hebrews 3 you will find again the writer establishing Jesus. Hebrews 3:1 says, "Therefore…consider the Apostle and High Priest of our confession, Christ Jesus." In other words, because Jesus was established as spoken about in Hebrews 1 and 2, now let's consider him as our Apostle and High Priest. The writer goes on to establish Jesus as greater than Moses. But as Moses led the Israelites out of Egypt their hearts were hardened, and they did not have faith that God would take them into the promised land. Therefore, they were not able to enter the rest God had intended for them. Hebrews 3:7-4:13 warns about not entering the rest. And it states that they did not enter because of their unbelief. This is the same disobedience of faith (unbelief) described in Hebrews 2:2-3. Here the writer is urging the audience not to enter into unbelief of Jesus, especially as our High Priest.

Hebrews 4:14 once again establishes Jesus as High Priest, but this time declares that He has passed through the heavens. "Therefore we are to come boldly to the throne of grace, that we may obtain mercy and find grace to help in time of need." (Heb. 4:16) But it doesn't stop there. The writer goes on to point out the qualifications for such a High Priest. He is taken from men and appointed on behalf of men to minister both gifts and sacrifices for sins.

But Jesus was different than the High Priests the Hebrews were accustomed to. Hebrews 5:5 and forward begins to establish Jesus as High Priest in the order of Melchizedek. We will get to the importance of this in a moment. However, in Hebrews 5:12-14 the writer is criticizing the audience because they have become "dull of hearing". They are "unskilled in the word of righteousness" and unready for the solid food that comes from the understanding of the righteousness established by Jesus. Romans 3:21-22 declares a "righteousness apart from the law" which is a "righteousness of God through the faith of Jesus Christ." To emphasize here, the writer is not correcting the reader because they don't have the proper understanding about Abraham's tithe to Melchizedek. He is correcting them in that they don't have the proper understanding about the right-standing that Jesus brings to us as High Priest.

Then the writer brings a warning to those "that have tasted the good word of God". If they fall away, it is "impossible" to renew them again to repentance (Heb. 6:1-6) This should strike attention and fear lest we get this teaching wrong! The writer then goes on to encourage the audience not to become "sluggish" in their assurance of Jesus.

If establishing Jesus as High Priest above Moses wasn't important enough for the reader to understand who Jesus is, in Hebrews 6:13 and forward the writer now goes on to establish Jesus greater than Father Abraham. He does this first by establishing how great Abraham was (and is) to God and the sureness of the blessing that He gave to Abraham. As the writer confirms this blessing that is established by God's Word alone, he states that we have this hope as an anchor. This hope "enters the Presence (of God) behind the veil, where the forerunner has entered for us, even Jesus." (Heb. 6:19-20a) The Hebrew people, knowing the law and procedures for entering behind the veil, would likely argue that this was impossible for Jesus to do. But the writer answers this immediately as he declares "even Jesus, having become High Priest forever according to the order of Melchizedek." (Heb. 6:20b).

So, let's talk about this Melchizedek. Hebrews 7 opens with this. Melchizedek was king of Salem and priest of the Most-High God. This is where the writer introduces the tithe that Abraham brought forward. But remember, this is all to establish who Jesus is, not to establish the tithe. After clarifying that he was without beginning or end of life, etc. Hebrews 7:4 says, "Now consider how great this man (Melchizedek) was." The writer is establishing Melchizedek as greater than Abraham, which is major in the Jewish faith! It also states that Levi paid tithes to Melchizedek through Abraham, as he was in "his loins". This also establishes that Melchizedek was higher than the Levitical priests as well. It is also important to note that Melchizedek is referred to as "priest" and not "High Priest". In other words, only Jesus would hold the position of High Priest in the order of Melchizedek. While as priest, Melchizedek would minister before the Lord. But only Jesus would have access to the Holy of Holies as High Priest.

We must also understand that while the Levites received tithes from fellow Israelites, the only tithe they brought was to minister to the Lord. In other words, the tribes of Israel were to bring ten percent of anything from the land (grain, fruit, and livestock) to the Levites. The Levites received these tithes and ninety percent was their inheritance. But ten percent was to be their tithe to the Lord. This tithe the Levites brought was never money, but it was only and always in the form of a blood or grain sacrifice. The blood sacrifice was to be without spot or blemish, the best of all the tithes. The Levitical High Priest would then bring the best of the "best tithe", once a year, and enter beyond the veil into the Holy of Holies with a blood offering for sin. The purpose was to bring a sacrifice to the Lord for the cleansing of conscious, so they could have access to God.

So, to reiterate what the writer is saying, Levi received tithes from his brothers, who were in Abraham's loins. But Levi, being the one to receive tithes, also paid tithes through

Abraham to Melchizedek. Note that the writer did not say that the brothers paid tithes through Abraham. Only Levi paid tithes through Abraham. This tithe by "Levi" was not money, but only livestock and grain. It had to be this, because God Himself established through the law that the tithe was not money, but blood and grain sacrifice. And it was the best of the tithes received from "his brothers". As this tithe was paid through Abraham it had to be, by definition, of the same type and kind as the Levitical tithe. In other words, if Abraham would have paid money, it would not have been the same tithe paid by Levi and his brothers. So Levi's tithe through Abraham would not have followed the Mosaic Law. When the writer inserted this statement he made it clear that the tithe was not money to those who were reading this (likely Messianic Jews). In addition, keeping with pattern and instruction that would follow in the law, the Hebrew people would completely understand that this tithe of Abraham's was not money, because no tithe was ever money. In following, as a tithe was brought to the High Priest, it would also have to be a tithe of the "best of the best". And it had to be something with blood that would be taken into the Holy of Holies. It would not be money, as money had no place on the altar. As priest, Melchizedek would receive the same type of tithe from Abraham and Levi that every priest would receive and minister before the Lord. This would not change, as the earthly temple was built and functioned as the exact replica of the heavenly temple. But, "if perfection were through the Levitical Priesthood, what further need was there that another priest should rise according to the order of Melchizedek." (Heb. 7:11) In other words, if Levi's tithe that was brought to Melchizedek through Abraham was sufficient, there would be no need for another to come. But as it did not bring perfection, Jesus had to come as High Priest to present the pure, unblemished tithe offering (himself). But Jesus did not come from the tribe of Levi, so he could not enter the earthly temple as High Priest based on the "…fleshly commandment". Therefore, as "He came from the tribe of Judah and was established according to the power of an endless life" (Heb. 7:16), it gave Him access into the heavenly temple, not the earthly temple.

So to be overly redundant, the writer states clearly that the tithe brought by Abraham to Melchizedek (which was the same type of tithe that Levi was instructed to bring) was not perfect. Therefore it was necessary for Jesus to come and bring the perfect tithe. When Jesus brought this tithe offering (himself), it brought perfection and put an end to the requirement, expectation and need for any other tithe to be brought. ***Any tithe offering other than Jesus' Blood is imperfect and is no longer needed nor accepted.*** Undeniably, this puts an end to tithing from a New Testament perspective.

Reading on, Hebrews 7:20-28 continues to establish Jesus not just as High Priest, but as High Priest forever in the order of Melchizedek. Then he writes:

"Now this is the main point of these things we are saying: We have such a High Priest" (Heb 8:1). This brings again the focus that it is not about the tithe, but it is about Jesus being established as High Priest. Then the writer goes on to describe the duties of the High Priest and that these were a "copy and shadow of the heavenly things" as Moses instructed. But Jesus has "obtained a more excellent ministry, inasmuch as He is also Mediator of a better covenant, which was established on better promises." (Heb. 8:6) The remaining portion of Hebrews 8 continues to describe how this is a greater covenant that God established through Jesus.

Hebrews 9 is describing the earthly sanctuary and the

services to be performed there. Again, it re-emphasizes the responsibility of the high priest in entering "once a year, not without blood, which he offered for himself and for the people's sins committed in ignorance." (Heb 9:7). The next statement is important: "The Holy Spirit indicating this, that the way into the Holiest of All was not yet made manifest while the first tabernacle was still standing." (Heb 9:8) It was only symbolic for that present time. But Christ came as High Priest of these good things to come, not with the blood of goats and calves, but with His own blood and entered into the "Most Holy Place" once for all. While it was necessary for "the copies of things in heaven" to be purified with blood of goats and lambs, the heavenly things must be covered with a better sacrifice. And Jesus is that better sacrifice, also spoken about in Malachi.

The point is this. First of all, it is established that the tithe is not money. While the Israelites brought a tithe of livestock and grain for provision of the Levitical priests, the ultimate reason was so that the Levites could minister continually to the Lord. The tithes that the Levites brought before the Lord were the best of the Israelite's tithes. They were to be unblemished, spotless, etc. This is the same type of tithe that Abraham brought, as it was established in the book of Hebrews that Levi brought the tithe through Abraham. This tithe was not about money but was about providing a blood sacrifice for the altar of the Lord. The writer of Hebrews was not establishing the tithe, but was establishing Jesus as higher than angels, higher than Moses, higher than Abraham, and in the order of Melchizedek.

The Levites did not have access to the heavenly temple and altar. They only had access to the "model" on earth. And then, they only had access to the earthly "Holy of Holies" once a year, and not without blood. Melchizedek had access to the Heavenly temple. I can say this because Jesus had access to the Heavenly Temple, as He was in the order of Melchizedek. If Melchizedek did not have access, then Jesus would not have had access either. This is one reason why it was important for Jesus to come in the order of Melchizedek. The picture is this: the Levites received tithes from their kinsman. Of those tithes they kept some for their provision as it was their inheritance from the Lord. But the ultimate reason that they received the tithes was for them to take the best of the tithe, their tithe, and present it to the Lord. This was to be an unblemished, spotless tithe offering. Once a year they would bring this pure tithe offering to the High Priest who would then go into the Most Sacred Place and bring a blood offering to the Lord for the sins of himself and the people. But here's Melchizedek, the Priest not in the line of Levi. He had different access and standing before God Most High. As the writer in Hebrews is laying this out, he is declaring that he holds a greater position than the Levitical High Priest, because he is receiving the tithe of the Levites' tithe.

This leads us to Hebrews 10. As Melchizedek received the tithe offering from Abraham to present a blood sacrifice before the Lord, Jesus says to the Father, "Sacrifice and offering You did not desire but a body You have prepared for Me. In burnt offerings and sacrifices for sin You had no pleasure." (Heb. 10:5-6). Then Jesus responds: "Then I said, 'Behold, I have come – in the volume of the book it is written of Me – to do Your will, O God." (Heb. 10:7) Jesus came to be the sacrificial lamb, the body that was prepared for God. The pure tithe offering that would be placed on the altar before God. I picture this (of course this is my interpretation): as Melchizedek receives Abraham's tithe and enters into the heavenly temple, the Lord God declares to Melchizedek, "Sacrifice and offering I did not desire but a body You (Jesus) have prepared for Me. In burnt offerings and sacrifices for sin I have no pleasure." Jesus remembered this as He left His heavenly throne.

Jesus came to earth as King of Kings and Lord of Lords. He, without doubt, came to establish God's Kingdom on earth. However, Jesus as King did not have access to the temple. Kings were not allowed to enter the temple, only priests. So God declared Jesus to not only be a priest, but High Priest; not in the line of Levi but in the line of Melchizedek. Remember, Levi only had access to the earthly temple. Melchizedek could enter into the heavenly temple.

So, as Jesus came to earth as King, he established His Kingdom on earth. But the work was not finished. He was sent also to give us access to God the Father. So He entered the Heavenly temple as High Priest established on the promise of an endless life. As Jesus entered the heavenly temple I envision Revelation 5 unfolding (my vision coupled with God's Word):

As all gathered around the throne of God, the angel asked, "Who is worthy to open the scroll?" No one in heaven or on the earth or under the earth was able to open the scroll, or to look at it. But then, as I wept, I hear a noise, a rustling, as Jesus approaches the sanctuary. As High Priest sworn by God Most High, He enters into the heavenly temple both as High Priest and as the spotless, unblemished, perfect Lamb who was slain. He walks past the brazen altar as silence falls on the gathering. As High Priest he enters into the Holy of Holies, beyond the veil. All eyes are on Him as He places His blood on the altar before His Father. Everyone turns to God Most High, watching for His response. The Father looks at His Son and says, "This is the unblemished, spotless sacrifice that I called for through my prophet Malachi. Now watch as I keep my promise". As

God moves His hand, there is a great shaking. The veil is ripped in two and the windows of heaven are flung wide upon. The uncontainable blessing that God promised, His Holy Spirit, is poured out upon all flesh. The heavens erupt with praise, crying out, "Worthy is the Lamb who was slain, to receive all power and riches and wisdom and strength and honor and glory and blessing!" And every creature in heaven and on earth and under the earth explode, saying "Blessing and honor and glory and power be to Him who sits on the throne, and to the Lamb, forever and ever!" Jesus turns and says, "It is finished. Behold, I give you the key to the kingdom of heaven. The key is My Blood. There is no other key. 'And whatever you bind on earth will be bound in heaven, and whatever you loose on earth will be loosed in heaven.'"

By His blood, the perfect tithe offering was received. It paid for our redemption. And Holy Spirit was poured out upon all flesh. Not only that, but we now have access to boldly enter into the throne room of God Most High. So as Christ came to establish His Kingdom on earth, He was raised as High Priest to establish our access. The key to the access is His Blood. Jesus, as the perfect tithe offering fulfilled the requirement and established it forever.

What God is Saying about This Message Today

While some may struggle with the importance and/or the validity of this message, it may be helpful to hear what God has been saying regarding this message. God wants His people to be free. He is grieved when His people are brought into captivity again. With that being said, below are a number of prophetic words released regarding the message in this book. While these words were released by well-known prophetic voices today, none were aware of this book or its message. However, I believe these prophetic messages direct the hearer to what the message of this book contains. While none of these prophetic words revealed the message itself, they all gave direction as to what God was bringing forth and what the Body of Christ should be looking and listening for.

Prophecies Regarding this message:

Years ago I felt the Lord speak to my heart, saying, "You are going to evangelize the church". I thought to myself that this was very strange (and perhaps a bit absurd). I had seen some areas where parts of the church had strayed from God's Word, but I had no idea of what He really meant by this at that time.

In 2008, as I wrestled with God about what I was uncovering in His Word about tithing, He began to reveal His truth and His heart regarding this. In 2010 He began prompting me to write a book about what He had shown me. Not being an author nor in a "prominent position" in the church I struggled with the question, "why me Lord, who am I that you would choose to reveal this to me?" Then, starting in 2011 God started speaking through His prophetic voices concerning this information (and my place in bringing it forward). This is in full realization that this is God's Word and God's Message, I do not take credit nor lift myself up, I am only trying to be an obedient vessel to bring forth what His heart is desiring at this time.

With that in mind, the following are a partial list of prophetic words spoken that are related to this message of Giving vs. Tithing. These words are spoken by many different prophetic voices that had no idea that God had me working on this message and was calling me to release it to the Body of Christ.

Keep in mind, many (if not most) yearn to hear from God, especially as it relates to what God's plan or assignment is for them. Some are blessed to hear a prophetic word spoken over them. This would be enough to get one's attention as God is speaking. When someone receives a second prophetic word regarding the same topic, it would really get their attention. However, if one were to receive as many words as are listed below (at least 7 personal prophetic words and many more than the 11 listed below for the "Body of Christ"), you would come to understand not only the significance but the importance of what God is speaking. This message is truly one that is on God's heart for the Body of Christ to receive at this time. While I maintain all of these messages, I have included the body of some of these in this section for the reader to grasp the heart of God regarding this word.

It is also interesting to note that the prophetic words that I personally received were given from 2011-2015 as I was learning, preparing, and writing this book. The book was sent to edit in October 2015 and we received the first copies of the book in December 2015 (the copyright date is 2016 to correspond with the official release date of this book).

The majority of the prophetic words released for the Body of Christ were given after the message of this book had already been completed. Please note: I do not claim that the prophetic words given for the "Body of Christ" were delivered with the knowledge of this message or the intention of supporting its conclusions. However, as I read these words it became evident to me that they, indeed, applied to the reformative message that this book brings.

I believe God was encouraging me in the times I needed it, to press on to the finish line to complete this work. Then God confirmed this work by releasing further prophetic words that underscored the importance He has placed on this message.

I have placed these words in close to chronological order to appreciate how this unfolded to me as a writer.

Listing of Prophetic Words related to the book "The Heart of Giving"

Personal Prophetic Words Spoken to the author about this message:

1. Sharon Stone: 3-9-2011
2. Barbara Wentroble: 3-10-2011
3. Prophetic Conference Ministry: two additional prophetic words: 3-10-2011
4. Sharon Stone: 3-11-2011
5. Cheryl Darr: July 2014
6. Roger Hyatt: April 2015
7. Sharon Heuton: May 2015

Corporate Prophetic Words spoken for Body of Christ that point to this message:

1. Kingsley Walker: Recalibration (April 2015)
2. Jo Ellen Stevens: "Breaking Foundations to Bring Restoration" (October 17,2015)
3. Grace Mills (Life Gate International Church): Shift in Understanding God's Word (Prophetic Word Delivered 11-27-2015)
4. Chuck Pierce: Church Shaking and Paradigm Shifts (from Chuck Pierce 1/6/2016 from Elijah List 1-12-2016 "A Month to Enter Your Path of Blessing!)
5. Dutch Sheets: Recalibration message (January 2016)
6. Cindy Jacobs: Shift in Understanding of God's Word (from Cindy Jacobs Word of the Lord for 2016)
7. Mary Bowen (Life Gate International Church) Leadership bringing a new fresh Ramah Word from God for the Body of Christ (4-24-16)
8. Kathy Walter: "The Angel in Bedford, UK: 'God Wants All People to be Free'" (May 8, 2016)
9. Doug Addison "2016 Prophetic Word: Get Ready for Realignments and New Assignments" OpenHeaven.com Voice of Prophecy 1/25/2016
10. Darren Canning, "A New Shift in Our Thoughts That Will Liberate Many" Elijah List 5-18-2016

Personal Prophetic Words

While the first four prophetic words listed above were given to me regarding this message, I have elected not to include them in this section. While these words were specifically about the book, they were more of a personal encouragement to me to continue pressing forward than they were a message to the body of Christ regarding the revelation and understanding.

Cheryl Darr

> "Steve, I sense that God has placed something major in your heart for the Body of Christ, that He is preparing you to bring forth a message; that you will be teaching people about the hidden things of God." July 2014

Roger Hyatt

> "Steve, you have stood in the shadows. That you have stood back, but God is calling you to step out. That He is going to use you in an area that you have never anticipated before. He's going to use you in ways that it's going to astound you, and you're going to find yourself talking to people that you never thought you would be talking to saying words that you never thought you would use. He's going to stretch you and move you into an area, and you're going to want to hold back, but the Lord would say, "Take the step forward and I will solidify the ground under your feet, and I will see that your path will be made straight. And I will lead you into a season to where you're going to encourage others, you're going to be a leader of men, you're going to show them the ways of God, and

people are going to look to you and say tell us about this that is your God." April 2015

Sharon Heuton

"Steve, I see you teaching in the church; I see that you are well versed in the Word of God. That the Lord has kept you hidden for a while, but there is something he has given you to share." I said that this is the fifth time someone has said this to me. She said, "you know what that means, it means that it is coming soon. That this is something important that the Lord has for you that will bring a shift, but that's why He has kept you hidden until the time is right and that time will be coming very soon. So just be ready to walk into it when the timing comes". May 2015

Corporate Prophetic Words for the Church

Kingsley Walker

"We are in a time of reset. It's a time of jubilee where everything is returning to the original intent and calibration. Revelation 21:4b-5a: "…for the former things have passed away." Then He who sat on the throne said, 'Behold, I make all things new." (March 2015)

"Sometimes we are trying to pull all of this new stuff from our past into our now. And God is trying to recalibrate us and get us reset so that things will work correctly in the new time…Jesus talked about this when He said, "You can't put new wine into old wineskins". …The two were not compatible…it was good for a time, but not for moving on. There was a great shift going on. He was trying to get them to recognize that some things you just can't bring forward. It's not that they're bad; they're good for this time, but just shift a little bit and allow God to do a new thing. How many churches, how many ministries, how many people in general have so loved where they were that when God was trying to shift them and move them into the next place or a next position He couldn't do it because they liked the old so much they wanted to stay there? Most of the time when there's a new move of God, the opposition is not so much the enemy as much as the old move of God. Those that are in a certain way or a certain understanding, they don't want to see the shift. I think right now we are about to see some new things released in the earth that we need to be willing to let God take us there. (Congregation responds with "Amen"). Kingsley, "I'm grateful for the agreement, but realize while we're saying that it means we are going to be tested on that. That means we're going to be recalibrated. We're going, "Yea, bring on the new!", but I'm just saying, you're going to be challenged, I promise you. You're going to be challenged in the way you perceive things. You're going to be challenged with the way you've been taught out of the Scriptures in the days to come. You will be challenged in how you functioned in previous times… We need to be prepared for the things that God is going to allow to come our direction, that they don't sink us but that they empower us to move forward in all He has for us." (excerpts from Kingsley Walker's teaching at Life Gate International Church 11/29/2015)

Jo Ellen Stevens

I heard the Lord say, "What seems to be shaking right now will truly turn to joy, as I take you out of your old way of doing things! I am about to come in and shake up and break up some old patterns, foundations, and ways of doing things in this hour and in this day! This generation coming up will be in need to see My raw power as many of you did in the beginning of your walks! I am stirring up the pot again!"

Reformation is Coming to the Church and to the

Nations Because I Am Blowing on Some Bad Foundations!

"The patterns and styles of your day are old, and I must again bring a reformation to My Church, for I am a God of the now and I am relevant to all generations! The way that you did things in the past will no longer work in this new season... Not only to My Church will I bring this change, but to your nation also.

"And I will again blow upon you, and what seems like a hard, fast wind, will be the wind that will come to shake some bad foundations and that which has been built upon them. A shifting, and a shaking! I am birthing the glorious Church in this hour and in this day!"

I Am Making My Angels Winds in this Hour

"I am making My angels winds at this time, and they shall turn over some of the tables of the money changers as they blow upon the earth. I am about to make My house a house of prayer for all nations, and joy and laughter will be in My house once again!"

I also saw angels coming as servants to bring scrolls to the people of God, and suddenly the people of God would receive these words from God's throne and would begin to speak about the reformation to come! These will be now words for this time! They will paint the vision so that they that hear it will be able to run with it! Jo Ellen Stevens (Elijah List 10/17/2015)

"Breaking Foundations to Bring Restoration"

Jo Ellen Stevens, Connersville, IN

Grace Mills

“Things are going to be different from now on. We’re going to see things that we haven’t seen before. The Scriptures are going to be taught different than they were before. It’s not that they were bad, but it was never getting new revelation. We’re getting a deeper depth of the Word. We’ve only just skimmed across the top of the Word of God. But it’s going to be more powerful and greater, as it says it’s sharper and more powerful than any two-edged sword. It’s going to cut into the hearts and souls, it’s going to pierce the very souls of men. But we have to be obedient just to give what God gives us; and receive when we hear the Word, even though we think we haven’t heard this before. But we will hear it again and again until we receive it, just like we have in the past. And God will not give up if we’ll be faithful.” (Grace Mills, Life Gate International Church 11/29/2015) (Author’s note: this word was released the week before the book “The Heart of Giving” was delivered to the Author. Life Gate International is the Author’s home church, and the members of the church were not aware of this book or of its message at this time.)

Chuck Pierce

"The heavens will shake, and the earth will quake. I am breaking up the fallow ground of your paradigms, and they are going to split wide open. It's time to plow the fallow ground. The time is NOW to plow that fallow ground. There is more than your mind has conceived – new patterns, new ways, and new means. The familiar will chain you down to an old thing and way, and you won't be ready for the breaking of a new day.

"Do not question, for you are hearing Me. Capture what you're hearing and bring it into obedience. You've been working with the iniquities of the ground, but Heaven now will shake and the earth will quake, and with what you've been working with I am ready to show you a new way to prosper and succeed. So start plowing and you will uncover the seeds to your future. You will return to divine patterns you've not seen clearly in the Word before; or you saw them and you didn't know how to apply it right. But now divine patterns are coming down!

"I will show you how to break open the heavens and shake the earth. You'll no longer be working with the iniquities of your forefathers. That will no longer be your paradigm. You'll no longer be working earth that is cursed, because the blessing is beginning to be uncovered. Plant your future and watch growth begin. (Chuck Pierce "A Month to Enter Your Path of Blessing! Key Prophecy: A New Sound of Movement! The Heavens Will Shake and the Earth Will Quake!" Chuck D. Pierce, Corinth, TX Elijah List 1/12/2016)

Dutch Sheets:

"At the start of the year, the Lord also spoke to me about this season we have stepped into, telling of spiritual recalibration and a great convergence within His church. He spoke of restoring our passion, our vision, our heart for service and our love for His Word."

"He is taking us back to the founding of our nation, affirming His covenantal promises with us, and equipping us with what we need to take out the giants of our day and shine as a city on a hill and light to the nations once again. It's going to be amazing!"

"Those who respond to what the Spirit is saying to the church in this hour, taking up the mantle of prayer, will become new wineskins filled with new wine. New paradigms, systems and structures will come into place to make way for what God is releasing into the Earth." (Dutch Sheets: "The Year of Joel 2:16" from Elijah List 3-25-2016)

Cindy Jacobs

"Concerning the church, a shift in understanding of the connection between tithes and offerings and blessing will cause poverty to be broken off many believers (see Malachi 3:8-10). Pastors will become bold and unashamed to teach on the subject of finances, and both the people and the church will be blessed." (From Cindy Jacobs Word of the Lord for 2016)

Mary Bowen

"The leadership (of this church) is bringing a new fresh Ramah Word from God for the Body of Christ." (Mary Bowen Life Gate International Church 4-24-2016) (Author's note: this message was brought to the Author (as a church elder) during a time of worship and prayer prior to her knowing of or receiving any information about the message of the book "The Heart of Giving")

Kathy Walter

"The Angel Who Said, "God Wants All People to be Free".

I was in Bedford with my group and we had a good first meeting on Friday evening. At the end of the meeting, I was standing and talking to a few people at the far side of the room when, out of the corner of my eye, I saw a flash of light. I knew that an angel had descended into the room on the other side. One person from my group, Carol, was standing near me. I turned to her and said, "Carol, there is an angel who came, and he is on the other side by the door; go over there and check it out." Carol went over while I finished talking to the people. About 10 minutes later, I went to see what Carol had discovered. The room was crowded and I made my way in the same direction as I had sent Carol.

When I got to the place near the door, Carol was standing there, but she was not there, if you understand what I mean. She was in a trance, caught up in the spirit, and so was not able to communicate with us. The presence of God was very strong, and the rest of us just stood and waited. Eventually, we had to leave the meeting and still Carol had not "come back." We carried her to the bus and then to the hotel, and we stayed in the hotel lobby until the anointing lifted from her. She told us that she went to the place in the meeting room to where I told her when she walked into a light. The light caught her up, away from the room, for a long time.

The light was an angel who was assigned to William Wilberforce's ministry. William Wilberforce spent 18 years tirelessly working in parliament to revoke the slave trade. He got a bill through the parliament nine times and was defeated. The tenth time it was passed overwhelmingly. It took another 26 years to ensure that slavery itself was completely abolished; when it finally occurred in 1833, Wilberforce died a few days later. Read this report:

"On July 26, 1833, the final passage of the emancipation bill was insured when a committee of the House of Commons worked out key details. Three days later, Wilberforce died. Parliament continued working out details of the measure, and later Buxton wrote, 'On the very night on which we were successfully engaged in the House of Commons in passing the clause of the Act of Emancipation...the spirit of our friend left the world. The day which was the termination of his labors was the termination of his life.'" (Christianity Today)

We did not know at the time that William used to go to Moggerhanger to rest and spend time with the Lord. Carol said that the angel told her he wanted *all people to be free.* Of course, true freedom can only be found in Jesus Christ. He is the only one who has power to deliver us from eternal death. He is the only one who is able to have power and dominion over sin. He is the only one who is the answer to living free from bondage. Others may offer peace and hope, but they are not able to deliver; only the eternal Deliverer is able to deliver us from the fear of death and Hell because He knows all things and is able to deliver and save.

Everyone Must be Led by the Holy Spirit

There is something special about Bedford. I love it there. William Wilberforce went there to rest. John Newton preached there and is buried there. He wrote amazing hymns like "Amazing Grace." John Bunyan was in prison right there, and that's where he began to write "Pilgrim's Progress," which has been translated into just about every readable language. Bedford is a very meaningful place for Christians. Why am I writing about this now? Well, on Thursday night, April 14th, around 11:00 PM, an angel came to my house; he was a golden color and was very bright. He was one of the angels assigned to William Wilberforce's ministry. That last week I couldn't stop reading about Bedford, and reading especially about Wilberforce. So, when the angel came, I knew it was a divine appointment. He didn't stay here long, but I asked him something and he spoke some things to me.

He said, "It's not good that any of God's children be under control." He said, "Everyone must be led by the Holy Spirit because He is their lifeline and no one else, although God may use someone. Each one being led by His voice is precious to God and no one should interfere. Leaders were to teach people to hear from God for themselves."(emphasis added)

In case you're thinking that he is saying everyone can do whatever he feels like, I am not saying that. The angel was talking to me personally, because he knows where I stand. We must all hear from God for ourselves, but we also must be open to others, because we can all get it wrong; none of us has everything down pat. In the end though, we must do what we feel God is telling us. We should not go where our conscience forbids.

The angel had told Carol when we were at the Bedford conference that he had keys for people to set God's people free. I asked him, "Do you have a key for me?" He responded, "You already have a key." He meant that I have truth that sets people free, which is really what my ministry is all about. Then he told me, "Be bold." I thought I was bold already, but when he said that I felt I really wasn't that bold and I sometimes keep back a lot of things." (Kathie Walters, Macon, GA "The Angel in Bedford, UK: 'God Wants All People to be Free'' Elijah List May 8, 2016)

Doug Addison

"This year will be a time of healing and breakthrough for those who have suffered unjustly. We will open the year with a purging of the things that are not of God. We are all walking through a John 15 experience in which God will be pruning things from our lives over the next few months.

The result of this time of deeper cleansing will be a closer relationship with God and you will have greater authority. If you remain in Me and My words remain in you, ask whatever you wish, and it will be done for you. John 15:7 NIV

Major Adjustment in Our Beliefs

God will be revealing to us the beliefs, values, and doctrines that are not for now. This will be a major adjustment for many people as God is moving

us away from mere tradition and revealing deeper revelation that will be needed to operate in the new things being released from Heaven this year. (emphasis added)

This will not create new doctrine necessarily, but we will all be challenged with how we express our faith. Expect to be stretched, as God will be pushing our faith to new levels.

Hold on, as God is going to challenge you; you will need to get these verses in your spirit: "I can do all things through Christ who strengthens me" (Philippians 4:13 NKJV), and, "...but with God all things are possible" (Matthew 19:26 NIV). God has mercy and compassion for all people. He is bringing His heart to us so that we too can operate in new levels of His love and mercy. (Doug Addison "2016 Prophetic Word: Get Ready for Realignments and New Assignments" OpenHeaven.com Voice of Prophecy 1/25/2016)

Darren Canning

"A New Turn Bringing Deliverance to Minds"

"This is the new turn that I believe we are all about to enter into. I feel strongly that there is coming a wave of the Presence to drive out all that is wrong in intellectualism in this hour. The philosophies that have entered into a generation and brought them far from the Cross of Christ will be exposed as the heresies they are. Jesus will shine brightly and His wisdom will appear brilliant and simple at the same time.

I cannot emphasize enough the well-being I felt as

I saw these candles being revealed to the hearts of men. I could see the very chains begin to fall as they entered into these new and brilliant thoughts. This path that is opening in this hour is going to be amazing. The light of God revealed to the hearts of men bringing freedom to all who embrace it. I believe that before we enter into the great reformation there has to be a shift in the thoughts of mankind. What God revealed in the past revivals was excellent and heavenly, but He wants to reveal more in this hour.

Who are the ones that will put themselves to the task to wait and listen to His voice? I sense the young men and women of this generation are about to rise.

I was in Howarth, England where a great revival took place under a couple of amazing reformers named John and Charles Wesley. I was told that as John spoke to a church in that town, 2000 people were present inside of the church, and then there were 6000 more standing outside, some of them on scaffolding to hear what this amazing preacher had to say. I asked a friend why this revival took place and they said, "John Wesley was not afraid to preach the Gospel even if it offended."

That is the heart of the reformer. There is fearlessness within them. I pray that you will become like this and that God's fire will begin to burn in you for the entire world to see." (Darren Canning, "A New Shift in Our Thoughts That Will Liberate Many" Elijah List 5-18-2016)

The Narrow Gate

Kriston Couchey writes of a vision/dream he had regarding the Narrow Gate. This vision/dream supports the premise of this book that much of the church has been led astray by following a list of rules to gain favor with God. But Jesus stands at the narrow gate inviting us to come and enter in:

> THE WROUGHT IRON GATE
>
> As I began to pray suddenly I found myself standing on a narrow path leading off into the distance. As I scanned further I could see the path led into the dark night to an unknown destination. As I walked this path I came upon a long line of people standing in the middle of the path. A man in the front of the line cried out, "You cannot go further unless you enter the narrow gate!" He stood before a narrow wrought iron gate and the people were attempting to go through. The top of the gate was fashioned from wrought iron and formed the words, "The Narrow Gate". This wrought iron banner was fastened so low down upon the gate that anyone desiring to enter had to crawl on their hands and knees fit beneath it, and then they still were required to squeeze between the narrow posts on either side.
>
> I scanned the path beyond the gate and noticed that as far as I could see was what seemed to be a carnival of sorts stretched out along the narrow path into the dark. To my surprise I saw men and women positioned along the road

shouting out instructions to the many souls traversing the road as they presided over a series of hurdles, doors, curtains, and obstacle courses blocking the path. At each obstacle someone would give instructions to those making the pilgrimage as to how to pass the obstacle. Finally I asked Father, "What is this gate and path with the obstacles all along the way?" He replied "This is the gate and path of religion. These hindrances on the path in front of people are stumbling blocks placed before them by men. Religion is a stumbling block that places requirements upon men that I never place on them. It attempts to get men to pay or work for what I have already freely given them."

I turned again to the path and saw that many of the obstacles on the path were created and erected by the very ones giving out "advice" as to how to overcome them. They had figured out how to turn the path of religion into an elaborate extortion scheme. These were receiving in return for their services; money, honor, titles, or position, etc. Something was received of everyone to pass an obstacle. When these received the appropriate payment, the pilgrim would be rewarded with the "secret" to overcoming, the "keys" to unlock doors, the "guidelines" on fasting, the "steps" to spiritual success, and on, and on. All of these purported to get you "closer" to God, become more like God, be pleasing to God and receive His blessing, or help you get to another spiritual level.

THE SUPERHIGHWAY

As I continued to gaze upon this religious charade, to my surprise I noticed that this "narrow path" that at first seemed to be the only path was simply one "lane" of a much bigger super highway that had many lanes on it. This road was very wide with hundreds of lanes being traveled upon by a multitude of people. Each religion had their own lane with their own stumbling blocks for the people that adhered to their ideologies. But, many of the other lanes were filled with people carelessly rushing down the road oblivious as to where they were headed. The lanes of the highway seemed to be divided between two different philosophies of travel. One philosophy of travel was religious engagement that lured people with levels of spiritual attainment and power. The other lured people with the philosophy that there was no absolute truth other than pleasing self. One philosophy was rooted in striving to be like God through requirements and laws. The other philosophy was rooted in believing that man was his own god and no law existed. These two philosophies formed into two distinct streams of humanity flowing in the same direction, to the same destination, and on the same road.

It was then Father spoke "This highway is so wide that those in the religious paths do not see that the lawless are on the same highway headed to the same destination. These two philosophies are manifestations of the tree of the knowledge of good and evil. Both are of the same tree, yet they manifest differently. Religion manifests as self-effort and self- righteousness. Lawlessness manifests as unchecked and unrestrained self-indulgence and self-expression. But son, I only showed you the highway in order to show you the TRUE Narrow Gate."

THE FOUNTAIN OF LIFE

As He finished speaking a light shone brightly from behind me and cast my shadow alongside the superhighway. Then a voice of as of many waters spoke from behind me saying "Turn around!" I turned to look and there stood Jesus shining in brilliant light. He was standing in the midst of a large fountain of water, and water flowed out from Him. As He spoke the waters rushed out with greater force and spread across the ground. "I AM the narrow gate. I AM the way! He who drinks of Me will never thirst again!" I immediately hit my knees in worship and began drinking from this fountain of life. Joy overwhelming burst from within me and I lost track of all time as I basked in His goodness and love. I awoke as if from a dream from my state of heavenly bliss and opened my eyes to a bright light like noonday. I found myself standing among a small gathering of people and realized the light was not coming from the sun, but emanating from the people standing with me. Even more shocking was the water flowing from everyone's belly, including my own. The water flowed in the same manner as the fountain that flowed from Jesus. When people spoke the fountain within them welled up with a greater flow that quenched the thirst of everyone around them and bathed them in light. The water was also the source of light. As it came from within each one it caused the person from which it flowed to and from to emanate light.

I turned around to see the super highway and to my amazement many of those on the road nearest us drawn by the light were on their knees scooping up and drinking the water as it flowed down around the small group gathered there. We began offering water freely to any willing to drink. Many who received the water were weary and downtrodden, but when they drank the water the transformation that came upon them was complete. Sorrow turned to joy, anxiety to peace, and fear to love. As the people were transformed they began to also overflow the water of life from their bellies and freely offer it to other thirsty souls. To as many as received what was offered, the water of life transformed them.

COME AND DRINK

We began walking among those on the highway offering water to all who would receive it. The people began to mob the water bearers for a drink. As a result, the explosion of light on the super highway caused many people to stop their journey to investigate what was happening. The light began to shine so brightly that the darkness shrouding the highway began to lift and it was clear to most that it lead to a precipice; anyone going over it would plummet to a certain death.

Again Father spoke, "Son, the stingy requirements of religion are not the path to life, nor is it found in simply pleasing self. Jesus IS the narrow gate, Jesus IS the path of life, and Jesus IS the light and water of life. The gateway to life is not narrow because it is hard to enter; it is narrow because Jesus is the only way to life. You must cease from your religious labors to enter into Him. His yoke is easy and his burden is light and you will find rest for your souls in His life giving flow. Only from Him, in Him and through Him can you obtain life. All who will drink of Christ receive abundant life; not someday, not through hard work, but NOW! Men either trust in what is already finished by embracing and receiving abundant life of Christ, or they follow another road which only leads to death.
The Spirit and Bride say come and drink that life."

In His Love,
Kriston Couchey
(Couchey, 2013)

The Story Behind the Journey

It becomes more and more apparent to the author that it is important not to base our thinking and understanding on our experiences alone. There is certainly evidence to support a myriad of opinions, especially when it comes to forming theological opinions and doctrines. It is important, however, to look at God's Word first and foremost regardless of what our experiences may suggest. "Faith is the substance of things hoped for, the evidence of things not seen" (Heb. 11:1).

With that in mind, it is intentional that this background is at the end rather than the beginning of this book as it is important to first examine and test all teachings with His Word. Having done this, this background is offered to gain an understanding of the authors "journey" as Holy Spirit revealed His Word.

As a Christian, I had long believed in the importance of tithing and giving of my time, talent, and possessions to serve God and His people. It seemed right that after what God had done for me through Christ, that I owed Him, or somehow needed to pay Him back. As a professional and throughout my career, I have had numerous occasions where I have had to trust God for my provision, wondering at times if I would be able to pay the bills, and in many instances, having to stagger bill payment because the income wasn't there to cover the bills. Having been instructed in the tithing requirements, the more challenging our finances became, the more I tried to tithe, and the more I felt guilty for those times I was not able to tithe. We were not living lavishly at all, but because of student loans, new practice loan debt service, and supporting our young family, we had very little money that wasn't already committed to other expenses. This created a lot of stress in my life, feeling I was not living up to the standard that I was taught God had called me to. I was desperately trying to provide both for my family's daily needs and keep the tithing obligation. As my practice grew, I found it easier to make the full tithe gift to the church, and at times I was able to give beyond the tithe (even up to 25 percent of income). God was providing for us, and by many standards, we were blessed, as our blessing went far beyond finances. However, while I was tithing, I continued to have financial challenges and certainly was not seeing the "blessing that would be so great I could not contain it" as taught in Malachi 3 about tithing and blessing. As a sidenote, the year that I discovered that I had tithed 25 percent was one of the weakest years financially. While God was gracious to provide for all our needs, I saw my practice revenues decline significantly. So I found myself trying to "give more" so I would open up myself for God's greater financial blessing.

I was also caught in the debate (with myself) of whether I was supposed to tithe on gross income or net income. Of course, there were different opinions on this, and my challenge was that, since I had to borrow a significant amount to pay for my education and open private practice, was I supposed to tithe on the amount that I borrowed (gross income) or on the amount after I paid my debt obligation (net)? There were times that I had to use borrowed money to pay basic bills (house, food, etc.). Was I to pay tithe on that portion and then pay tithe on the income I received to pay back the loans? As one might anticipate, I was conflicted about this.

I could not find any specific direction in God's Word and I discovered there were varying opinions on what figure I should use to calculate the tithe. I felt that perhaps my not reaching a financial blessing was still my fault because of my shortcomings. Was I doing something wrong, even if I wasn't aware of it, or was it regarding the tithe payment which I was now making but had fallen short in the past. Perhaps there was something else in my life that I didn't get right with God, or even perhaps I was tithing on the wrong amount. There was also the debate as to where the tithe should go. We continued to support many Christian organizations in addition to our local church, but the questions became "What is the storehouse?" and "Who was the 'Levitical priesthood' that we are supposed to take the tithe to?" Of course, this answer depended upon who you asked. And I questioned that if I was giving to the wrong "storehouse," perhaps God was withholding my blessing.

I also saw a dichotomy in the "operation" of the church with His people. Let me explain with an example. Consider a set of twins, both whom lost their jobs. Both are Christians attending a "tithe-following church." One paid their tithe faithfully. The other, while giving regularly, was not able to keep the full tithe commitment because of the need to use money to feed and provide for the family. As they both sought prayer for new employment, the leaders also prayed and instructed. To the one who tithed, they declared that the enemy was attacking this child of God and commanded Satan to take his hands off, that he has brought forth his tithe and as a result has the blessing of God. The other twin was told that the reason that he was in this situation was because he did not tithe, that he had robbed God and was under a curse. Both loved God, but it was hard to imagine that given the same situation, one was attacked by Satan and the other was being judged by God. Was God's love so conditional and judgmental to the one in need while not strong enough to withstand the attack of the enemy and keep His promise as declared in the tithing principle to the other?

Furthermore, I observed time and time again the situation where a God loving Christian faithfully paid the tithe according to the principle commonly taught and continued to struggle financially while a nonbeliever in the same situation pays no tithe and is financially "blessed" greater than the child of God. I couldn't grasp how our God would not hold to His Word of blessing the tither, even if it was just as equally as the nonbeliever. If His Word said it, He would fulfill it. Why are so many tithing Christians living in financial distress?

As I continued to seek the Lord in this matter, I was led to question the validity of tithing. I began to realize that if God's Word was so clear about the requirement for the New Testament Christian to tithe, there surely would not be such a debate and "gray area" about the details and specifics about the process and requirement. As Holy Spirit guided me, His Word became clearer (as you have discovered through this study). I realized that the requirement of tithing by the New Testament Christian is not supported biblically and actually opposes the grace of God through Jesus.

Be certain, I struggled with these findings greatly because I was taught and believed ten percent was God's and tithing was necessary to fulfill God's requirement and to receive His blessing. I also believed that I would be cursed if I did not tithe (Malachi 3:8–10). In this struggle I was directed to dig deep into the book of Malachi to assess what God was really saying and to whom he was saying it, as we learned earlier.

In addition, as my investigation into God's Word continued, I realized that what I was learning was quite contrary to the deeply grounded teaching in the church today. I was challenged greatly with this, first because this teaching was contrary to what my previous understanding and stance was on this subject (I had taught, lead, and followed this teaching whole heartedly). Secondly, because the doctrine of tithing is wide spread and firmly entrenched in the church. How could so many well-known and respected prophets, evangelists, apostles, leaders, and members of the body of Christ be mistaken on this issue?

As I continued to struggle with God, I asked that if this revelation was really accurate according to the truth of His Word, was He really calling me to bring the correct teaching into the church? I wondered, *Who am I that You would ask me to bring this forward, not being an ordained pastor?* As I continued to "question God" regarding this, I looked again to the Malachi passage, particularly where God says, "Test me in this," and my wife and I began to pray, "God, if this is truly your word for the church, we need confirmation" (not testing God but simply asking for confirmation). My wife and I continued to give financially as God directed us, but not giving according to the tithing principle. We continued to pray throughout the entire year of 2009 as I continued on this discovery, understanding that when the truth of God is spoken, there is a demonstration of power.

One may be reminded that 2009 in the United States unfolded as a very difficult economic time for many people, being likened to the worst recession since the Great Depression. As I continued to pray over this, I asked God if He would confirm what He was showing me by dealing with my finances. I totally relied upon Him for my provision, sustenance, and growth of my practice. I even discontinued the external marketing practices that had helped us attract new patients into our practice prior to this point and simply rested in my prayer that God would either confirm or disprove what He was showing me and calling me to do.

Throughout the year, God continued to provide a supernatural provision and increase beyond my expectations, and as the year 2009 finished, I found that He brought forward the best year I had ever seen in my practice, increasing it by thirty percent. This increase occurred even while other comparable practices were "thankful to have lost only ten percent" of their practice (as told to me by a practice consultant). Please understand this, I do not boast of this, but if I boast, I boast in the Lord and what He did, giving Him all the glory. The increase had not been of my own effort (as I actually reduced my effort) but was to underscore the importance of taking heed to what God revealed in His Word at that time.

God continues to pour out His blessing through Grace and the work of Jesus as we rest in His promise and continue to claim this blessing not out of what we can do or have done but only by the blood of Jesus.

In the midst of this journey, I received a prophetic word from the Lord.

> *I felt that the Lord would say*, "You have indeed been redeemed from the curse of the law. You are no longer a slave to the law of sin and death but rather are freely bound to righteousness by grace which is through faith. This is a free gift given to you and paid for in full by the blood of My Son. It is fully and freely available for you. It is not something that you can earn. It is not something that you can work for by any means. It is not as a debt that you should pay nor a tax that you owe. Nor is it a loan that you should (or could) pay back. It is a free gift. Simply receive it in and through the love that I have for you. And when you have fully received, you will see rivers of living water flowing through you and from your belly. In these living waters, you will find love, joy, peace, patience, kindness, goodness, gentleness, faithfulness and self-control. In these waters, live. In these waters, give. In these waters, move and have your being. In these waters, rest and know that My work is complete. Receive this gift, for it is unconditional *love* that I have for you."

References

Arnold, G. J. (2009). *Church History and Tithing*. Retrieved September 26, 2015, from Tithing Today: http://www.newtestamentgiving.com/index.htm

askelm/tithing. (2015). Retrieved September 29, 2015, from askelm.com: http:// www.askelm.com/tithing/thi003.htm

Bolender, M. (2011). *When the Cross Became a Sword.* Indianapolis: Merrill Bolender-Psalm 71:18.

Couchey, K. (2013, March 16). *OpenHeaven.com Forum Voice of Prophecy*. Retrieved from Open Heaven Digest: http://www.openheaven.com/forums/forum_posts.asp?TID=42905

Douglas Harper Historian. (n.d.). Dictionary.com. *Online Etymology Dictionary*. Retrieved October 05, 2015, from http://dictionary. reference.com/browse/prosperity

Houghton Mifflin Company. (2005). "indulgence". *The American Heritage® New Dictionary of Cultural Literacy, Third Edition.* . Retrieved October 5, 2015, from Dictionary.com: http://dictionaryreference.com/ browse/indulgence.

Houghton Mifflin Company. (2005). *"meat."* , The American Heritage® New Dictionary of Cultural Literacy, Third Edition. . Retrieved October 05, 2015, from Dictionary.com: http://dictionary.reference.com/ browse/meat

Johnson, B. (2015, September 25). *Bill Johnson Quotes*. Retrieved September 25, 2015, from Christianquotes2: https://sites.google.com/site/christianquotes2/home/projects

Life Application Bible. (1991). *Life Application® Bible.* Wheaton, IL: Life Application® Bible Copyright ©1988, 1989, 1990, 1991 by Tyndale House Publishers, Inc. Wheaton, IL 60189. Holy Bible, New International Version® Copyright© 1973, 1978, 1984, by

International Bible Society. Notes and Bible Helps copyright©1988, 1989,.

Monroe, M. (2004). *Rediscovering the Kingdom.* Shippensburg, PA: Destiny Image® Publishers, Inc.

preparing for eternity. (2015). Retrieved September 26, 2015, from preparing for eternity: http://www.preparingforeternity.com/mosevs10.htm

Random House, Inc. (2015, October 05). Dictionary.com Unabridged. Retrieved from http://dictionary.reference.com/browse/ alien

Reformation Heritage Books. (2014). *The Reformation Heritage KJV Study Bible.* Grand Rapids, MI: 2 The Reformation Heritage KJV Study Bible Copyright ©2014 by Reformation Heritage Books, Grand Rapids MI 49525 pgs. 1679,1680.

Smith, S. M., Zelon, D., Hayes, N. (Writers), & Carter, T. (Director). (2014). *Where the Game Stands Tall* [Motion Picture].

webmd. (2015, September 25). *webmd.com.* Retrieved September 25, 2015, from webmd.com: http://www.webmd.com/heart-disease/guide/exercise-healthy-heart

Webster's Collegiate Dictionary. (1948). *Webster's Collegiate Dictionary Fifth Edition.* Springfield, MA: G&C Merriam Co. Publishers.

wikipedia. (2009, April 14). *wikipedia.* Retrieved from wikipedia: https://en.wikipedia.org/wiki/Martin_Luther_and_antisemitism